TERESA OF AVILA

The Progress of a Soul

TERESA OF AVILA

The Progress of a Soul

—

Cathleen Medwick

IMAGE BOOKS

DOUBLEDAY

New York London Toronto Sydney Auckland

AN IMAGE BOOK
PUBLISHED BY DOUBLEDAY
a division of Random House, Inc.
1540 Broadway, New York, New York 10036

IMAGE, DOUBLEDAY, and the portrayal of a deer drinking from a stream are
trademarks of Doubleday, a division of Random House, Inc.

The Library of Congress has cataloged the 1999 hardcover as follows:
Medwick, Cathleen.
Teresa of Avila: the progress of a soul / Cathleen Medwick.
p.   cm.
Includes bibliographical references and index.
1. Teresa of Avila, Saint, 1515–1582.   2. Christian saints—Spain—Avila—Biography.
I. Title.
BX4700.T4M38   1999
282'.092—dc21
CIP

ISBN 0–385–50129–3

First Image Books Edition: February 2001

5   7   9   10   8   6

For Jeff, Lucy, and Peter,
and in memory of my mother and father

Contents

Introduction

—

In the Cornaro Chapel of the Church of Santa Maria della Vittoria in Rome is a masterpiece of baroque theater. Inside an altar niche, on a billowy white marble cloud, is the figure of a nun who looks as if she has just fainted, or is about to. Her eyes are lidded, her mouth half open in pain—or ecstasy. Her body is limp. Nearby is a serenely smiling angel who, with one hand, gently lifts the cloth of the nun's habit and with the other aims an arrow at her heart. The marble gentlemen seated in the balconies, or prie-dieux, on either side of the altarpiece seem to be discussing this divine tableau, while, backlit by celestial golden rays, the nun and her companion are poised in silent rapture. The viewer too is transfixed: just the effect intended by Gian Lorenzo Bernini, a sculptor known for wringing high emotion from stone.

The central player in Bernini's drama is Saint Teresa of Avila—Teresa de Jesús, as she named herself in religion—a sixteenth-century Spanish mystic and reformer. The event depicted in Bernini's sculptural group is known in the Catholic Church as the transverberation, and it refers to a recurring vision of an angel that Teresa described in the *Libro de la vida*, the book of her life. "In his hands I saw a large golden spear," she wrote,

> and at its iron tip there seemed to be a point of fire. I felt as if he plunged this into my heart several times, so that it penetrated all the way to my entrails. When he drew it out, he seemed to draw them out with it, and left me totally inflamed with a great love for God. The pain was so severe, it made me moan several times. The sweetness of this intense pain is so extreme, there is

no wanting it to end, and the soul is not satisfied with anything less than God.

This was one of many occasions when Teresa experienced an ecstasy, or rapture, which mystics describe as an irruption of the sacred into everyday life. Sometimes she dropped to the floor and was frozen in position for hours, unable to speak. At other times she conversed with God directly, a dangerous practice, the Inquisition often having its ear to the door. Her superiors, who worried about diabolic intervention, made her account for every voice and vision that came to her, as well as for the sins that might have engendered them; that was how she came to write the *Vida*, which is one of the lesser-known masterpieces of Renaissance literature. The Inquisition appropriated the book, but she went on to write others—the *Camino de perfección* (*The Way of Perfection*), *Libro de las fundaciones* (*Foundations*), *Moradas del castillo interior* (*The Interior Castle*)—as well as minor works and numerous letters. Her seminal work, in her own opinion, was the ongoing reform of the Carmelite order, an enterprise that required all of her personal and organizational skills.

What made her such a problem for her contemporaries, and for people who came across her legend in later centuries, was her flamboyant presence: not only the way she attracted attention with her raptures but also the way she instituted her reforms. She persuaded rich and pious women to open their hearts and houses to her; she wrote cajoling letters to powerful men, including King Philip II of Spain; she extracted permission to make her monastic foundations in towns that were overstocked with them already. She traveled across Castile and even into Andalusia, by mule and by covered wagon, spending nights at inns or under the stars when she should have been safely immured in a convent, as nuns were required to be. She inspired criticism for her brashness and admiration for her single-mindedness: as far as Teresa was concerned, everything she did was for the glory of God. She had a working knowledge of finance and law, and was a skilled negotiator. Sometimes, when she was right in the middle of a meeting, she would be overtaken by one of her raptures, which she found annoying and embarrassing. She prayed to God to put a stop to them. (He did.) She was an extremely businesslike mystic.

For the last fifteen years of her life, she traveled almost continually, making as many foundations as she could, despite persistent health problems and snowballing opposition from both civic and ecclesiastic authorities. Her dedication to a life of prayer and self-abnegation made conventional nuns and friars look self-indulgent, and they could not forgive her for that.

By the time she died—still on the road—in 1582, she was widely (though not universally) venerated as a saint. That she was officially declared one by the church, after years of debate before and during her canonization proceedings, could be considered a miracle of jurisprudence. Her ecstasies were a sticking point; not everyone agreed that they were divinely inspired. And her practice of instructing her nuns in the techniques of silent prayer—a very private form of devotion—struck critics as subversive of church authority. Perhaps worst of all, though she was a woman and a nun, she moved through the world with assurance, like a man. Yet, her partisans argued, she was always obedient (in her fashion) and furthered the goals of the Catholic Reformation by reviving the spiritual values of her order. In the end, the church stamped its approval on her life and on her mystical teachings as well. In 1622 she was canonized, and in 1970 she became a Doctor of the Church, the first woman ever to receive that distinction.

Some of the people who knew Teresa well may have had their doubts about her sanctity. Her human flaws are fully evident in her letters, which are replete with passion, not all of it holy. Though saints are not angels, as the poet Phyllis McGinley once pointed out, still, a saint-watcher today might observe that female saints, in general, often *seem* angelic—or at least above reproach. Sainthood is not gender-neutral. A man might renounce his sensory pleasures, as Saint Augustine did after a profligate youth, and be admired for his self-control. Like a boutonniere, his prior sin only sets off his holiness. A fallen woman, on the other hand—a Saint Mary Magdalene—must wear her sin like a scarlet letter, a mark of shame. Except in the case of widows, female saints are celebrated for their lifelong virginity—their *integritas*. They are also demonstrably humble, obedient, and penitent, scorning the needs of the flesh. Saint Lucy is said to have gouged out her eyes when a suitor admired them; Saint Catherine of Siena sheared off her beautiful long hair. Saint Teresa was more moderate, but she did shoot down a gentleman who admired her shapely foot by telling him to "take a good look—this is the last time you'll ever see it."

And yet she didn't exactly fit the mold. Or, more accurately, it took a lot of adjusting to squeeze her into it. Her history was ambiguous. Though she was very devout, especially in girlhood, as a teenager she leaned toward frivolous pursuits like dancing and dressing up. In fact, she made such an impression in her finery that one orange dress with black velvet trim was dusted off at her beatification and folded into her legend. After a dangerous flirtation, she was sent to a convent school where she contracted a mysterious ailment and was sent home. Fearing for her soul, she finally convinced herself to become a nun. Her extraordinary experiences at prayer, along with her amazing recovery from a catastrophic illness, soon made her a local celebrity. In the convent parlor during visiting hours, her witty, serious conversation attracted society women (and certain men) who liked their spirituality with style.

Though she tried to contain herself, her personality was expansive. Her warmth, her moodiness, her temper, her occasional pettiness, her sense of humor, her appetite for good food ("there is a time for penance," she famously remarked, "and a time for partridge"), her emotional attachment to certain male confessors struck critics as inappropriate for a reformer who advocated hemp sandals, veils, and silence in her convents. But in order to create oases of spirituality, she did have to embrace the world to some degree. She always said her dream was to live the reclusive monastic life she had fought so hard to institute for others. She considered obedience the greatest of virtues, but in order to follow God's orders, she sometimes had to find circuitous ways of obeying her superiors. Her critics called this a penchant for subterfuge. In a sense, becoming a saint made an honest woman of her.

Many of Teresa's modern admirers have been women, often devout or lapsed Catholics who see in her a pattern for living an energized life of the spirit and sometimes for renewing their faith. She has also had her detractors, usually men who find her mystical experiences unorthodox, if not patently erotic. "If this is divine love," remarked one laconic eighteenth-century Frenchman, eyeing the Bernini altarpiece, "I have known it well." Among Teresa's most eloquent critics was the seventeenth-century satirist Francisco de Quevedo, who in his essay "Su espada por Santiago" (His Sword for Santiago) scorned Teresa as too feminine to share the honor of patron saint of Spain with the warlike Santiago Matamoros, Saint James the Moorslayer. Quevedo wryly disputed even her miracles, conceding, for example, that if she had indeed expedited King Philip II's release from purgatory, she had made a serious mistake.

During the next several centuries, Teresa's reputation took many turns, for better but mostly for worse. Her fortunes tended to parallel those of Spain itself, where she came to be seen, at least by traditional Catholics obsessed with religious and even racial "purity," as La Santa de la Raza, the saint of the race. Spaniards had always considered themselves a people apart from the rest of Europe, even when their Habsburg rulers swallowed up much of the continent. This psychic separatism had as much to do with geography (culture as cul-de-sac) as with the Spaniard's peculiar sense of a heroic and tragic national destiny. The Black Legend, Europe's and later America's gloss of the Spanish character as arrogant, bloody-minded, and fanatically religious, was based not only on its inquisitorial practices but also on the Spaniards' own opinion of themselves. The word "desperado," as Miguel de Unamuno remarked in *The Tragic Sense of Life in Men and Nations*, derives from the Spanish word *desesperado:* desperate, combative, suicidal. Sixteenth-century Spaniards, like those who came before and after them, were famously proud and passionate, dreamers who refused to disown their dreams even on the brink of death. They were also realists, which meant that they were more willing than most people to suffer the consequences of their mistakes. "We find ourselves," the historian Américo Castro wrote, "facing a history that at once affirms and destroys itself in one swan song after another." This penchant for high drama irked even the most intemperate Europeans. "Those Spaniards, those Spaniards!" Friederich Nietzsche was said to have remarked. "Those are men who wanted to be too much."

The Spanish tragedy was, in the end, the human one. Death was the stark truth that no one, not even a king, could escape, and so the Spaniard embraced it, some would say ghoulishly; he or she would say stoically. King Philip II's palace of the Escorial had none of the sunlit glory of a Versailles; it was a sober monument and a tomb. "We apprehend here," wrote José Ortega y Gasset of the great grim walls of the palace, "the Spanish essence, that subterranean spring from which has bubbled up the history of Europe's most abnormal people."

To a civilization with such a dark cast of mind, saints were the ultimate heroes. They had lived in the world but overcome its temptations through heroic piety, which had bought them eternal life. They had passed the test, beaten the system. Even their mortal remains were holy: a piece of hair or a sliver of bone could mediate with the world beyond and help the soul get a grip on salvation. King Philip himself had a massive collection of relics from around the world, including a hair from Christ's beard and the head of Saint Jerome (the king's collection boasted 103 heads in all). Relics were sanctity incarnate, spoils of the spirit's war with the flesh.

Given this obsession with mortality, it's no wonder that Saint Teresa, a champion on the spiritual battlefield—facing death with resolution every day of her life, braving the terrors of the world while tasting the joys of heaven—came to seem even more Spanish than Santiago, who had only had to fight marauding Moors. As La Santa de la Raza, she came to epitomize a Spain where traditional piety was under siege from without and within. During the civil war of 1936–39, the fascist forces chose Teresa, not Santiago, as the defender of the Catholic realm.

The idea that she was a wild-eyed, raving "papist" had always been a given in Protestant Europe and especially in England, where her mystical raptures seemed ill-mannered at best. But even there she had her champions, notably the seventeenth-century poet Richard Crashaw, whose baroque interpretation of ecstasy in his cycle of Teresa poems repelled puritanical readers (and still does). The poet's apparent delirium ("By all thy brim-fill'd Bowles of feirce desire / By thy last Morning's draught of liquid fire; / By the full kingdome of that finall kisse / that seiz'd thy parting Soul, & seal'd thee his") seemed to these rational Englishmen the inevitable consequence of emotional excess and bad faith. In a book called *Mysticism and Catholicism* (1925), Hugh E. M. Stutfield stated the obvious, that "the saner Protestant does not think that it is necessary in order to be pious to remain in a state of perpetual transports." He deplored the (generic) Catholic mystic's "dreary round of celestial billing and cooing, inexpressible raptures, ineffably sweet caresses, 'abysses of delectation and illumination'—all described in language that is equally trite, cheap, suburban."

Others profoundly disagreed. George Eliot, who made Teresa the genius loci of her novel *Middlemarch*, lamented that no Saint Teresa could flourish in repressive Victorian society. Vita Sackville-West, in a little-known work called *The Eagle and the Dove*, thought that a potent personality like Teresa's could flourish anywhere. She hoped to dispense once and for all with "the prototype of the hysterical, emotional woman writhing in a frenzy of morbid devotion at the foot of the Crucifix" (for which she partially blamed Richard Crashaw) and replace her with the "sane, vigorous, intelligent, humorous Spaniard" who had a lot in common with the independent woman of the mid-twentieth century.

In France, where Teresa's reforms had taken root in the seventeenth century, thanks to the persistent efforts of her followers, and where holy socialites like Madame Acarie had made spiritual ecstasy de rigueur, the findings of Jean-Martin de Charcot, director of the Salpêtrière mental hospital for women in Paris, struck deep and hard. Charcot theorized that women who manifested extreme religious responses—ecstasies and stigmata as well as physical illnesses—were suffering from delusions. Hysteria, he maintained, was a disease originating in the womb and often manifesting itself as religious excitement. For his three-volume *Iconographie photographique de la Salpêtrière*, published between 1876 and 1880, Charcot photographed the women he was treating for hysteria in poses labeled "Ecstatic State," "Beatitude," and "Crucifixion." His purpose was to pinpoint the moment at which pathology dovetailed with religious fervor—the moment he thought Bernini had immortalized in stone.

Sigmund Freud's colleague Josef Breuer, no stranger to the Parisian *charcoterie*, dubbed Teresa "the patron saint of hysteria"—though he did admit that she was "a woman of genius with great practical capacity" (*Studies on Hysteria*, 1893–1895). Almost a century later the "French Freud,"

Jacques Lacan, remarked decisively in his essay "God and the *Jouissance* of T/he Woman," that "you have only to go and look at Bernini's statue in Rome to understand immediately that she's coming, there's no doubt about it." It took a modern feminist theorist, Luce Irigaray, to point out the absurdity of drawing conclusions about Saint Teresa from a piece of marble—and one sculpted by a man, at that.

Frenchwomen have always admired Teresa's strengths, as have certain Frenchmen, especially the *décadents* of the late-nineteenth century. "That magnificent and terrible saint frightens me," sighed a character named Durtal in J. K. Huysmans's *En route*. "I have read her works, and, do you know, she gives me the idea of a stainless lily, but a metallic lily, forged of wrought iron. . . ." As the feminist movement of the mid-twentieth century gained momentum, so did expressions of approval for the much maligned female saint. Simone de Beauvoir celebrated the sheer erotic force of Teresa's spirituality: "She is not the slave of her nerves and her hormones," de Beauvoir announced in *The Second Sex*, explaining that "one must admire . . . the intensity of a faith that penetrates to the most intimate regions of her flesh." What had been Teresa's vice was becoming her virtue, at least in some quarters.

Over the last decade or so, Teresa has become a feminist icon on both sides of the Atlantic, not only because she has come to represent the missing link between female sexuality and spirituality but also because of her ability to function, albeit obliquely, within a male-dominated hierarchy. A 1990 study by Alison Weber of the University of Virginia, *Teresa of Avila and the Rhetoric of Femininity*, describes a verbal strategy of self-abasement that enabled Teresa to accomplish her objectives without upsetting the status quo. Carole Slade's *St. Teresa of Avila: Author of a Heroic Life* (1995) depicts the saint as a woman with "a lively appreciation of the ludicrous contradictions in everyday life," who, by means of her *Vida*, constructs a version of herself the Inquisition can live with. By these standards the nun of Avila seems surprisingly modern, a rational woman living life on her own terms. She seems familiar and accessible, as she has in every country and century that has cast a critical eye on her.

All the same, she remains a Spaniard, with sixteenth-century views on the world and God. She believes in supernatural forces she can't control but may be able to influence. She trusts her abilities, but only because God (and not the devil) endows her with them. She is a daughter of her church and pointedly on loan to those who recognize her as a soul mate. Like other religious figures from the remote past, she has a kind of untouchability, coming briefly forward via a new translation of her work or another biography, then receding behind convent walls, where she belongs.

This book is an attempt to take a look at the saint as she makes her end run through the twentieth century. The writer, whose background is not Catholic, but Jewish, has no claim on her except for a desire to see her as she was, a soul in progress toward a very specific and elusive goal. As a Spanish nun, Teresa had only one legitimate direction in life: the true north of saints. She knew that her sinful human nature would keep pulling her off course and that only faith, calibrated by grace, could put her back on the road to God. This book attempts to follow her on a journey that, with all its unexpected deviations, was as full of wonder and terror as any ocean voyage through uncharted seas.

TERESA OF AVILA

The Progress of a Soul

Prologue: *First Views*

—

In the summer of 1583 Jerónimo Gracián de la Madre de Dios, the provincial of the Discalced Carmelites and a close friend of Teresa de Jesús', made his way to the convent at Alba de Tormes, where the founder had died the previous fall and been hastily (some said unceremoniously) buried. The ailing sixty-seven-year-old Teresa had traveled to this convent at the insistence of one of her patrons, the duchess of Alba, whose daughter-in-law was about to give birth. An event like this would be enhanced by the famous nun's presence. The sisters, who knew that their guest was mortally ill, had enthusiastically prepared a sickbed for her in a cell with a view of the cloister. Teresa was closely attended. She couldn't utter a word without its being whispered throughout the convent. Her death throes were enshrined in memory: if she really were a saint, that would be apparent by the manner of her death and by the events that followed it.

Most witnesses agreed that she died reciting the *Miserere*, asking forgiveness for her sins. Soon after, an inexplicably sweet scent permeated the convent—only a nun with sinus problems failed to detect it. A beautiful light filled the room; someone saw a dove fly up from the bedside. A leafless tree within the cloister burst into bloom. A bedridden sister was cured at the point of death. It didn't take more than this to convince the faithful of Alba that they had a saint on the premises. Teresa was buried on the spot—there was barely time for ceremonial observances—so that her remains would bless the convent for all time. Her body was dressed in a fresh habit and covered with a gorgeous pall of silk brocade. She was fussed over (though her face was covered by the Carmelite's black veil, her "alabaster" foot could still be kissed), then placed in a simple pine box and stuffed into a deep grave beneath an archway in the chapel. Masons were called in to seal the grave well with stones, bricks, and mortar, making it virtually impenetrable.

But Gracián was not to be deterred. His secret plan, hatched with officials of Teresa's native city of Avila, was to transport her body home. The nuns of Alba, innocent of his intentions, urged him to exhume her: if Teresa were a saint, that was the only way to know for sure. As the masons began to hack away at the walls, the same sweet scent, suggestive of lilies, filled the air. This would be the odor of sanctity. As the corpse was withdrawn, the party could see that it was intact, though caked with mud and moss. (The coffin lid had caved in during that rough interment.) So the body was, in the language of the church, incorruptible. Gracián and the others took her gently to a bed where they could examine her. Francisco de Ribera, who would be Teresa's first biographer, took notes, as did Gracián. She was so perfectly preserved, the latter wrote, that he retired to another room while the others undressed her and covered her with a sheet. When he returned, he took a closer look and was surprised to see how full and firm her breasts were. Then he got out his saw. He severed her left hand, which of all the pieces of the freshly unearthed saint that were destined to travel far was the most prized: it was said to cure jealousy and indigestion. Gracián later deposited the hand at Avila, reserving the little finger for himself.

He had to leave the rest of her at Alba—for the time being. But he and others continued to wrangle over the precious corpse. Teresa was exhumed five times, and always a piece or two were spirited away—a foot, an eye, a collarbone. Her damaged heart (in which some pilgrims see signs of the angel's handiwork) is displayed in an ornate reliquary case at Alba. Her right foot and upper jaw are in Rome, a bit of her cheek in Madrid. Other pieces of her flesh migrated to Brussels, Paris, and Mexico. A finger complete with rings is one of the prime attractions at San José de Avila, the first of Teresa's seventeen foundations. Her left hand continued its bizarre journey: General Francisco Franco kept it beside him until his death.

With the blessing of the Discalced Carmelites at Avila, Gracián returned to Alba in 1585. Consoling the sisters of Alba with the gift of an arm—as easy to cut through as a piece of cheese, said Gregorio Nacianceno, the priest who reluctantly performed the surgery—Gracián's delegation spirited away the now somewhat puffy but still whole and fragrant corpse to the convent of San José. When the duchess of Alba heard of this, she was inconsolable and the duke was furious. Warning the nuns to guard the arm with their lives, the powerful duke took his grievance to the pope and back Teresa came to Alba, where (notwithstanding a few more exhumations) she stayed. Ribera saw her again in 1588. She was still intact, if a little bent and the color of dates. He wrote, "When one raises the body up, it is sufficient to support it with a hand behind the back for it to remain upright; one can dress and undress it as if it were living." He could still see the three little moles on her face.

A woman who spent her life being scrutinized and revered, and her death being peered at and worshiped, has been dissected by more than one admirer. Gracián can hardly be blamed for his matter-of-fact surgery: he was just facilitating the process of Teresa's transfiguration from holy woman to saint. (The more revealing gesture was his appropriation of her finger, which he always carried with him. It was stolen in the early 1590s, when Gracián was captured by Barbary pirates, but he bought it back from them.) The impulse to claim a piece of divinity is powerful, and from the beginning of Teresa's postmortem history, people drew from her what they needed to make a case for her sanctity and to get close enough to read for themselves the holiness in her flesh and bones. So María de San José and María de San Jerónimo, two Carmelites who had known her well, chronicled Teresa's appearance for posterity, extracting the saint from her corporeal self. The Jesuit Ribera, describing her in his biography of 1590, took her apart again, holding up her idealized features to the light of his sixteenth-century day.

The authorized version was this: she had a clear, almost translucent skin; hair that was pure black and shiny. She had rounded, black, and brilliant eyes with dark, reddish brows. The nose was well placed, not too long or short, and slightly inclined downward. The upper lip was thin and delicate; the lower, full and slightly drooping. Teresa had three strategically set moles that gave a certain interest to her face (the very moles that could still be seen six years after her death). She was more plump than thin, more tall than short. She had tiny hands and elegant, well-proportioned feet, as admired in life as when they peeped out from under her lavish shroud in death.

Her contemporaries, who read these features like a map, agreed that her face was perfectly symmetrical, and that made her always look young, even though her demeanor was serious. She had an easy, persuasive way about her, but those thick brows suggested firmness and moderation. Her head sat easily on a short, straight neck, which gave her an air of resolution and confidence. She was naturally robust and looked healthy in spite of her frequent illnesses.

Teresa sat for her portrait in 1576, when she was sixty-one years old. The painter's name was Juan de la Miseria, and he made her a stolid, watchful nun, not likely to be felled by a bolt of lightning, much less an angel's spear. This portrait does give the salient features, except for the black hair, safely tucked beneath the nun's wimple. Beneath the bushy eyebrows are the rounded eyes, the three moles, the full lower lip—and no beauty whatsoever. ("God forgive you, Fray Juan," Teresa reportedly snapped when she viewed the portrait, "you've made me a bleary-eyed old hag!") It is this image, or something like it, that adorns many of the books and trinkets sold at Avila, where *la santa* is a prime tourist industry. In 1982, during the quattrocentennial observance of Teresa's death, which was marked in Spain by scholarly convocations and a TV miniseries, an admirer could buy a plastic television that lights up, showing a view of the city of Avila and a figurine of Fray Juan's impenetrable saint.

Bernini gave the world a marble mystic who swoons divinely. She has one recognizable feature, the delicate foot that dangles beneath her disheveled habit. Her lidded eyes are an oddity: the saint is more typically shown examining what is before her—a cherub, a sacred dove descending, the book of her own life. Sometimes she writes, but without looking at the pages. (She always said God gave her dictation.) A portrait attributed to Diego Velázquez has her holding her book with one elongated hand, while the other balances a pen as if it were a teacup, and the saint's intelligent eyes assess the divine light reflected on her face.

In almost every extant image, Teresa appears as an alert woman who stands upright even while enraptured. As the art critic Irving Lavin points out in *Bernini and the Unity of the Visual Arts*, Teresa was sometimes shown reeling back as if struck in the chest. But the sculptor's visceral image of a woman whose body "seems to contract violently at the abdomen in a kind of paroxysm of the solar plexus" was something new. Or it was a reminder of something old, the deep discomfort that reports of Teresa's ecstasies caused among the least spiritually adventurous of her contemporaries.

Juan de la Miseria's 1576 portrait of Teresa de Jesús at the
age of sixty-one

It was and still is hard to reconcile Bernini's swooning mystic with Fray
Juan's iron maiden, a pragmatic woman who founded seventeen convents
and was as adept at finding God in the kitchen, "among the pots and pans"
(in her words), as at the altar. Teresa liked to view herself from a distance,
and would refer to herself laconically as "this saint." Her own raptures
made her impatient, and she never encouraged ecstatic behavior in her
nuns, suggesting that they find more useful occupations. She fully agreed
with her contemporaries that women were prone to emotional excess, and
she confessed to being *flaca y ruin* herself—a typically worthless female.
Until very recently her admirers echoed the church's judgment that she triumphed over her enemies and her own weak flesh because her spirit was
varonil. Pope Gregory XV's Bull of Canonization praised her for subduing
her female nature, a compliment that would have pleased her. But still,
conflicting images of Teresa raise questions about her character. Was she
heroic or histrionic: a saint encased in the armor of humility, or an unstable
woman, brown as a date, propped up by the ardor of faith?

Chapter 1: *Expeditions*

———

Teresa de Ahumada began the first of her many journeys at the age of seven. This was not the usual thing for a well-off Castilian girl in 1522. She lived in Avila, a city of walls within walls: ancient ramparts, built to guard against Moorish invaders from the barren, windswept countryside; church and monastery walls, erected as bulwarks of the faith; and the facades of houses, designed to keep strangers out and family members (especially women) in. A girl like Teresa lived most of her early life in a domestic fortress that looked impregnable from the street but opened interiorly onto patios. She played with her sisters and brothers there and with a select group of relatives whose visits her father allowed. Properly attended, she ventured out to attend Mass and public festivals, but most of the time she stayed home with her mother, who managed a household full of children and servants. If she had been taught to read, a girl might while away the long afternoons with the *Flos Sanctorum*, a popular retelling of the lives of the saints. By the time she entered her teens, she could look forward to marriage and to a life congruent with the one she knew.

The young Teresa had other plans, based on hopes that in those times seemed realistic. Her religion had taught her that life on earth was only a test: if she was chaste and virtuous, she would someday ascend to heaven; if she was immodest and sinful, she would descend to hell. That was the truth, and no one she knew of had ever questioned it. Being a practical-minded, enterprising child, Teresa thought she might find a way to skip the preliminaries. She thought of Saint Catherine writhing on her wheel, of Saint Lawrence burning slowly on his grill, and, most of all, of Vicente, Cristeta, and Sabina, the child martyrs of Avila, who in Roman times had endured blow after blow from their heathen torturers because they had refused to bow to pagan idols. The lovely basilica of San Vicente, just out-

A detail from an anonymous eighteenth-century painting of Teresa and her older brother Rodrigo seeking martyrdom in the "land of the Moors"

side the city walls, had been built in their honor. These martyrs, all devout opportunists (just like Teresa herself), had bought passage to heaven with their life's blood. To a girl with an eye for a bargain, this seemed a reasonable price to pay.

She knew that the world was only an illusion. *La vida es sueño*—life is a dream—was a phrase familiar to every Castilian, young and old. But heaven, as she whispered to her eleven-year-old brother, Rodrigo, while they read inspiring stories to one another in their father's library, was *para siempre, siempre,* forever and ever. If they could just make their way to the land of the Moors (which Teresa thought must be somewhere beyond the treacherous Sierra de Avila), they could shed their own innocent blood for God. Teresa and her brother would burst upon the infidel, proclaim themselves Christians, and promptly get their heads cut off. From there the only place to go was up.

Rodrigo had to agree; he didn't really have a choice. So one day his sister packed some raisins in a handkerchief, took the docile boy by the hand, and led him away to glory. Stealing from the house at dawn, they hurried through the narrow cobbled streets, finally passing through the gate and over the Adaja bridge—just as, many centuries before, the sixty brave knights of Avila had marched out the Puerta de la Malaventura to become hostages and have their heads boiled in oil. Emerging alone from that inviolable fortress city, the children must have felt their smallness beneath the vast open sky. Rodrigo probably cringed. Teresa, who was afraid of nothing except damnation, must have been exhilarated as she drank in the endless view. Ahead were valleys strewn with white boulders that could have dropped from the moon, and beyond that, the distant mountains, where Christians and Moors had crossed swords long ago.

The children were just walking along the dusty road to Salamanca—not quite as far as legend has carried them—when their uncle Francisco arrived on horseback and carried them home. Confronted by their parents, Rodrigo complained (not without justification) that *la niña*, the little one, had made him do it. And *la niña* had no excuse: the logic that had propelled her made no sense to anyone else. Alonso de Cepeda, her father, was a pious man, but for him religion was a duty rather than an adventure. Her mother, Alonso's second wife Beatriz de Ahumada, was a weary young woman with a taste for chivalric romance, which she found exclusively in books. Her household was not where she looked for excitement, and she was distressed to find it there. All she wanted was to raise Alonso's progeny (including two children from his first marriage) in a sheltered environment where each day's activities seemed preordained and the rules of comportment immutable. Having her children disappear for any length of time and for any reason was enough to send her straight to bed, where she usually passed much of her time.

Teresa may have felt remorse about disturbing the peace at home, though she never mentions it in her *Vida*, where she is always quick to find fault with her own motives. In any case, the crisis passed, and the would-be martyr was soon busily at work in the family orchard, building stone hermitages where she—and her siblings, if they obeyed their prioress—could savor the austerities of monastic life.

Expeditions

. . .

This is how the story begins. The hagiographer distills its essence: the young girl's heavenly aspiration, her nascent sanctity, her gift for self-sacrifice. The hope of all humanity, sweet as a raisin in a young girl's hand. The story is told and retold like a medieval *chanson de geste;* the walls of the chivalric city are breached by pilgrims wanting to evoke the saint's presence by enshrining her past. Avila, a bustling marketplace and a hotbed of politics, is for the purposes of legend the city of *cantos y santos*—of stones and saints.

There is another beginning that belongs to devotees of sacred genealogy. That story opens with a paean to Teresa's aristocratic lineage, her impeccable descent from the Ahumada family, with its ancient crest of a burning (hence *humo,* smoke) tower; the Cepeda, sprung from a hero of the siege of Gibraltar; the Sánchez . . . but here revisionists pick up the thread. Sánchez was a common name in Castile; it was also the name of many *conversos,* Jews who, since the persecutions of the fourteenth century, had tried to protect themselves by converting to Christianity, as had Teresa's grandfather, the Toledan Juan. Like many of the city's "New Christians," Juan Sánchez had made a name and fortune for himself in a city once famous for its tolerance, where Christians, Muslims, and Jews had thrived in close proximity. In the thirteenth century King Alfonso X (Alfonso the Wise) had invited Jewish and Moorish intellectuals to court, where they pooled their talents to make spectacular advances in literature, philosophy, and science. But times had changed. *Convivencia*—the fruitful coexistence of races and religions—was over for good. Spanish Christians had come to resent perceived and actual Jewish wealth and influence, perhaps even more than they had feared Muslim aggression. After Ferdinand and Isabella expelled the Jews—specifically, those who wouldn't convert to Christianity—in 1492, resentment modulated into scorn, as the Inquisition pursued its mission of sniffing out "judaizers," *conversos* who clung secretly to their ancestral identities. The Inquisition's handling of such "criminals" was famously brutal, and Juan Sánchez wasn't eager to experience it. So he took advantage of an Edict of Grace that promised milder punishments to sinners who came forward and confessed. Juan accused himself of crimes that undermined the church—probably customs like washing on the Jewish Sabbath or refusing to eat pork. He was tried and convicted, and sentenced to be paraded through town, along with his children, on successive Fridays. For this event each member of the family was required to wear the robe of shame, a yellow *sambenito* marked with a large green cross and tongues of flame. As punishments went, this was a light one, though no Castilian could ever take public humiliation in stride.

Juan was resourceful, though, and managed to relocate his family to Avila, where a relative had a business in silks and woolens. By the year 1500 Juan Sánchez had won a *pleito de hidalguia*, a legal petition that granted him the status of *hidalgo*, or gentleman. That title of convenience (easily obtainable by those who could afford it) not only exempted him from taxation but also made it legal for him to collect certain revenues for the crown. In Castile, where tax collecting had long been the province of Jews, too intense an interest in money was considered the sign of a base nature. A Christian gentleman would never stoop so low. So a new kind of noble had to be invented, one who gladly and efficiently feathered the royal nest. Juan couldn't have been better equipped for the task. He was by all accounts an agreeable man, but he had no social standing. The success of his *pleito* enabled him to append the title of "don" to his name, which guaranteed him a certain amount of respect in his adopted city, and to ally his children, when the time came, with families of bona fide "Old Christian" blood. In Spain in those days, a really noble family was one that could boast *limpieza de sangre,* which was defined in legal statutes as blood without the "taint" of Jewish or Moorish admixture. That was beyond Juan Sánchez's power to obtain. But the *pleito* vouchsafed him (on paper at least) an untarnished Christian lineage. And since not very many Castilians could really lay claim to *limpieza de sangre*—some of the noblest Old Christian families had been intermarrying with *conversos* for years—Juan could be content with its legal equivalent. Just to be on the safe side, he appended his wife's brother's surname, Cepeda, to his own.

One of Juan's sons was Alonso, a morose young man who called himself Alonso de Pina for a while, then Alonso de Cepeda. He arrived in Avila with memories of Toledo fresh in his mind, though by the time he reached adulthood, he had the solace of money and prestige. Juan used his personal and financial skills to introduce his son to Avila's most influential citizens, including officials of the church, and this, along with substantial capital, enabled Alonso to marry Catalina del Peso, a farmer's daughter with a pedigree to trade for wealth. To establish the two of them in style, Alonso bought a compound called the Casas de la Moneda (which had once been a mint) in a desirable neighborhood at the edge of what had once been the Jewish quarter. The place was austerely elegant, with several buildings grouped around patios and gardens where the servants would tend to the livestock, laundering, and other domestic work. There was plenty of room there for an *hidalgo*'s family to grow and thrive.

Catalina died after two years of marriage, leaving her husband with a couple of young children, María and Juan. After a period of mourning he married Beatriz de Ahumada, a fourteen-year-old cousin of his first wife's. The biographer Victoria Lincoln, who did a prodigious amount of detective work on Teresa's family, reports that during their courtship, Beatriz became pregnant by Alonso and that her mother was dead set against the match. Teresa de las Cuevas—a country woman who signed her name with a cross, her "mark"—had plenty of family pride and prejudice. She tried to void the engagement by having it declared illegal on the basis that Beatriz and the late Catalina had been cousins. But Alonso used his connections to buy a dispensation from the church, and the marriage took place. Once again Alonso forged his link with an Old Christian family, and this one had a special attribute. During the eleventh-century *reconquista*, when the Christians recaptured Castile from the Moors, men from a family called Ahumada had reputedly defended a tower, fighting their way through the smoke and flames and winning (among other prizes) the right to their distinctive family crest. This was now Alonso's to hold high.

Alonso and Beatriz had a country wedding at the Ahumada family property at Gotarrendura, where shortly afterward, Beatriz gave birth to her first child, who was named Hernando. Alonso soon had a bit of luck. The duke of Alba had been ordered to pocket the Pyrenean kingdom of Navarre for King Ferdinand, and he needed a fighting force of Castilian nobility to do so. Alonso rode off to what turned out to be a brief and successful war. At last he had the one thing his *hidalgo*'s heart still longed for: a piece of the valiant history from which Avila had risen, stone by stone.

Beatriz de Ahumada soldiered on to produce nine more children, a tour of duty that left her enervated and worn. She was still a young woman when, just before dawn on March 28, 1515, she gave birth to her third child and first girl, to be named Teresa after that recalcitrant maternal grandmother.

. . .

She was a vain and vivacious girl with a divine agenda. This was not unusual, though it seems to be in retrospect, which is the vantage point from which saints' lives must be viewed. At the time she was growing up, Avila was a lively, though still semirural, city famous for its wool production (like most Castilian cities), where commerce lived arm in arm with faith. Outside the ancient battlements, sheep grazed on the hillsides; the river Adaja curled around the city's feet. Inside the walls, wagons clattered down narrow streets that opened onto *plazas* teeming with life. In the Mercado Grande and the Mercado Chico, the city's two main marketplaces, people shopped and gossiped over the noise of roving entertainers, the chiming of church bells, and the clang of pots and pans made by Avila's *morisco* (converted Muslim) artisans. Skeins of merino wool passed from hand to hand, as did bolts of bright silk, locally grown pears and grapes, trout and partridge and plump pigs ready for roasting—a Castilian delicacy. Trade was brisk in shops much like the one off the Mercado Chico, where Teresa's grandfather Juan Sánchez had made his fortune in silks and woolens. It was in the Mercado Grande, in 1491, that a group of Toledan Jews who had confessed under torture to the gruesome murder of a Christian child—known as the Santo Niño de la Guardia—were burned at the stake.

Avila's most prestigious families could trace their roots back to the *reconquista;* the rest of the nobility, which (like Alonso de Cepeda) couldn't, tried to procure family crests and legends to go along with them. Even though most of the elite families—including the Mendozas (whose numbers included the bishop of Avila) and, arguably, the powerful Bracamontes—lacked perfect pedigrees, *converso* ancestry was for the most part a closely guarded secret. Many of Teresa's biographers think she knew the truth about her background. If she did, it was probably not through her father, a man invested in obliterating his past.

The wealthiest families made a point of bankrolling religious festivals, which were frequent and well attended. This won them social and political prestige, not to mention a chance at eternal bliss. Benefactors of religious orders endowed chapels with crypts where family members could be interred and Masses said (around the clock, in some cases) for their souls. In Teresa's later life as a reformer, she often had to deal with wealthy patrons who made excessive demands on her nuns' time by requiring unremitting prayers for the souls of dead relations. A person's residence, in death as in life, was a clue to his or her social identity.

For the living, a house could be a sign of *hidalguia,* noble descent. In Avila de los Caballeros (Avila of the Knights), many of the finest houses had been built close by, and even into, the city's walls, so that centuries later their occupants had easy access to the ramparts—including those who had never seen a field of battle. A man like Alonso de Cepeda made sure his home bespoke his valor and his piety. Over the arched doorway, emblazoned on a shield of stone, the family crests (in Alonso's case, the combined crests of the Cepeda and Ahumada) staked his claim to ancient nobility. The stone facades, the massive doors decorated with iron spikes (sometimes gilded), the tiny barred windows protected his honor and his wealth. Inside the house, devotional paintings relieved the pallor of the whitewashed walls, and tapestries helped guard against drafts. Over the chilly floors were laid Flemish carpets, on which were scattered fine embroidered silk cushions. As in Moorish houses, family and visitors sat on these cross-legged, while the head of the household and important guests used the straight-backed chairs with tooled leather seats. (As historian Américo Castro has noted, "Spain, rich in all types of art, has never invented, in truth, a single comfortable piece of furniture.") Massive oak tables and cabinets, wrought-iron chandeliers, and other stately furnishings testified that their owner was a man of consequence.

So did his wife, who was, again as in Moorish households, a closely held asset. Her value hinged not only on the dowry she brought to the marriage—though this was extremely important—but also on her modest and prudent behavior. She had to be, as the theologian and humanist Luis de León defined her in a treatise, *la perfecta casada,* the perfect wife, skilled at managing the servants, as well as at other tasks like spinning wool and flax and making the family's clothes. Perfectly attired and coiffed, she appeared by her husband's side at social and religious functions. If any man insulted or (worst case) seduced her, that was a mortal blow to the family's honor; her husband had to avenge it, even to the death. No wonder he wanted to hide her away—a task made easier by the fact that she had very few places to go. She had no formal education and no role in municipal life. She could take an interest (depending on her resources, sometimes a very active one) in religious foundations and charitable works, but otherwise she went out infrequently and never alone. Her head had to be covered when she left the house, and so she often wore her hooded cloak. A veil (another Moorish survival) could be problematic: the *tapado de medio ojo*, the veil arranged to reveal one eye, could enable a woman to flirt.

The paradox of domestic life for a woman of Avila was that even though her own life was circumscribed, she lived in the city of *hazañas* (heroic deeds), famous for its history of daring sorties and conquests. A girl like Teresa de Ahumada was regaled from early childhood with stories about men and even women of legend: Jimena Blázquez, for example, epitomized the *mujer fuerte*, the woman equal in valor to a man. Once when the men were off to war and a horde of invaders approached the city walls, she dressed the women of Avila in false beards, hats, and armor, then ordered them up to the ramparts, where they drove away the heathen by loudly rattling their kitchen utensils. Even if she couldn't become a soldier or do missionary service in the Americas, the *mujer fuerte* could still suffer for the faith, as the female saints of the *Flos Sanctorum* had done. And if she couldn't become a martyr, she could at least channel her heroic impulses by joining a religious order, renouncing the comforts (such as they were) of home and marriage. This was a sacrifice that a girl with an eye to her future could make.

The hermitages in the orchard tumbled down, and the would-be prioress began to turn her attention elsewhere. She was growing up, and romance was flowing in her veins. She devoured her mother's books of chivalry, especially the one all of Europe was reading, the *Amadís de Gaula*. This was the story, in four books, of a knight who was brave, handsome, and cunning, and as pious as he needed to be. Amadís was in love with Oriana, a ravishingly beautiful and provisionally chaste maiden. He performed miraculous feats (like pulling a magic sword from its scabbard) in the name of honor and virtue, which Oriana rewarded, clandestinely, with her love. His passion distracted him for a time from heroic deeds, but he recovered his strength and courage to champion the honor of God.

For Doña Teresa de Ahumada, the *Amadís* was a delight and a revelation. Its tales of holy valor and amorous intrigue were proof that courage and strategy paid off if enough willpower was applied—a lesson that she apparently never forgot. The *Amadís*, with its devout seductions, seems not to have shocked Teresa any more than it did two of its other avid readers, Ignatius of Loyola and King Philip II. All three of them conflated religious fervor with chivalric love. The young girl was so stimulated by her reading that she decided to write a romance along with her brother and co-conspirator Don Rodrigo de Cepeda. Their youthful effort, which they called *The Knight of Avila*, is tactfully glossed over by hagiographers, who focus instead on her piety as she stood at the threshold of adult life.

After her mother died giving birth to her tenth child, at the age of thirty-three, the thirteen-year-old Teresa grieved before a statue of the Virgin Mary and begged her to fill the vacancy. "It seems to me that, even though I did this in all simplicity," she writes in her *Vida*, "it did me good, because whenever I have put myself in the hands of the sovereign Virgin, she has always helped me, and in the end she has brought me close to her." Teresa's veneration of Mary, fixed during that early crisis, could have easily lured her away from frivolous pastimes. But it didn't. She was ripe for new experiences, sacred or secular; her adolescent mind barely made such distinctions.

As the years passed, Teresa "began to be aware of the natural attributes which the Lord had given me—which people said were considerable." (Or as the French biographer Louis Bertrand put it in 1927, "She was beautiful. And she knew it.") Teresa de Ahumada was a magnet for attention, a sociable girl who could never help liking people, as long as they liked her. She wore dangling earrings and ropy necklaces, dabbed on perfume, and piled her hair on top of her head in the style of the young empress Isabella of Portugal. "I began to wear fancy things, since I wanted to be attractive, and to fuss with my hands and my hair," she writes. "I used perfumes and all the silly baubles I could get hold of—not a few, because I was very particular." On occasion—say, a festival or a family entertainment—she put on something dramatic (that celestial orange dress, with its black velvet braid) and danced a galliard or a pavane. Her lively young cousins often came to visit; in the name of hospitality, Alonso couldn't turn them away, even though he frowned on gaiety. But one of these relatives turned out to be a schemer. From the few hints dropped in Teresa's *Vida* (which makes short work of her early years), it sounds as if this woman engineered a flirtation between the girl and a male cousin (only Vita Sackville-West suspects a female one), with a servant as go-between. People began to talk.

Teresa says she almost lost her honor, or *honra*—a word that could mean many things. It virtually always meant family pride or reputation (no sixteenth-century Spaniard distinguished between the two). To an Old Christian, *honra* also meant *limpieza de sangre*, innate nobility that informed all behavior, from simple manners to deportment in battle. To a moralist, it had to include the idea of integrity, an inviolable code of conduct. To a teenage girl, *honra* hinged on chastity, the basis for the world's opinion of her and for what today might be called her self-esteem. *Honra* was always fragile, "a clear, transparent glass," as the playwright and poet Lope de Vega wrote: "A breath's enough to cloud it over." Teresa explains in the *Vida* how the devil tempted her so that she *almost* lost her *honra*, but how her good inclinations (which she understood to be a gift from heaven) prevailed.

That wasn't quite enough for Alonso. He had lost his wife; his prim older daughter, María, Teresa's half sister, had just married and left home. Clearly the young girl could not be left without a female watchdog. It was the summer of 1531. Teresa was sixteen and in her glory. There was a lot going on that would keep her from serious pursuits—for example, the arrival of Empress Isabella and her three-year-old son, Prince Philip, who had come to Avila to ceremonially exchange his childish clothes for the

A modern view of the walls and city of Avila

regal ones befitting the heir to the Spanish throne. These were boom times for Spain. Charles V's empire, his Habsburg birthright, encompassed much of Europe, including Naples and Milan. Across the seas, Hernán Cortés had conquered Mexico; Francisco Pizarro was making inroads into Peru. The city of Avila was poised to embark on months of festivities to mark the young prince's investiture—glamorous processions and other royal fanfare—and there was nothing Teresa enjoyed more. That was when Alonso decided to pack her off to a nearby Augustinian convent that ran a kind of finishing school for genteel young woman boarders, preparing them for a devout domestic life. Alonso handled the situation delicately. If he hadn't, the rumors about his daughter might have spun out of control. "This was done in such a discreet way," she explains, "that only I and a relative knew about it, because they waited for the perfect moment, when no one would think it was strange." The moment came right after María's wedding, "when it wasn't appropriate for me to be left on my own, without a mother."

Teresa couldn't have been glad to go away, although she writes that she was fed up with her own reckless behavior. She had never stopped wanting to be good. So in the middle of everything, Avila's celebrations and her own exuberant sortie into womanhood, she went off to live the life of a nun.

Chapter 2: *Perils*

—

At the convent of Santa María de Gracia, where she worried at first that gossip might have preceded her, Teresa decided to give up her worldly ways. That wasn't so hard after only a week or so of discomfort (or so she says; her sense of time was never exact). But embracing a life of prayer was. It wasn't that she felt uneasy in the convent. As she remembers, "Everyone liked me, because the Lord gave me the gift of pleasing people wherever I happened to be." Whatever was transpiring inwardly, Teresa always knew how to handle herself. She might have been happier if the friends she had left behind hadn't kept sending her messages, piquing her never-dormant curiosity. It seemed like intrigue followed wherever she went, and she had to struggle to remember what it had been like—way back in childhood— not to be wicked at all.

More than a year passed, and Teresa adapted herself to a life that was piously routine. While she and the other girls said their prayers and perfected their embroidery, they watched the nuns of Santa María de Gracia perfect their souls. It was a sobering experience. These women practiced austerities that little Teresa, with her backyard hermitages, had never dreamed of and couldn't even now aspire to. She wanted only to pray fervently, dissolving in tears as some of the other students did, at the thought of Christ's Passion. But Teresa never dissolved. She was a hard-praying, dry-eyed realist with (it seemed) very little to offer her God. "If I saw anyone weeping while she prayed, or doing some other virtuous thing, I became very envious," she writes. She was soothed by the company of an older nun called Doña María de Briceño, who had also been sixteen when she entered the convent; she must have been a sympathetic listener. But Teresa didn't really want to be a nun any more than she wanted to be married—and those were the only alternatives a girl in her position could choose. She could become a wife, consigned to virtual slavery by her husband (about which Teresa the prioress had something to say later on) and the unceasing agony of childbirth until perhaps, like her own mother, she died young. Or she could take the veil. If she was careful about her choice of a convent, she might have some freedom there. Well-heeled nuns in "mitigated" convents (i.e., those that had been allowed to mitigate their austerities by papal decree) could have their own furnished suites, some jewelry, and even lapdogs. But her days could be as dry as dust, especially if, as she suspected was the case, she lacked the inner resources for prayer.

It was a quandary from which she was rescued, after nineteen months, by a mysterious illness—the first of many in her long life. She was overcome by fainting fits and a high fever, but no ailment the bewildered doctors could identify. The nuns at Santa María de Gracia were alarmed; they had no idea what to do with her, so they sent her home. After a while she improved enough to be sent on a recuperative journey to her sister's house in the countryside. María and her husband, the rigidly polite Martín de Guzmán, had a place at Castellanos de la Cañada, not very far from Avila, where it was felt the fresh air and food might help her get back her strength. Since the journey by wagon and mule on bumpy mountain roads would be uncomfortable (though for a person who had been cooped up in a convent and a sickbed, probably something to look forward to), it made sense for Teresa to stop along the way at her uncle Pedro de Cepeda's house at Hortigosa, a rural hamlet.

Uncle Pedro was Alonso's brother. Dryer than the desert where his hero, Saint Jerome, had lived as a hermit, Pedro had little use for the world. But he seems not to have minded his niece's company or the chance to improve her soul. One of his few indulgences was allowing himself to be read to, and even though Teresa didn't much like his books, she pretended she did—she was that eager to please. And in spite of herself, she was stirred by the trumpet call of Saint Jerome's *Letters*, where religion was a holy war, complete with knights, infidels, and heroic action. She could hardly have resisted that. As Teresa recounts in the *Vida*, during conversations with her pious uncle, she "began to grasp the truth which I had heard as a child, that all is nothing, and that the world is vanity and on the verge of ending. And I began to be afraid that if I had died right then, I would have gone to hell. Even though I couldn't make myself want to become a nun, I saw that that was the best and safest thing to do; and so, little by little, I decided to bully myself into doing it."

This was not a conversion experience—a deep and transformative apprehension of the truth of faith—but it did put the fear of God into her. She reasoned that a convent couldn't be a worse place than purgatory, and as things stood now, she was sure to go straight to hell. As arguments went, this one might have been persuasive, but it didn't do much to relieve her anxiety. During the subsequent brief visit with María, Teresa became more and more fretful and ill. The symptoms that had alarmed the nuns at the Augustinian convent began recurring as Teresa worried over the state of her soul. Eventually the fits and fever grew so severe and so unremitting that her father had to retrieve her. This daughter, for all her adventurousness, kept creeping back into the family nest. Once there, she began as before to recover; then she set to work persuading him to let her become a nun.

Alonso was not an easy man. He had very set ideas about behavior and social identity, not at all unusual for a man of his time and place. Ortega y Gasset writes in *Invertebrate Spain* about the posture he calls *altanería,* pride or loftiness expressed by a literal drawing-up of the neck and head, "or at least the muscular beginning of this," an attitude that shored up Alonso's fragile persona. He was also known for his somber cast of mind, which was probably exacerbated by his having been shamed as a child before the population of Toledo. Adults who as children endured much less humiliation than that have been known to overprize their dignity (another reading of *honra*).

Alonso had all but escaped his past when it ambushed him in the course of a lawsuit in 1519, one year before the revolt of the Comuneros, the civil uprising that pitted the Castilian nobility—and eventually other citizens, rich and poor—against Charles V, who had just been made Holy Roman Emperor and needed funds for his European wars. Alonso and his three brothers refused to pay taxes within the province of Avila on the grounds that they were *hidalgos* and therefore exempt from taxation. The Cepeda brothers made their claim in hopes that their connection with an influential official would guarantee success in court. But there were unforeseen complications. Some people did indeed testify that the brothers were perfect *hidalgos,* as evidenced by their sterling behavior. But others (including

Alonso's first wife's brother-in-law) provided graphic descriptions of the family's public disgrace in Toledo. As if this weren't bad enough, the case dragged on and on, delayed by the Comuneros rebellion, which was headquartered at Avila. Though the Cepedas eventually won their case, Alonso's discomfort must have lingered. As secure as his position now was, he could never let down his guard.

He had to protect his family name: that was a given for any Castilian gentleman. The question was how to go about it. If he wanted to safeguard precious objects, he might put them in a *vargueño,* a monolithic (though highly decorated) fall-front cabinet that opened to reveal a profusion of inner compartments—an apt metaphor for the Spaniard's soul. Protecting a daughter was a more delicate operation, requiring a search for the proper husband (that is, for a prestigious family to marry her into) and usually a substantial investment of capital for the dowry. Alonso was well equipped to take on such a project. But Teresa refused to cooperate, saying she would never become a wife, perfect or otherwise (though in one of the nicer ironies of literature, Luis de León, future author of *La perfecta casada,* would become the first editor of Saint Teresa's works).

Her solution, which she pressed on her father unremittingly, was that she enter the convent of the Encarnación, newly built on the site of an old Jewish cemetery just outside the city's walls. Her good friend Juana Suárez was already a novice there. But Alonso hated the idea. He had probably heard rumors about life at the Encarnación, a convent that observed the mitigated rule, where some nuns enjoyed more freedom than married women. They could leave the convent to visit friends and relatives, and they could have visitors, even men. In fact, nuns were known to carry on lengthy flirtations with suitors. This, of course, would be intolerable to a man like Alonso. Besides, Teresa was attractive and well-off; she could make a match with some scion of a good Old Christian family, enhancing the *honra* (as he must have defined it) of the Cepeda y Ahumada. What Alonso said to his daughter and to the friends she got to intercede for her, was, "Over my dead body." Or, as Teresa writes, "The most that we could get from him was that I could do what I wanted after his death."

She seems to have admired her father. He refused to keep slaves, behaved decently to servants, and never slandered a soul. She respected his wishes when she could. Still, one November dawn in 1535, and with the help of one of her brothers (possibly the oldest, Juan, though legend has it as Antonio) whom she had convinced that he wanted to be a friar, the twenty-year-old made her way to the Encarnación. This time she did feel some remorse; at least she is pretty sure she did. She tries to record these inner events faithfully: "I remember—and I think that this is the truth—that when I left my father's house I was feeling so tormented, I doubt I'll feel any worse when I die. It seemed as if all the bones in my body were being pulled apart." At this point, she explains, she had no love for God to counteract her pain at leaving home. But her fear of damnation and her *determinación* (tenacity) spurred her on.

It wasn't all that daring a journey compared with those that others were taking. In those days Avila was sending its ambitious young men off to the Indies as *conquistadores*. A number of Teresa's brothers, including Rodrigo—who had presumably outgrown his timidity—made the long and dangerous voyage across the seas, where they would fight for the glory of the faith and be enriched by victory and gold. It must have rankled Teresa when Rodrigo set sail, especially since he cavalierly gave up his future inheritance in her favor so that she could marry well.

Juana Suárez had been alerted and was waiting to welcome her friend. The Encarnación wasn't a sea journey away, just a little beyond the ramparts, with a view to the distant hills. From this quiet retreat, with its sunny cloister and abundant orchard, Teresa's spirit could forge ahead. She, too, gave up her inheritance, turning over Rodrigo's bequest to her little sister Juana. Bowing to the inevitable, Alonso relented and agreed to the customary dowry, providing the convent with an annual supply of grain (or, in a dry season, gold ducats), bedding, books, and gifts for the other nuns. He also furnished fine linens and woolens, the Cepeda family's stock in trade. Teresa herself got two black habits—one of fine serge, the other a little coarser—as well as three underskirts, a sheepskin cloak, veils, underwear, and shoes. After her yearlong novitiate, Doña Teresa (the title *doña*, which she would retain even as a nun, was a nod to her social standing) would be given a suite of her own on two levels, with a connecting staircase, guest room, and private oratory.

The rest should have been easy, or at least predictable. Doña Teresa should have prayed long and earnestly, worked at humbling menial tasks—mopping the floors, sweeping the rooms—and taken her recreation, which for a nun in her position was not infrequent, with her sisters in religion. In fact, all the signs, when she entered the convent, were good. "God turned the dryness in my soul into a very great tenderness," she writes. "Everything about the religious life delighted me, and the truth is that sometimes when I was sweeping the floor at a time of day when I used to be busy indulging and adorning myself, and realized that I was now free from all that, I felt a thrill, which surprised me because I couldn't understand where it came from."

On the other hand, she suffered. Her illness, first experienced at Santa María de Gracia, came back in force. This time she offers an explanation: "The change in my life and diet endangered my health, so that even though I was quite happy, that wasn't enough. I began to faint more often, and the pain in my heart grew so intense that it scared everyone around me."

It was a curious statement: happiness *no bastó*, it wasn't enough. As she confessed in the first sentence of her *Vida*, having virtuous parents hadn't been enough to make her good. (It would have been, "if I hadn't been so wicked.") She hadn't loved God enough to assuage the pain of leaving her family. Now, apparently, she didn't love Him enough to deserve his favor. Such compunctions suggest that Teresa's conception of *honra* had a broader base, even at that early point in her life, than concern about her reputation. Her *honra* hinged, as it did in later years, on the dynamic of her relationship with God.

Because she considered herself such a hard case, Teresa felt she deserved her maladies, and she did what she could to increase her suffering. And the means were available to her in a culture that made a virtue of self-punishment. A wealthy man might put on a *cilicio*—a painful hair shirt—beneath the fine linen one his wife had woven for his pleasure. Penitents marching in religious processions, or kneeling in their private oratories, might keep a supply of scourges with which to flog themselves, often severely. (Teresa kept her *disciplina* with her even when she traveled.) The question was not whether to castigate oneself, but how and how much to do it. Extravagant penance could be a sign of pride.

Displaying her usual *determinación*, Teresa not only flogged herself but—as witnesses later testified at her canonization proceedings—she wore her *cilicio* and tied nettles to her wrists. Even then, she felt it wasn't enough. Once when it was her turn to care for a nun who was so ill that she "had open sores on her stomach . . . through which she voided everything she ate," Teresa wasn't at all disgusted. On the contrary, "I envied her patience, and asked God if He could give me some—and then send me whatever sickness would let me be of service to Him." (Her response was more moderate on this occasion than that of Saint Catherine of Siena, who forced herself to drink the pus of the invalid she was nursing.) Within two years Teresa's prayers were answered: "Though my illness wasn't the same as hers, I don't think it was any less painful or hard to suffer through."

The young nun rapidly declined, and when conventional remedies (bleeding, poultices, scorpion oil) failed, the convent agreed with Alonso to try a more radical approach. The alternative medicine of the 1530s was practiced by a *curandera,* or healer—a woman who administered her herbal remedies via an often grueling regimen of purges. Such a woman practiced in a small country town called Becedas, not far from Castellanos de la Cañada, where María lived. And so, for the second time in as many years, Teresa's bags were packed.

It was now winter; it was almost always winter in Castile, except in summer, which was as brutal as it was brief. *Nueve meses de invierno y tres de infierno*—nine months of winter and three of hell—was an accurate forecast. The harshness of the climate, bright sun pounding on dry, rocky soil, was said to make flinty characters and to inspire the greatest extremes of emotion. Teresa seemed proof of that. Travel in winter being difficult, it was deemed wise for her to stay for a month or so at María's. Again she stopped off at Hortigosa, and this time dived headlong into Uncle Pedro's library. She began to read *El tercer abecedario* (*The Third Spiritual Alphabet*) by Francisco de Osuna, a Franciscan mystical writer. This was a highly readable workbook for those who wanted to learn how to pray, with an eye to achieving what Osuna called *recogimiento,* or recollection. That might be described as a state of spiritual composure: the intellect and senses working in harmony to block out the world and respond to God's love. Osuna's homespun prose got at the gist of Teresa's problem: "The fisherman, intent on the little float on his line to notice when fish bite, worries about his business, thinking only of the fish he has already caught or is about to catch. I do not think that anyone can find God, regardless of the road he follows, unless he has this determination and anxious concern. It is not the road that matters, only that we single-mindedly set out for God."

The itinerant young Teresa, armed with just such *determinación* and anxious concern, couldn't put the book down. Finally Uncle Pedro made a gift of it, and tucking it under her arm, she traveled on to María's, where virtually nothing was likely to distract her. "I began to spend time alone," she writes, "to confess often, and to start on the road of prayer, with this book as my guide. Because I found no other guide—I mean, no confessor who understood me—though I kept looking for one for twenty years."

Teresa couldn't have picked a better time to take up this kind of reading: Spain was just then awash with how-to books on inner spirituality, the result of changes occurring both at home and abroad. By the late 1530s, as the reforms of Luther and Calvin were sweeping across Europe, the Spanish church—following the lead of the militantly pious Charles V—was energetically trying to reform itself. Abuses were rampant: members of the clergy had enriched themselves through benefices and real estate (which was exempt from taxes) and were living like grandees. Some monks and nuns, free to come and go from their monasteries, were behaving scandalously. Like Ferdinand and Isabella before him, the emperor longed for the days when the clergy's interests had been strictly spiritual, and he tried to legislate a return by the religious orders to the more austere practices of the early church. Lay Catholics and devout religious, caught up in the momentum of reform and eager to enhance their own spirituality, were now embracing the vogue of private, interior devotion, taking their cues from the *Enchiridion,* or *Manual of a Christian Knight,* by the Dutch humanist Desiderius Erasmus. This book, even more popular in Spain than in the rest of Europe, would be censored later on when the Inquisition thought it detected links with Protestant theology; but for now, Spanish Catholics eagerly absorbed Erasmus's thoughts on "mental" prayer—a refreshing change from the more public, less reflective "vocal" prayer long sanctioned by Rome.

The demand for mystical treatises to guide the novice on his or her individual path toward God was insatiable: Osuna's *Tercer abecedario* was a favorite; so were Alonso de Madrid's *Arte para servir a Dios* (*The Art of Serving God*) and Bernardino de Laredo's *Subida del Monte Sión* (*The Ascent of Mount Zion*), both of which Teresa read. Additional guidance was sought from *beatas,* or holy women, like Mari Díaz of Avila, and from holy men like the Franciscan ascetic Pedro de Alcántara, who were consulted by peasants and aristocrats alike. The courtly Ignatius Loyola, laid up after being wounded in battle, began reading the lives of the saints and other religious texts, which transformed him into a Christian soldier. He renounced his previous life and wrote his wildly popular *Spiritual Exercises*. Francisco de Borja, the duke of Gandia, gave up family wealth and influence to join the Jesuit order after viewing Empress Isabella's horribly decayed body from her funeral cortege. As so often happened, thoughts of death led to a rude spiritual awakening.

The idea of an intimate relationship between the soul and God was not alien to Spain, where *iluminismo*, defined as interior enlightenment, was a long-established tradition. In Castile, groups of *alumbrados*, or enlightened ones, rejected empty devotional practices in favor of more personal approaches to prayer. But some ecstatic visionaries were taking spiritual experience to new extremes. Refusing to settle for anything less than customized instruction from God, they were increasingly viewed as a threat to the established church. What was more (as the Inquisition began to notice with satisfaction), many of these visionaries were *conversos*, the very people who were under suspicion of heresy in the first place. They were also—in disproportionate numbers—women, who fainted away as raptures swept them literally off their feet. Since everyone agreed that women had no intelligence and that *conversos* had no *honra*, observers assumed that these raptures were the devil's work. The inquisitors knew what to do next.

Teresa was exactly right to seek out a guide to prayer. It was dangerous not to. And she had no desire at all to stray from her church's teachings, only to grasp them better and use them to get closer to God. Prayer wasn't a straight road up; it was usually a winding path, full of detours and obstacles. A person should not (as one branch of the *alumbrados* did) practice a form of meditation called *dejamiento*, a kind of blissful abandon. What that led to was a belief that nothing the person did was a sin, because God was a silent partner. *Recogimiento*, which Osuna recommended and the church sanctioned (for the time being), was more active and perhaps more suited to a woman with a surplus of mental energy. What Osuna taught, and Teresa learned with alacrity, was something that might be defined as spiritual fitness: a kind of alert praying, a limbering up and bracing of the faculties to weather God's onslaught of love.

Teresa went to Becedas for her cure in the spring of 1539 with a sense of her own heightened prowess. Reading Osuna, she had somewhat prematurely experienced the prayer of quiet, a state of outward serenity and interior activity—and even, she thought, the prayer of union, a sense of oneness with God that is usually reserved for advanced contemplatives. Bolstered by such apparent successes, she was impatient (as she was throughout her life) to find a confessor who understood her and could help her advance even further. "I have always been attracted by learning," she writes in the *Vida* as she looks back on this period from middle age, "though half-educated confessors have done a great deal of harm to my soul." She didn't suffer fools gladly. In fact, she writes with some irritability in her *Vida*, even after years of experience, she'd rather confess to good men who know nothing than to those who know just a little. "Because then they don't trust themselves, and I'm not likely to trust them."

The ill young woman arrived in Becedas with every spiritual ambition intact. She may have had some sense of herself as an attractive invalid—being famously "particular" about cleanliness and orderliness, she wouldn't have arrived in disarray. So she must have presented an alluring image to the man she chose as her confessor, a village priest named Pedro Hernández, who was not as scholarly as he seemed and was in need of some confessing himself. He told Teresa he was having an affair with a woman in the town, and what's more, everyone knew about it. He was ashamed; he was enchanted, literally, by the copper amulet the woman made him wear. The devil had seduced him, yet he was still saying Mass. He had lost his *honra*, and now he was risking his soul.

Teresa felt sorry for him. He was probably the first man who had begged for her counsel, and she was flattered. She had always loved to be admired. "I felt very sorry for him, because I liked him quite a lot; and I was so worldly and blind that I considered myself virtuous for being grateful and loyal to anyone who cared about me." It was an impulse she would fight later on: to cling to human friendships when God's friendship was all she needed. But for now she was content to be indignant with the woman who had bewitched her poor priest ("to satisfy her needs and the passion the devil incites in her, a woman will stop at nothing"). Teresa recounts how her own virtuous example convinced the fellow to relinquish his amulet (there was the dramatic gesture of throwing it into the river), after which he seemed to awaken from a long sleep. He gave the temptress up and became a new man just in time, as it turned out; he died the following year.

The town of Becedas must have been dazzled. Of course the priest would have advertised his miraculous redemption. And the young visitor from the city must have been lionized, which could not have been a humbling experience. A nun who had come so far so fast, who was pretty and wan and had rescued a lost soul, might have returned home in glory, trailing a reputation for piety and good sense. She might have succumbed to her own charms and spent her life advising wealthy but indiscreet men and women to mend their ways. And she might have been forgotten—if only she hadn't become so ill.

The *curandera* was sapping Teresa's strength with concoctions that made her vomit uncontrollably, and she was soon in a desperate state. Even though she makes a point throughout the *Vida* of saying how bad her memory is, and even though she forgets to mention details at times and circles back to them later, her illness is one subject on which she has perfect clarity:

> The medicines were so potent that after two months I was half dead, and the terrible pain in my heart, which I was there to be cured of, was much worse, so that I sometimes felt as if sharp teeth were gripping it—I was afraid I was going mad. I had no strength—the idea of eating repelled me, all I could do was drink a little—and I was always feverish, and wasted, because for nearly a month they had been purging me every day. My nerves were so shrivelled that they started to contract, which hurt so unbearably that I couldn't get any rest, day or night: utter misery.

Teresa went home, where she was surrounded by frantic doctors and relatives. Her pain was constant, and no one could diagnose it or give her any relief. The doctors conferred and quarreled and finally agreed that she was consumptive. Teresa says that didn't worry her. From a spiritual point of view, the only thing that mattered was how she endured her agony and how she used it to focus her thoughts on God.

She was more than ever inclined to pray. "All my conversation," she writes, "was with God." She was surprised at how patiently she could suffer—reading the Book of Job had helped. But she wanted to confess: there were offenses she had committed, things her confessors considered trivial, but she did not. She had to account for them. But her father, thinking how intense and potentially debilitating an experience confession would be for his daughter, refused to let her.

The result was disastrous. On the night of his refusal she became cataleptic and remained in that state for over four days. Almost everyone thought she was dying, and the nuns at the Encarnación prepared her grave. They kept her coffin open and ready. Thinking her dead, they wrapped her in a shroud and even sealed her eyelids with wax in preparation for her final journey. Alonso was plaintive: *"Esta hija no es para enterrar,"* he kept repeating, "This daughter is not for burying."

Suddenly on the fourth day she opened her eyes (caked as they were with wax) and asked again to confess. Alonso agreed—eagerly, one must suppose. At this point in one of Teresa's chivalric romances, the heroine might have shaken off her fever and been miraculously restored to health. But Teresa was physically wrecked. In the *Vida* she describes her illness's aftermath in the minutest detail. Realist that she was, she would never have dreamed of shying away from the memory of her own ravaged flesh: "My tongue was bitten to pieces; since I was so weak and hadn't eaten, not even water would go down my throat. My bones felt as if they had been dislocated, and my brain was totally confused. I was twisted up in a knot from all those days of torture, and couldn't move my arm, foot, hand, or head, any more than if I had been a corpse. I think that all I could move was one finger of my right hand."

If God is in the details, then these must be filled with divine instruction. Teresa seems to be most interested here in showing how she kept her faith despite her torment and even continued to enjoy the practice of prayer. At first her body couldn't be touched, the pain was so excruciating—she had to be lifted in a sheet. But when things got a little better, she was ready to return to the convent, where "instead of the corpse they were expecting they received a living soul, but a body that was worse than dead, so that it was painful to look at. . . . I was nothing but bones."

Under the circumstances, it is reasonable to wonder how Teresa's intense and conflicted religiosity might have affected her health. Long after she emerged from this crisis, she was plagued by illness, and (as one of the many doctors who considered her case pointed out) its etiology was complex beyond belief. She had too many symptoms for any single disease. In the course of her surprisingly long life, she repeatedly experienced fevers, chest pain, jaw and tooth pain, backaches, noises and throbbing in her head, palsy and paralysis, attacks of nerves and nausea. For fear that the nausea would keep her from receiving Communion, she induced vomiting regularly, with the help of an olive twig—a strategy (not uncommon among religious women) that historian Rudolph M. Bell describes as "holy anorexia." Physicians who examined Teresa suspected heart disease, consumption, malaria, and a laundry list of other ailments. Given the perspective of time and no hope of examining the patient, physicians over the next several centuries diagnosed everything from cerebral meningitis to hysterical epilepsy. With the dawn of the modern era came the conviction, at least among practitioners of the budding science of psychoanalysis, that her misery was self-induced. Breuer's famous description of her as the "patron saint of hysteria" was less an original opinion than a witty reiteration of a received idea.

After years of defensive diagnoses from those who feared for Teresa's sanctity, her most assiduous twentieth-century biographers, Efrén de la Madre de Dios, O.C.D., and Otger Steggink, O. Carm., asked some doctors to review the medical evidence (such as it was). On the basis of their opinions, the two Carmelites decided that the saint's maladies were, for the most part, psychosomatic. Because her three-year paralysis didn't cause any muscular degeneration, that condition seemed most likely to have been triggered by neurosis. Then again, the Becedas "cure" might have done some real somatic damage. The sensation of her bones and nerves being pulled apart, for example, could have been caused by severe dehydration. Teresa might also have had a thyroid problem and, at the end of her life, metastasized uterine cancer, as evidenced by her constant back pain and by the blood found on her sheets after she died.

It must have seemed plausible to these Carmelite scholars that spirituality can coexist with neurosis, as can intellectual clarity, business acumen, and common sense. Even Breuer had to admit that the neurotic Saint Teresa was also "a woman of genius with great practical capacity." One of her admirers went further, suggesting that whatever its origins (he leaned toward hysterical epilepsy), her suffering was most importantly "a painful stimulant, not unlike the grain of sand which is introduced into the oyster and becomes the cause and center of a pearl." Teresa might have argued the point. She thanked God for her illness, but only because she welcomed trials. In fact, the busier she became, the more her infirmities got in her way. "I always thought I could serve God much better if I recovered," she wrote, though with some qualms about second-guessing his divine plan for her. She resolved to function brilliantly in God's service, illness or no illness— as she did for over four decades. From her perspective, good health was as rare and wonderful as a balmy day in Castile.

Chapter 3: *Discoveries*

—

It was eight months before Teresa could move (she still had only the use of her little finger) and three years before she could crawl. In spiritual terms it was opportunity. She tried to take advantage of it, praying and confessing as often as she could. She did miss her solitude (there was no chance of being able to pray alone in the infirmary), but as she was always surrounded by other nuns, she began to talk about God "in a way that edified the other sisters," who were amazed at how patient and wise their invalid had become. She made rules for herself—to avoid gossip, for example—and, as always, people imitated her: unusual behavior in a convent that had aways been a beehive of intrigue.

Into this serene environment came doubt, as usual. Teresa felt like a fraud: as far as she could tell, she was no less wretched than she had ever been. She had the leisure (if it can be called that) to pick apart her life and find the twisted threads that ruined its fabric. But she couldn't repair it. As her health began to improve, her spiritual malaise intensified. She felt inept at prayer. In effect, she had replaced one form of paralysis with another. "So I began to go from distraction to distraction, from vanity to vanity, from one occasion of sin to the next, letting my soul be corrupted by so many vanities that I was ashamed to turn to God, in that intimate friendship that comes with prayer." She did turn to Saint Joseph—San José—who was much revered in Spain at the time, for help in this crisis, but even her veneration of him was flawed. She marked his feast day at the convent by funding a lavish celebration, and displayed "more vanity than spirituality, I was so eager to make a brilliant impression."

Instead of courting solitude, the attractive convalescent began to receive socially prominent visitors behind the parlor grille. These people came to see her out of curiosity and were soon enchanted by what biographer Louis Bertrand calls her "pure *coquetry* of humility." The Encarnación became a salon. Teresa was far more comfortable now discussing the art of prayer than she was trying to master it, and her conversation was *graciosa,* filled with a merry shrewdness that is the Spanish equivalent of *esprit.* She had read all the latest books and could discuss them comfortably. She had a gift for listening, so visitors vied for her attention, and even the other nuns enjoyed her knack for tailoring her interests to their needs. Wealthy widows in need of consolation invited her home to freshen their souls.

In those days *galanteos de monjas,* flirtations with nuns by devoted (though not necessarily devout) suitors, often occurred at convents like this one, where the nuns were not strictly enclosed. Teresa disapproved of those sisters who arranged nocturnal conversations with their admirers "through the chinks" of the convent walls. She wished these women's parents had placed them in houses that would watch over them more carefully. Her own behavior seemed at first glance to be beyond reproach. Thanks to her charismatic presence, the Encarnación was gaining attention and, as a result, much-needed funding. But during her hours in the parlor, Teresa began to have all-too-pleasant "conversations" with someone who, for reasons she will only hint at, was so dangerous to her *honra* that during one visit Christ showed up and glowered at her. His meaning was unmistakable. "I saw Him more clearly with the eyes of the soul than I could ever have seen Him with the eyes of the body," she writes. She didn't understand at the time that this was what theologians called an "imaginative" vision—not because it was unreal, but because it had a kind of physicality that "intellectual" visions, those that allow a perception of God not connected to any image, did not. She stopped receiving her caller for a while, but then the devil (who was always lurking, as in morality plays) made light of the incident. So did the other nuns, who thought that Teresa's fashionable visitor could only enhance her reputation. Teresa, for her part, may have taken pleasure in counseling a man who, like her poor bewitched priest in Becedas, might be made less sinful through her care. Apparently, though, this was not happening, because one day a huge and hideous toad, or something that looked like one, hopped through the room (she says even her visitor saw it), and though Teresa understood this to be a second warning, she ignored it too.

So things went on for years. Teresa continued to observe herself with a ruthless eye and found that she had become not only sinful but (even more surprisingly) ordinary. She was behaving like almost everyone else. Meanwhile, her father, Alonso, who visited her from time to time at the convent, had plunged headlong into religion. He was probably already suffering from the debilitating illness that would kill him. Teresa couldn't bring herself to lie to him about her spiritual progress, so she explained that she had been too ill to pray. Alonso felt sorry for her, though not so much that he was about to waste his time commiserating through the grille. He was a man of business, and now his only business was to save his soul.

After her father died ("like an angel"), Teresa was caught up in the worldliest of pursuits—settling his heavily indebted estate. (He had made some unwise real estate deals that almost decimated the family's wealth.) Whether or not he appreciated Teresa's talent for prayer, Alonso had correctly assessed her talent for administration and made her one of his executors. She had her brothers to deal with and her coexecutor, Martín de Guzmán, her sister María's husband, who made aggressive claims on his wife's behalf, even though Teresa had inveigled two of her brothers into throwing their bequests María's way. In spite of her efforts, the case went to court, where lawyers consumed most of what was left of Alonso's estate. Her immersion in the byzantine legal system of Castile can't have enhanced Teresa's appreciation for nonmonastic life, but it gave her expertise that would be valuable later on.

With the estate finally settled, Teresa had her own badly neglected spiritual claims to attend to. Death had served its usual function of bringing the living up short. She turned to her father's confessor, a Dominican called Vicente Barrón, who told her what she already knew: that her soul hung in the balance. He urged her to pray, and since all she had ever really wanted was this kind of unambiguous direction, she began to try again.

The more she prayed, the more she understood her faults. The trouble was that she was at cross-purposes with herself. "Everything that had to do with God gave me tremendous pleasure; but the things of the world captivated me." She couldn't relinquish prayer (and never again would), but she also refused to deprive her senses, "and so I couldn't shut myself within myself (which was my whole way of proceeding in prayer) without shutting a thousand vanities in with me." In spiritual as well as in domestic life, a

Castilian woman was supposed to crave enclosure, a private and protected space. But Teresa's nature was too expansive; it kept pulling her out into the world. What was worse, considering this obvious failure, was that God kept rewarding her efforts. As she reminds Him in one of the many swift prayers that underpin the *Vida,* "You punished me with the most subtle and painful punishment, since You knew very well what would hurt me the most: You punished my sins with great favors." The worse she behaved, the better God seemed to like her. She tried to deserve this approval, only to slip back into her usual ways. Every failure increased her anxiety.

"I spent almost twenty years on this stormy sea, falling and rising, then falling again." She remembers the worst times; the best ones (including a whole year in which she managed to avoid worldly distractions) are much less vivid to her. For the purposes of her *Vida,* which is meant to be a meticulous account of her spiritual progress, she calculates that she spent eighteen of the twenty-eight years since she first began to pray bobbing between the world's attractions and God's. She considers this a terrible record but also reasons that it might be the very thing to help those who are struggling with prayer: if God will stick with someone like her, He will stick with anyone.

The line that Teresa walks when she remembers her sins and God's mercies is a very thin and difficult one. What her reader may see is an engaging, intelligent, and reasonably devout woman with a healthy appetite for life. But she asks the reader to see that woman differently: as a confused and preening sensualist who is taking her first steps toward hell. Throughout the *Vida,* Teresa disparages herself as a *mujercilla,* a worthless little woman. As she puts it, "Just the thought that I am a woman is enough to make my wings fall off—how much worse, the thought that I'm a *wicked* woman!" Modern readers have wondered if Teresa really saw herself that way, or if she was presenting an image of herself—inferior, weak, womanly—that the men who would examine her life through her *Vida* could recognize and finally forgive. Teresa did live at a time when women who seemed spiritually independent and self-confident could be viewed as potentially heretical, so she could well have been spoon-feeding her readers a palatable version of herself. But in her most private moments, when she was face to face with God and her own exacting judgment, she also saw, sometimes with blinding clarity, the difference between the woman she was and the woman God needed her to be. She knew that she was prone to temptation and often succumbed to it, and yet the world admired her. So when she insisted on her failings, she was reminding her readers—as well as reminding Teresa the nun, who always needed reminding—that appearances deceived.

It was essential for her to be *desengañada,* disillusioned—not in the sense of being deprived of hopes and dreams, but of having her illusions brushed away so that she could see the truth. The soul, as Fray Luis de León wrote in his introduction to her works, needed to be *"desengañada de lo que la falsa imaginación le ofrecía"*—stripped of its fantasies. Teresa admitted her strengths, notably her courage ("it's obvious that God has given me more than a woman's share of it"), but she also worried that she might be prone to illusions sent expressly by the devil, who relished women in particular as his prey. The devil had been very busy in Spain lately, and Teresa was frankly afraid. An abbess from Córdoba named Magdalena de la Cruz had been taken in and had taken in many others, including the queen herself. Having confessed that her ecstasies were faked and that she had made a pact with the devil, Magdalena had been convicted by the Inquisition. That was enough to make anyone take precautions. Teresa began recruiting *letrados,* learned men, as her confessors (Osuna had strongly recommended this), roping them in like steers whether they wanted to help her or not. Only men could get enough education in that society to distinguish truths from lies, and Teresa craved the advantage of their insight. In her view a woman had no more business venturing out alone on the road to God than she had leaving her house without an escort—which was not to say she couldn't leave. Who led on this adventurous highway and who followed was another matter. Teresa's ability to get what she needed from men would serve her well in her later career as a founder, and it was essential to her spiritual life as well.

In 1554, when she was almost forty years old and had spent half of her life fighting her own worst impulses, Teresa finally experienced some relief. She had gone into an oratory, where someone had left a very moving image of the wounded Christ. It was as if she had never seen such a thing before. Suddenly she was on the floor in "a great flood of tears," and by the time she got up again, she felt more at peace than she had felt in decades, and was sure that God had infused her with strength. This was a classic conversion experience, like the one she had encountered in her reading of Saint Augustine's *Confessions,* newly translated into Spanish; Teresa had been one of the first to read it. She couldn't help but identify with the flagrantly sinful young man who confessed so furiously and well. She felt that God was with her despite her imperfections, "that He was within me, or that I was totally engulfed in Him." This wasn't a vision, she assures her readers, who are likely to distrust such experiences, especially when women have them: "I believe it is called mystical theology," she writes with some ingenuousness. "The soul is suspended in such a way that it seems completely outside itself."

Before this, Teresa had tried to feel the presence of God by mentally summoning up images: Christ in the garden of Gethsemane was a good one. She found that books, which had always been a great source of comfort, helped her focus her thoughts. When she didn't have books, she could meditate on fields, water, or flowers, which "made me alert and recollected, and served as a book." But this new way of praying was different, much less strenuous. The mind wasn't "working" at all. Teresa's description of the process is notable for its tortuous phrasing and careful hesitations: "The will loves; the memory, it seems to me, is almost lost; and the intellect, I think, stops functioning, though it isn't lost—what I mean is that it doesn't work, but seems to be astonished at all the things it understands, because God wants it to realize that it understands nothing about what He is showing it." Which is to say, the mind understands that it understands nothing at all, and that is the beginning of true humility—a tricky proposition.

Teresa has a lot to say about humility, which does not come very easily to her. On the one hand, the human soul is small and wretched, and can do nothing under its own steam—God is the only mover. No amount of fasting or self-flagellation or praying through the night will change that. On the other hand, there is the danger of false humility. The devil tries to entrap the soul whenever possible, "making it seem as if pride is instilling such strong desires to be like the saints and crave martyrdom." But (as every Castilian knows) small efforts bring small rewards. God is "the friend of courageous souls, as long as they behave humbly, not trusting themselves at all." Humbly but energetically: the person who proceeds too cautiously on the road to prayer ("at the pace of a hen") can hardly expect to make rapid progress. "That's no way to achieve freedom of spirit. . . . I tried it myself, and would still be at it today if the good Lord hadn't shown me a shortcut."

Like most shortcuts, it is an unexpected but logical discovery. All the soul has to do is reach with all its might toward God. Whatever happens next, which can be anything from an onrush of mystical rapture to years of aridity in prayer, is up to God. The soul's responsibility is to keep pressing toward its destination and to accept what comes (or doesn't, though Teresa believes it will). That is where courage and humility unite.

During most of this early period, Teresa had to wrestle alone with the nuances of prayer, though she cast around frantically for advice. The devil had deluded her once with the notion that she should quit praying until she was free from sin. ("Oh, what a wrong road this hope led me down! The devil would have held it out to me until Judgment Day, then carried me off to hell!") But after Padre Barrón frightened her into praying again, she was even more confused. God had begun to grant her favors, even though she didn't deserve them—or did she? "This is the trick the devil plays. When a soul sees that it is close to God, and recognizes the difference between the good things in heaven and what is available on earth, and how much love the Lord is showing it, that love brings a confident, secure feeling that the soul cannot fall away from what it enjoys. . . . With this confidence the devil robs it of the ability to think less of itself."

The confessors at the Encarnación had trouble following all this, but Teresa had heard about one man who she thought might be able to help her: a fiery preacher named Gaspar Daza, who had become a local celebrity by traveling great distances to save the souls of rural peasants. Teresa arranged to meet him with the help of Francisco de Salcedo, a wealthy and pious family friend. Salcedo, who was known about town as the *caballero santo* for his holiness (even though, as Teresa remarks, and frequently, he was married), was worried that she might be diabolically deceived. He convinced the overextended Daza to take her on.

Daza seems to have done so with a vengeance. "I told him about my soul and my prayers," Teresa writes, "but he wouldn't hear my confession. He said he was very busy, and so he was." Hearing her confession, at this point, would have required hours of sifting through Teresa's minute analysis of her motives and influences, as in: "The delight and sweetness that I felt was so great, that often I didn't have the strength to resist it. On the other hand I was sure that this came from God, especially when I was praying. . . . But as soon as I was a bit distracted, I went back to feeling afraid, and wondering if the devil might be suspending my understanding, making me think that this was a good thing."

Daza didn't have time to hear it. In effect, he told her to shape up, which was hardly the kind of discreet and subtle direction she was hoping for. She writes that he was treating her as if she had the strength to do what he wanted, whereas she was just a lucky beginner in prayer. Teresa doesn't presume to criticize him directly, so she explains that she *would* have been able to meet his expectations if only she had been better than she was. But Daza was so critical about those *cosillas,* those "little things" that she did in spite of herself, that she was deeply upset. "I'm sure that if I hadn't spoken with anyone but him, my soul would never, I believe, have improved. . . . I'm sometimes amazed that, as a person with a special gift for leading souls toward God, he wasn't given an understanding of my soul, or a desire to take command of it."

The *caballero santo* had to do his best to comfort the anxious nun, and he asked her to tell him exactly what was happening to her when she prayed. She couldn't express it, so she underlined a passage in Bernardino de Laredo's *Subida del Monte Sión* that exactly mirrored her most intense experience, the one in which she felt as if she had achieved the prayer of union, or oneness with God. No exercise of logic could make this seem a likely event; she had not paid her spiritual dues. Salcedo consulted with Daza, and the two decided that Teresa really must be suffering delusions. It was the devil's work after all. She needed more help than they could give her. Luckily, a Jesuit college—that is, a residence where young men were prepared for future membership in the Society of Jesus—had opened nearby at San Gil; Teresa had had her eye on it even before she consulted Salcedo. She knew that among the Jesuits she was bound to find a *letrado,* a learned man who could read her soul.

Diego de Cetina was the first. After him would come an army of others, most often Jesuits, but also Dominicans and even a Carmelite here and there. Those who understood her tried to direct her. Those who were frightened by her unconventional experiences in prayer tried to change her course, but that turned out to be difficult—not because Teresa wanted to disobey them, but because, as she often pointed out, God was directing her as well.

After an initial outburst of tears over Salcedo and Daza's verdict, which made her fear for her soul, she composed herself with the thought that God would never abandon such a faithful friend. She started writing an account (now lost) of her spiritual condition, and that depressed her because she couldn't think of much to say that was good. She began focusing more and more on prayer and withdrawing from her usual activities; but the more she turned inward, the more uncomfortable convent life became—especially when, despite her efforts to be discreet, the other nuns found out that she was arranging to see a Jesuit confessor. They said she wanted to be a saint, even though she wasn't much of a nun, and that others were much holier than she was. In all humility Teresa had to agree with them. But as she struggled with the riddle that a wretch like her was being favored by God, she heard his voice—not, as she says, with her ears, but somewhere within her—saying, "Do not look too deeply into this, but serve Me." It was the first of many experiences called locutions; they would be less surprising later on.

Teresa's confessor was encouraging. He told her that she didn't know much about prayer, but that God was obviously helping her along. Maybe He meant to use her to help others. So it was important for her to pray regularly, beginning each time with a meditation on an incident of Christ's Passion, and to practice self-mortification. (At this point, she says, she hardly knew the meaning of the word.) She should resist God's favors, by violent means if necessary, while she enhanced her skills. "How wonderful it is to understand a soul!" Teresa writes, voicing her relief at finding such an insightful confessor. Diego de Cetina was young, and not especially brilliant, but Teresa had little basis for comparison. The only thing that puzzled her about his direction was that when she criticized certain bad habits, he "seemed to treat the whole matter very lightly." Naturally, this motivated her to change her behavior. She renounced distractions and practiced every kind of penance her confessor prescribed for her, even some that she found unappealing. The more she resisted God's gifts, "the more the Lord enveloped me in that sweetness and glory, so that it seemed to me I was completely surrounded by it, and couldn't escape it."

Discoveries

Things were going well, at least from Teresa's point of view, when the influential Jesuit (and future saint) Francisco de Borja came to town. He was soon introduced to Teresa, who was glad as usual to bare her soul to an intelligent man. Borja had experienced some divine favors himself, and was inclined to agree with Cetina except on one matter: he thought that Teresa had resisted God's favors long enough. Everyone was relieved. Coincidentally or not, following Borja's arrival, Cetina was transferred from town. Teresa was stricken. She was afraid she would return to her old ways. "It was as if my soul was left in a desert, fearful and depressed; I didn't know what would become of me." She was also in an awkward position at the Encarnación: having had one Jesuit confessor and not having been assigned another, she would be very conspicuously alone.

Salcedo took her under his wing again and arranged for Teresa to move in temporarily with a well-off widow called Guiomar de Ulloa. Doña Guiomar, whose name Teresa always wrote as Yomar, was devout in a girlishly enthusiastic way. She surrounded herself with holy people, not just the Jesuits of San Gil, but the ascetic Mari Díaz, who at this time was living (as austerely as possible) in Doña Guiomar's lavish household, which was equipped with oratories. In no time Teresa was introduced to her new Jesuit confessor, Juan de Prádanos, who "dealt with me quite skillfully, but gently." She was not a woman who responded well to brutal handling. "Because my soul wasn't strong at all, but very delicate, especially with regard to giving up certain friendships." (The dangerous convent visitor was still a presence in her life.) Prádanos thought she should lay this matter of friendships before God while reciting the hymn "Veni, Creator Spiritus." This strategy appealed to Teresa, who was always looking for direct approaches to God. And she got her answer with characteristic swiftness. Having spent most of the day in prayer, she began to recite the hymn, and "a rapture came over me so suddenly that it almost lifted me out of myself. There was no doubt about it, because it was very obvious. That was the first time the Lord gave me the favor of rapture. I heard these words: 'Now I want you to speak not with men but with angels.' "

That was all she needed to hear. She didn't give up all human friendships—that would have been too literal a response to God's mandate and against her own nature. But there are angels and there are angels. "I have never again been able to commit myself to a friendship, or take any comfort in, or feel a special love, except for people who clearly love and are trying to serve Him," she writes. She began to see friendships as tandem vehicles moving expeditiously toward God.

Juan de Prádanos became ill; Teresa and Yomar nursed him very attentively until at last he recovered and was transferred to Valladolid, a city in northern Castile. Once again the transfer of one of Teresa's confessors coincided with a visit from Francisco de Borja, who may have sensed that Teresa was again on unstable ground. Now she had begun to have ecstasies that whisked her soul away from her body, just like those foolish *alumbrados*. Sooner or later such behavior, especially in a nun, would bring the Inquisition to her door. She needed to disappear, and so was sent to visit her younger sister Juana in the town of Alba de Tormes.

After a month or two away, Teresa returned to the Encarnación, where the mood must have been anticipatory, news of her spiritual escapades traveling faster than she could. The woman who came back was no longer of two minds about the world and God. But inside the convent and out, people were of two minds about her.

Chapter 4: *Gold*

—

It seems only natural, when Teresa describes her spiritual adventures, to place her at the center of a tableau. As she recites the "Veni, Creator," she hears God's voice coursing through her like her life's blood. She is rapt with delight. Her body is still, her eyes close; she listens. At her side, Yomar shivers with excitement while, in the shadows, her confessor observes Teresa carefully and makes a note or two. Outside the doors, Yomar's servants begin to stitch the elaborate brocade of rumor that will envelop Teresa from this time on, wherever she goes.

In fact, Teresa's first experience of the mystical state called rapture, or ecstasy *(arrobamiento)*, may have happened in the privacy of her "cell" at Yomar's house or in one of the oratories. She doesn't say. But it was by its nature a public event of tremendous interest to Avilans searching (as many were) for a human conduit to God. Teresa knew this to be the case. She never wanted to make her raptures public, unlike those *mujercillas* who seemed to be collapsing with religious fervor on every street corner. She thought such displays were ridiculous, coining the word *abobamientos* (*bobo* means fool). But she perceived that God, whatever his reasons, wanted her raptures to be observed, and besides, she couldn't conceal them. Usually she became immobilized, fixed to the spot where she had just been praying or having a conversation. Legend has it that at least once while praying in chapel, she rose about a foot and a half off the ground. Another time, after receiving Communion, she grabbed at the bars of the grille to keep from levitating but went up anyway—an embarrassing interruption of her normal routine.

After she returned to the Encarnación, she was assigned a new confessor from San Gil named Baltasar Alvarez. At this point, no one was permitted to hear her confession who hadn't first been approved by Salcedo and Daza. If the devil were whispering in Teresa's ear, a skilled confessor had to bring that fact to light, questioning his penitent until she revealed more than she knew. The twenty-five-year-old Alvarez took on the assignment, and Teresa was grateful because she *was* fighting the devil, at least hypothetically. She knew the devil could impersonate God and that even devout believers could be deceived. By the time they realized what was happening, it was often too late. The inquisitorial approach would be to presume guilt until innocence was proved, and as a woman of her time, Teresa thought that approach reasonable. Supposing that the devil were speaking, what kinds of things would he say? How would his words make the hearer feel? Could the effects be the same as when God spoke? Teresa examines her experiences with the doggedness of a scientist, analyzing causes and effects. She looks for distinguishing characteristics and often asks the same question several ways, in case there are several answers:

> It sometimes happens that the intellect and the soul are so troubled and distracted that they couldn't put together a coherent sentence, and yet the soul finds itself being served up impressive speeches that it couldn't concoct by itself, even if it were completely recollected—and at the first word, as I said, the soul is thoroughly transformed. If it is in a rapture, especially, and if its faculties are suspended, how can it possibly understand things that have never occurred to it before? How can those things come to it at a time when the memory is hardly functioning, and the imagination is more or less stunned?

Her answer is that when a soul trusts God rather than itself, God makes himself understood. It does no good to resist a divine locution, because it will come anyway, and—an important distinction—it will leave only good effects behind. By contrast, "locutions from the devil not only do no good, but leave bad effects behind. . . . The soul is left feeling a great dryness, and also a certain disquiet. . . . The soul seems to resist, and is upset and tormented without knowing why, because what is said isn't evil, but good." Maybe, she muses, one kind of spirit recognizes another. Still, the devil's gifts can mimic God's, seeming to bring "a sweet, strong, impressive, delightful, and calm refreshment" that is hard to refuse. Clearly it takes a soul with delicate perceptions and vast experience to distinguish the false from the true.

What an inexperienced soul needs most, Teresa explains to the *letrados* reading her book, is backup—a second line of defense. That comes in the form of church doctrine. "I am very sure," she proclaims (no hesitation here), "that the devil will not deceive—God won't permit him to deceive— a soul that doesn't trust itself at all, but is supported by its faith, and is absolutely certain it would die a thousand deaths for any single article of it." This is a crucial statement for her to make because her readers must be convinced that she is not, and never has been, a heretic. In case any authority should miss the point, she hastens to clarify: "And with this love of the faith that God then instills in it, which is a strong, vital love, the soul always tries to conform to the Church's tenets, asking advice from one person and another, like someone who is already so grounded in these truths that no imaginable revelation—even if it saw the heavens open—would cause it to swerve one inch from Church doctrine."

The soul that would adhere to church doctrine "even if it saw the heavens open" would be obedient (some would say to a fault) and therefore protected from sin. By contrast, any soul that even allowed itself to wonder if what it learned—presumably from God—might be right and the church's teachings wrong would be giving the devil an opening. This would be immediately apparent because whenever the devil is involved, "everything good seems to run away and hide from the soul, leaving it peevish and agitated and with no good effects. Because even though it may seem to have good desires, they are weak; and the humility that is left behind is false, troubled, and lacking in gentleness."

Having posited all this, Teresa goes on to the subject of obeying superiors, which can be a sticking point with her. Obedience, as the mystical writer Francisco de Osuna had pointed out in his *Tercer abecedario,* is "the royal way. . . . All the holy desert fathers walked this road." It is essential to rely on a *letrado* and (she emphasizes) "not hide anything from him, so no harm can come—although plenty has come to me because of the excessive fears of some people." As much as Teresa *wishes* she could count on her superiors, she is too much of a realist to pretend that she hasn't sometimes been misled. For example, at one point, five or six "great servants of God" met about her difficult case and decided that she shouldn't take Communion so frequently (like her father, Alonso, they thought the experience got her too worked up—and she did enjoy Communion inordinately), that she should spend less time alone, and that she should find some activities to distract her. They seem to have treated the middle-aged Teresa like an overwrought adolescent. She thought they were condescending, and sensed that they were laughing at her behind closed doors.

"When I spoke to them about my experiences, I thought they were making fun of me, as if it were all my imagination. . . . My confessor constantly comforted me, even though he was on their side." Teresa persisted in liking Alvarez, who had only been testing her—or so he would give her to understand after he came around to her way of thinking. In the meantime, he told her that the devil couldn't hurt her if she trusted God, but she was still distressed, as much by her apparent lack of humility as by the terrifying idea that all her experiences might be illusory.

She was trying hard to be obedient. This meant being extremely flexible, since "It always happened that when the Lord ordered me to do one thing during prayer, and then the confessor gave me a different order, that very same Lord would come back and tell me to obey the confessor. Then His Majesty would bring the man around to giving the same order as His." She diligently prayed, as Alvarez instructed her, to be led heavenward by a less dubious path than her current one, so lush with mystical graces. Her locutions were now occurring frequently, yet the way she was going felt right. "I saw that this road led to heaven, and that I had been on the way to hell. I couldn't make myself want to take a different path, or believe that the devil was tricking me—even though I did everything I could to want the first and to believe the second. But it was out of my hands."

Again she was experiencing what she called "heart trouble," and she suffered almost continuously, from physical as much as from spiritual distress. She had almost exhausted her resources when she heard God say, " 'Don't be afraid, daughter. I am here, and I will not abandon you.' " Her confidence flooded back. She thought about God's power—how He could quiet an angry sea in a minute—and saw how ridiculous her fears had been. "What have I been thinking of?" she asked herself. "What am I afraid of?" Even if there were devils, how much power could they possibly have against such an opponent? "I took a cross in my hand, and God really seemed to give me courage, because in a little while I found myself so changed that I wouldn't have been afraid to wrestle with devils—it seemed

I could easily beat them all down with that cross, and so I said, 'Okay, come on, all of you. I'm a servant of the Lord—let's see what you can do to me.' "

She never did have to fight off a legion of devils, though she often had to ignore them. The truth is that Teresa's devils frightened her superiors more than they did her. The confessor who instructed her to snap her fingers or spit when she had a vision (even if she was sure the approach was from God) was much more insecure than Teresa was. "How these devils frighten us," she writes, "because we're asking to be frightened, through our attachment to honors, property, pleasures." She continues, "I don't understand these fears. We exclaim: 'The devil! The devil!', when we could be exclaiming: 'God! God!' and making the devil tremble. Oh yes—because we already know that he can't move a muscle without the Lord's go-ahead." If God is powerful and good, there's no doubt He will protect those who depend on Him. This isn't revelation but common sense. "What's going on here?" she writes with astonishment at the general misconception. "Without a doubt, I'm more afraid of those who are so scared of the devil than I am of the devil himself." And rightly so.

In 1559 Fernando de Valdés, the Inquisitor General of Spain and a fervent champion of conformity, published an Index of banned books that included almost every spiritual treatise published in Spanish and most of Teresa's favorites, including Osuna's *Tercer abecedario*. Even Francisco de Borja's *Obras del cristiano* was on Valdés's list. Teresa was crushed; for a forty-four-year-old woman who drank in books with enormous pleasure, depending on them to focus her thoughts on prayer when everything else failed, such deprivation was hard to accept. But then she understood God to say to her, " 'Do not be upset, because I will give you a living book.' " The meaning of this locution became clear some time later, when she saw Christ at her side, "or, to put it better, I was conscious of Him, because I saw nothing with the eyes of the body or the eyes of the soul." She just knew Christ was near. He stayed at her right hand, watching her. It was a complete surprise, she says, because being so ignorant, she had no idea that such visions were possible. It seemed wise to go straight to Baltasar Alvarez, who did his best to cope with this latest challenge: "He asked me in what form I had seen Him, and I answered that I had not seen Him. He asked me how I knew it was Christ, and I answered that I didn't know how, but that I couldn't help being aware of Him being beside me, that I had plainly seen and felt it, and that when I prayed my soul was now much more deeply and consistently recollected."

This kind of vision, she later found out, was rare and, from the devil's point of view, inimitable. So, of course it is hard for her, an untutored woman, to describe it ("men of learning will explain it better"). All she can do is make comparisons. Teresa sometimes seems like a resourceful translator, conveying thoughts for which her own language has no words:

> If a person claims to be like someone who is in the dark, unable to see the person right next to her; or if the person claims to be like someone who is blind, that's not the way it is. There is some similarity, but not much, because a person in the dark can perceive with the other senses, or hear the other person speak or move, or touch him. This is not how it is in this case, and there is no perception of darkness, but the vision is transmitted by means of a knowledge brighter than the sun. I don't mean that any sun is actually seen, or any brightness, but there is a light which, even though it isn't seen, illuminates the understanding.

Alvarez was in an unenviable position. If he allowed himself to believe what Teresa was saying (and her logic was always hard to resist), he might be condoning just the sort of behavior that set the machinery of the Inquisition in motion. It was now June of 1559. In May an *auto de fe* was held at Valladolid, at which the condemned heretic Agustín Cazalla (who had had a passing interest in Teresa) recanted and was garroted before being burned at the stake. Alvarez had to protect not only his penitent but himself: he could be considered guilty by association. His defensive strategy was to subject this nun, who was becoming more and more intricately bound by her beliefs, to an inquisition of his own.

" 'Who said that it was Jesus Christ?' " Teresa's answer is typically straightforward: " 'He often tells me so Himself.' " And even before He tells her, she understands who it is. If she were blind and was told that a *particular* person was beside her, she couldn't confirm it. But this kind of seeing, or not seeing, allows a positive identification. The truth is imprinted on her soul, much as it is when God instructs her with language that is beyond words. She doesn't have to work to assimilate this knowledge: "It is as if food has been put in our stomachs without our eating it or knowing how it got there. We know very well that it's there, even though we don't know what kind of food it is or how it got into us." It is, she continues, as if a person who never learned to read and has never studied is suddenly filled with knowledge. Again Teresa exploits her imperfections: if someone as ignorant as she can see and hear and know such truths, how can they not have come from God?

To his credit, Alvarez tried manfully to make sense of what she was telling him. What finally enlightened him, though, was having his own vision of Christ. Teresa gently teased him about that (" 'how do you know it was Christ?' "), and as time went by, he became a more committed friend to her.

As she struggled to make herself understood, she was more and more frequently deluged with visions. First she saw Christ's hands, ravishingly beautiful. A few days later she saw his face. At first she couldn't fathom why the revelation was so gradual. "But I finally I realized that His Majesty was catering to my weak nature. May He be blessed forever. A creature as base and vile as I am would not have been able to stand all this glory at once."

Such a reaction might seem overmodest at first; on the other hand, there is nothing like an undiluted view of divinity to make a person feel small. Teresa says she felt ashamed to be receiving these favors, which kept growing greater. Pretty soon she saw—"with the eyes of the soul"—the body of the resurrected Christ, a vision so exquisite that she can hardly bring herself to describe it. But out of obedience (and a zest for clarification) she must: "It isn't a dazzling radiance but a soft whiteness and infused radiance, which delights the eyes so much, they're never tired by it. . . . This light is so different from what we are used to that the sun's brightness seems very dim by comparison. . . . Afterwards, we don't want to open our eyes again. It's like seeing a very clear stream running over a crystal bed that reflects the sun, and then a very muddy stream, running beneath a clouded sky."

In case her reader misinterprets, she goes on to say that this light is nothing like sunlight; it seems to the soul to be more natural and makes sunlight appear artificial. If she tried to imagine such light, she could never do it. Nor could she reproduce its effects, which are so soothing. Think of the difference, she suggests, between an attempt at sleep and the real thing, which refreshes the brain and restores the soul. "I made this argument, among others, when they told me—as they often did—that my visions were from the devil and were completely unreal."

By this time Teresa was facing a virtual army of skeptics (one having told another, "so that they all ended up knowing, even though I had only told my confessor, and certain others he had asked me to tell"). She had to convince them that her visions were authentic. When one argument didn't work, she tried another. She was tireless in her efforts to convey the gist of her experience (the reality was inexpressible) to these men who, as she never omits to say, were far more learned than she was. If they had told her that someone she knew very well wasn't really himself, she would have believed them, she promised, because of course they knew better. But if that person had left her some jewels, and she had become rich, though previously poor, how could she believe she was deluded, however much she wanted to? And she had those jewels—the wonderful changes that had occurred within her soul. Her confessor could testify to that.

And so he did, as well as he could, given the fact that he didn't trust his own reactions and his oveseers didn't especially trust him. They warned Alvarez not to let the devil get the upper hand. The worst thing that could happen (putting aside the fate of Teresa's soul for a moment) would be for the Inquisition to question her before her superiors had thought to do so. They might be dragged down with her. So these *letrados* grilled Teresa at length, she said, as if she were Martin Luther himself. And because "I talked carelessly about certain matters, which they took in the wrong sense," they accused her of a lack of humility. "They would ask me some questions, which I would answer frankly and without thinking. Then they thought I was trying to instruct them because I considered myself wise." No matter how hard she tried, there was no way to undo the damage, and Teresa was made to pay for her indiscretion. The most she says—and it is a lot under the circumstances—is that "the opposition of good men to a weak and wretched and fearful little woman like me sounds like nothing when I describe it like this—and yet, of all the terrible trials I've undergone in the course of my life, this was one of the very worst." She hopes that God was served by her misery; her critics were, of course, only after her good.

Some of them wanted to have her exorcised. That didn't bother her, she says. But when she realized that people were avoiding hearing her confession, she became alarmed. Confession had always grounded her, and she couldn't continue to make progress without it. She turned to God for reassurance: "I would go and complain to Him about all my trials, and I always emerged from prayer comforted, and feeling strong." Alvarez consoled her, too, though less efficiently. And when she couldn't see him she was handed over to another confessor, the one who ordered her to snap her fingers at her visions as a sign of contempt for the devil's work. She couldn't always obey—it upset her too much. This confessor also demanded that she make the sign of the cross when a vision occurred, but since that was almost continually, she took to carrying around a crucifix. Once when she was holding the wooden cross of a rosary, Christ took it out of her hand and returned it studded with four large stones, "much more precious than diamonds," on which were incised the five wounds of Christ. No one else could see them, though she could never again see that cross as it had been before.

She continued to be as docile as she could, and God continued to give her good strong explanations to pass along to her critics. At the same time, she began to be consumed with a longing for divine favors. She wasn't looking for some inchoate impression: she wanted to see what color Christ's eyes were. But the harder she looked, the less she saw, and the more impassioned she became: "I saw that I was dying of the desire to see God, and I didn't know where to look for that other life, except in death. Such powerful impulses of love came over me. . . . I didn't know what to do, because nothing satisfied me, and I couldn't contain myself; I really felt as if my soul were being torn away. Oh, how crafty the Lord is, what subtle skills You practice on Your miserable slave! You hide from me, and inflict on me, through Your love, so delectable a death that the soul doesn't ever want to distance itself from it."

This was a turning point for Teresa, not only in mystical terms but also linguistically. From her early readings of chivalric romance and her later readings of Spanish mystics, she knew that love had its own vernacular. The troubadours, devotees of what C. S. Lewis called the "religion" of courtly love, had written about women so chaste and inaccessible that loving them was a delicious pain, a tender enslavement. Religious poets had aimed their identical oxymorons at a loving but elusive God. As the

French critic Denis de Rougement pointed out in his study *Love in the Western World,* the very air a European breathed from the early Middle Ages on was charged with devotion to one idealized love object or another, conventionally expressed in such figures as Teresa employs here. Mortally wounded knights, transfixed by amorous desire, stole metaphorically into both the *casa,* where a woman like Teresa's mother, Doña Beatriz, passed the sultry hours dreaming of romantic adventure, and the cloister, where a woman like Teresa found herself dreaming of spiritual betrothal to Christ.

This customized language of love and the kind of experience it conveyed were so universal by Teresa's day as to have become almost banal. That is why, after her quick and emphatic prayer, she stresses that when she describes the true impetus of prayer, she is not describing that "restlessness of the heart, or those feelings of devotion that happen often and seem to stifle the spirit, because they can't be pent up. This is a lower form of prayer, and these quickenings should be averted by gently gathering them up inside oneself and calming the soul." She has seen any number of sincerely religious people give way to such restless longings, and she isn't unsympathetic. "This sort of prayer," she writes, "is like the violent sobbing of children. They seem to be about to choke, but their onrush of emotion stops right away if they are given something to drink." (Teresa the prioress would later prescribe equally simple remedies for her more excitable nuns.) In the case of religious enthusiasm, the cause might be physical or emotional; one should always check. "Reason should rein in these feelings, because they may just result from our human nature. . . . So the child has to be calmed with a loving caress, which will elicit its love gently, and not, as they say, with an iron fist."

It is interesting that whenever Teresa wants to bring her reader back to earth, she uses homely comparisons; and though these must have served (as critics often theorize) to remind her erudite readers of her humble— that is, nonthreatening—female identity, they also got her point across as swiftly and unambiguously as possible. Teresa was a pragmatist through and through; she always made use of the material she had at hand. "This love," she writes, "must be contained, so it doesn't boil over like a stew pot when too much wood has been put on the fire. The fuel needs to be used judiciously, and an attempt has to be made to put out the flames with gentle tears, and not with painful sobbing that comes from those emotions I've described, which do a lot of harm."

Women, as she often observes, can get carried away by their emotions. She herself has boiled over in the past and been left too enervated and confused even to pray. That's why it is important to prevent violent outbursts and let spiritual changes occur in a more gradual way. Having said all this as prosaically as she can, she now has to make an important distinction. "The true impulses," she writes, "are as different as they can be. We don't put the wood on the fire ourselves, but it seems that once the fire is made, we're suddenly thrown into it to be consumed." Now she is describing an experience that isn't controlled by human passions, because its origin is divine; no mortal impulse can affect it. And here she cuts in smoothly with a description of rapture that alludes to her most celebrated (and least homely) experience:

> The soul doesn't try to feel the pain of being wounded by the Lord's absence, but sometimes an arrow is plunged into its most vital organs, its entrails and heart, so that the soul doesn't know what is happening, or what it wants. It fully understands that it desires God, and that the arrow seems to have been dipped in some poisonous herb so that it will hate itself, out of love for the Lord, and would willingly give up its life for Him. There's no way to exaggerate or describe how God wounds the soul, or how He causes it the most excruciating pain, so that it loses awareness of itself—but this pain is so sweet that none of life's pleasures can bring more delight. The soul, as I've said, would always want to be dying of this malady.

Teresa had many well-tested weapons in her arsenal of explanations. That arrow had done service for Eros, the Greek god of love, and the poisonous herb (as a love potion) had conquered Tristan, the hero of Béroul's twelfth-century romance. Just as the wound of love or the flaming heart would be automatically understood in the literature of courtly love as emblems of passionate devotion, these same figures in mystical literature were evidence of the divine invasion by which God put his brand on the soul.

A rapture such as the one Teresa describes above can have levels of intensity. So there may be periods of relative calm when the soul performs some penances ("but feels nothing, no more pain from drawing its own blood than if it were a corpse"). But when the experience is really intense, the soul is stricken, and the body is too. It is just like having a critical illness, another matter Teresa knows about firsthand. "There's nothing to do, because the whole body contracts, and the feet and arms can't move at all. If standing, the person sits down, like a thing that is carried from place to place, and can't even breathe, but can only moan weakly. Inside is where the pain is felt."

Comparisons with her earlier description of the illness that almost killed her are inevitable here, and Teresa's critics have not been remiss. There are the contraction of muscles and limbs, the paralysis, the helplessness, the unspeakable pain. But there is also an essential difference between the two debilitating states. What is missing in the physical crisis is the sweetness of the pain and its resolution through love. A critically ill person tries to endure her pain and recover. But the spiritual invalid savors her pain, which is indistinguishable from pleasure and may climax in death—the answer to her prayers.

The passage in Teresa's *Vida* that Bernini dramatized in marble, that the baroque English poet Richard Crashaw enshrined in a trio of poems, and that over the centuries has scandalized any number of orthodox readers from prelates to pathologists was just another of the struggling nun's attempts to bare her soul to her wary examiners. The rapture occurred more than once, and her description is as exact as she can make it; there is no margin for error here. What comes through, as elsewhere in Teresa's writings, is passion viewed beneath the lens of reason, a crystal under glass:

> It pleased our Lord that I should sometimes see this vision. Very close to me, on my left, an angel appeared in human form, which is not how I usually perceive them—though I do once in a while. Even though angels often appear to me, I don't actually see them, except in the way I mentioned earlier. But our Lord willed that I should see this vision in the following way: he was not tall but short, and very beautiful, and his face was so aflame that he seemed to be one of those superior angels who look like

they are completely on fire. They must be the ones called cherubim—they don't tell me their names—but I am very aware that in heaven there is such a difference between some angels and others, and between these and still others, that I would not know how to explain it. In his hands I saw a large golden spear, and at its iron tip there seemed to be a point of fire. I felt as if he plunged this into my heart several times, so that it penetrated all the way to my entrails. When he drew it out, he seemed to draw them out with it, and left me totally inflamed with a great love for God. The pain was so severe, it made me moan several times. The sweetness of this intense pain is so extreme, there is no wanting it to end, and the soul isn't satisfied with anything less than God. This pain is not physical, but spiritual, even though the body has a share in it— in fact, a large share. So delicate is this exchange between God and the soul that I pray God, in his goodness, to give a taste of it to anyone who thinks I am lying.

This was an extraordinary experience, to say the least, but Teresa couldn't be more matter-of-fact. She is *desengañada,* having no illusions about her readers' likely response to her narrative. All she can do is make the necessary distinctions, and God will do the rest. The first thing she explains is that she doesn't "usually" see angels this way, though she often has visions of them; but those visions are the intellectual ones she described earlier, when she was aware of a presence but didn't actually "see" it. This vision, then, was unusual. She thinks the angel was a cherub, but she wouldn't know, not being learned. (What she depicts here is, according to biographer Francisco de Ribera, a higher kind of angel called a seraph, and he changes the word in her text.) The spear was gold with an iron tip (that is how closely she looked at it), red-hot. The angel plunged it into her heart, all the way to her entrails, again and again. She felt eviscerated by each withdrawal, and the pain, which "made me moan several times," was almost too sweet to bear, yet left her wanting more. It left her, as she says, consumed by her own love for God, one heat generating another.

By this point of the narrative any reader, however cloistered, must have noticed an unmistakable correlation between Teresa's rapture and others of a less transcendent kind. So she takes a moment to say that "this pain isn't physical, but spiritual, even though the body has a share of it—in fact, a large share." Her point is that the experience is not *essentially*, but only accidentally, physical. Far from being naive, she is clearly aware of the suspicions her description will raise. If she were less scrupulous (or less devout), she might decide to soften its impact. But she is bent on reporting her vision accurately, no matter how alarming its content. The pragmatist in her sees nothing to be alarmed about. As she writes elsewhere, "We are not angels but have bodies," and bodies respond as they can.

Teresa does not linger on this question of physicality, but moves to a point of greater importance to her, which is that the exchange between God and the soul is (despite its sudden intensity) extremely delicate, *suave*—literally, smooth. It is, like courtly love, a very accomplished kind of wooing, filled with amenities. The angel in Bernini's work smiles kindly, and this is in keeping with Teresa's description of a loving act. Such reciprocity is key to her own perception of her relationship with God, which is at once a burning passion and a gracious, considerate friendship. All of that is what Teresa means by love.

If Bernini's marble gentlemen in the Cornaro Chapel could speak, they would no doubt argue, as so many men (fewer women) have since, about the nature of Teresa's transverberation. Some would cite inspiring precedents: the sensuous rhapsody of the biblical Song of Solomon, or Saint Bernard's painstaking explication of its bliss ("there comes an unexpected infusion of grace, our breast expands as it were, and our interior is filled with an overflowing love"), or its recasting in the lyrics of the *Cántico espiritual* by Teresa's friend and confessor, San Juan de la Cruz (Saint John of the Cross). Spiritual marriage, the perfect, lasting union between the soul and God, to which Teresa aspired—though she achieved it only later in life—would be a familiar concept to the gentlemen in the balconies, who are educated men and might have read the writings of the medieval mystics Heinrich Suso or Richard of St. Victor. The *Dialogue* of the Italian saint and Teresa's fellow Doctor of the Church, Catherine of Siena ("in so knowing me the soul catches fire with unspeakable love, which in turn brings continual pain") might be submitted as evidence that true holiness can break free of the fetters of sex, as it does in the lives and works of other ecstatic women—Hildegard of Bingen, for example, or Julian of Norwich.

The Ecstasy of St. Teresa, c. 1650, by Gian Lorenzo Bernini, in the Cornaro Chapel of Santa Maria della Vittoria, Rome

But even if they admired such precedents, these gentlemen might look askance (as so many Italians did) at extravagant displays of Spanish religiosity by sinners like Magdalena de la Cruz, who admitted that her ecstasies were inspired by the devil; or the *alumbrada* Francisca Hernández, who treated her male disciples to rapture of an essentially physical kind. Who could really say that Teresa of Avila wasn't a woman of that stripe?

In fairness to those witnesses—and to Teresa's countrymen who had doubts about her holiness while she lived—a woman with such suspicious tendencies must have been hard to fathom or believe. In Spain, the problem was a particularly thorny one. For the sake of his soul and of his *honra*, a sixteenth-century Spaniard had to be wary of deceit. Faced with what seemed like transcendent glory, he sometimes had to look away.

Chapter 5: *A Glimpse of Hell*

For most practical purposes Teresa spent her life among women, but her spiritual welfare resided with men. Fledgling confessors (including Cetina, Prádanos, and Alvarez) were ringed by men of experience like Salcedo, Daza, and Borja, who watched Teresa's every move. The circle grew wider; more opinions were sought. (She herself never tired of seeking them.) Sometimes the men who considered her case were unmoved, but at other times she got lucky. Experienced theologians like the Dominican Pedro Ibáñez elicited precise accounts of her soul, the kind she ached to provide. García de Toledo, the confessor who ordered her to write the *Vida*, became as much a disciple as a guide. Domingo Báñez, another learned Dominican, became her adviser in tricky spiritual and political situations.

As her experiences in prayer grew more and more intense, Teresa found that she was walking around "in a kind of stupor." Pain and bliss were all she wanted. The raptures came on strongly, "so overwhelming that I couldn't resist them even though I wasn't alone." Everyone was talking. Teresa seemed to have lost her faculties, a bad sign: the last thing the Encarnación needed was a crazed ecstatic nun attracting attention. Her advisers were not pleased, and she was distraught. As usual, Doña Guiomar stepped into the breach. Governed by emotion rather than intellect (though she was, according to her loyal friend, "an intelligent and extremely perceptive woman"), Yomar's role in Teresa's life was always to propel the action forward. When she heard that a holy man had come to town, "without saying a word to me she got my provincial's permission for me to stay at her house for a week, so that I could meet with him more easily." Intrigue came naturally to Yomar, and Teresa herself (as later events showed) had a weakness for it.

She went to visit her friend, who must have wrapped herself for a time in mystery before introducing her to Fray Pedro de Alcántara, the Franciscan ascetic who preached poverty and reform. He was famous for his austerities, living as he did in a grim, inhospitable cell, with hardly enough space to move. His bare feet were gnarled, his clothing threadbare and much too tight, his body caked with dirt. When Teresa met him, he was very old and extremely thin. He looked as if he were made of twisted roots. Fray Pedro slept sitting up, with his head on a log nailed to the wall, and only for an hour and a half a night. When Teresa came to see him, he didn't exactly look at her (or at any woman; he liked to say that for him they were just walking trees). And yet, she writes, "even with all this sanctity, he was very affable, though he didn't say much unless he was answering questions. At those times he was very delightful, because he had a lively intelligence."

Teresa came to him in confusion. She understood why it made sense to experience physical pain with spiritual pleasure. But spiritual pain and pleasure at once—what she had felt during the vision of the angel—still made no sense to her. She told Fray Pedro what had been going on: the kinds of visions she'd had, the warnings and instructions from her advisers, the irresistible impulses of love. She held nothing back and, anticipating objections as usual, argued against herself. But Fray Pedro believed her instantly; he was no stranger to ecstasies. "Almost from the start, I saw that he understood me from his own experience, and that was all I needed." Because at that time, she explains, "I couldn't understand myself then the way I do now. . . . Then I needed someone who had personally gone through everything I had, and could tell me what it was." She had to have explanations. Otherwise, how could she know if she was on the right path?

Fray Pedro explained it all, especially the visions—that is, the ones she saw with the eyes of the soul. He told her not to worry, but to praise God for all these favors. After he discovered that she really was brave (one of the few virtues that Teresa never minds mentioning), he actually enjoyed talking with her. What she had experienced, "the opposition of good people," was "one of the greatest trials in the world," he explained, and "I still had lots of them to look forward to." She would need someone around who understood, but (he could assure her) there was no one like that in town. He would do what he could to help her—and so he did. He spoke to the men whose opinions mattered, including Teresa's confessor and "that married gentleman," Salcedo. It is easy to picture the irresolute young Alvarez faced with a wild-haired, leathery, scolding ascetic of great repute. He "hardly needed this advice," Teresa reports generously. Salcedo wasn't altogether convinced, but at least "what he heard kept him from frightening me so much." Fray Pedro could make anyone squirm, even a *caballero santo*.

Teresa continued to consult with the old man for years, and he advised her on important matters. It was a lasting friendship. The two had an unconventional rapport that allowed him to appear to her, in spirit, right before his death, which she then predicted to him. After he died, the conversations just continued. In fact, she notes serenely, "the Lord was pleased to let me have more to do with him since his death than when he was alive."

Besieged by visions and raptures, desperately trying to steer a straight course toward heaven, Teresa spoke less with men than with angels—and less with women than with men. As disapproving as some of her advisers were, at least they were concerned about her spiritual health. A few of the nuns she lived with were sympathetic, others were frightened, and the rest were simply annoyed. They had to endure her wild displays and hear, from buzzing visitors if not from one another, about the dubious favors that God had bestowed on her. Most of these women lacked even the minimal education that inept confessors had and were in no position to evaluate her experience. They could only judge by what they saw. And in spite of Teresa's best efforts, they saw a lot. The devil was acting up, tormenting her not only in private but in public: "Once I was in an oratory, and he appeared at my left, in an abominable form. I was especially aware of his mouth, because he spoke to me, and it was terrifying. It seemed as if a great flame shot out of his body, which was completely bright and didn't cast a shadow. He told me in a scary voice that I really had escaped his clutches, but that he would catch me in the end."

Perhaps it was the devil's lack of divine inspiration that made him appear, virtually every time Teresa saw him, in the tritest way imaginable. Here he did everything but twirl his mustache; another time he showed up as "a most hideous little blackamoor snarling as if in despair that what he had tried to win, he'd lost." Teresa laughed that time, but on other occasions the devil got under her skin, making her thrash about uncontrollably. The nuns who witnessed this were terrified, as they were when she pretended that nothing was wrong, but they distinctly smelled brimstone—a very unpleasant odor. Luckily, holy water drove the devil away, and Teresa often had to sprinkle it liberally: for example, when she was trying to read one night and the devil kept landing on her book.

She had more trouble when she was alone, and the devil tempted her with false humility—as when she doubted herself and feared that she was trying to delude "all those good men." False humility, she explains, constricts soul and body, creating a dryness of spirit, while true humility is tranquil. Even when the soul is ashamed of doing too little for God, it feels deeply comforted. One of the devil's nastier techniques is the surprise attack. While she is trying to focus on prayer, "suddenly my mind is fixated on things that at any other time would make me laugh. The devil mixes up my thoughts every which way he wants to, and chains up the soul so that it no longer controls itself, and can't think about a thing except the idiotic thoughts he brings it. . . . Sometimes it seems as if devils are playing ball with the soul, and it can't free itself from their power."

When this happens, she feels dead to the world and to God. Love is lukewarm. She can't pray or read. "To speak with anyone is worse, because the devil makes me so temperamental they all think I want to gobble them up." This kind of behavior can't have increased her popularity in the convent, and it drove her confessors crazy. "Saintly though they were," she writes a bit acidly, "they scolded me so harshly that when I told them about it afterward, even they were amazed."

Sometimes she can't even think straight. Her intentions are good, but "this intellect is so wild that it seems like nothing so much as a raving maniac, and nobody can chain it down." But somehow she does manage to step back, let her mind do what it wants, and then God steps in and "enchains this madman in perfect contemplation."

Teresa doesn't say how long it took for things to calm down, only that she had one awful experience that brought everything to a head and was the impetus for a crucial change in her life. One day while she was at prayer, she suddenly felt that she was in hell. She saw the place that her sins had reserved for her, a black hole. This passage and one that follows it read like a diabolic inversion of sacred imagery. Instead of the marble saint ensconced in its niche, there is the flesh-and-blood sinner stuffed into a hole in the wall: "The entrance seemed to me like an alley, narrow and very long, or like an oven, very low and dark and confining. The ground appeared to be filthy, muddy water, with a pestilential odor and infested with evil vermin. At the end of the alley, part of the wall was hollowed out, like a cupboard, and I saw that I was wedged into it." Everything was pitch-black; there was no light or air, no place to move. The walls, she writes, closed in on themselves and smothered everything inside them. A woman who prized her freedom (which is another way of saying she herself defined its boundaries) could have no severer punishment. As usual, when describing an emotionally overwhelming experience, Teresa links it to the pain of extreme illness: "I felt a fire inside my soul. . . . The physical pain was so unbearable that even though in this life I have been wracked by the greatest pain (the worst, the doctors say, that a person can suffer here on earth and still live, since all my nerves contracted when I was paralyzed, and I went through plenty of other agonies of many kinds, including some, as I've said, caused by the devil)—still, they were all nothing compared with what I felt there, especially since I knew that they would be endless and unremitting."

Misery *para siempre* was not what she had ever imagined for herself. This feeling of oppression and suffocation was more than she could stand. So was the sensation of "the soul being continuously torn from the body." She couldn't see her torturer, she writes, "but I felt myself burning and crumbling up, and I tell you, that fire and interior despair were the worst of all."

It wasn't as if Teresa questioned the justice of her infernal punishment or God's mercy in allowing her to preview it. Only God could have enabled her to see in that total darkness, and only as much as concerned her. She couldn't make out the rest of hell, which she had learned about in books but never viscerally imagined. Now, she thought, she would shrug off all the agonies of this life, having already endured something much worse. She had been brave before; now, as far as the world was concerned, she would be fearless.

The thing that bothered Teresa most, after her round-trip to hell, was that the devil was snagging so many other souls, those of the "Lutherans" (which was how she referred to the French Calvinist Huguenots) in particular. She wanted to rescue these lost souls, sacrifice herself if she could for their salvation. Even if that was impossible, she had to do something penitential. Obviously her efforts up to now had been inadequate. "My spirit was not at ease, though the uneasiness wasn't troubling, but delightful. I clearly saw that it came from God, and that His Majesty had given my soul this ardor so that it could digest other, heartier food than it was eating."

Earlier, Teresa had compared her spiritual satisfactions to the feeling of being full, but not knowing how the food had entered her body. Now, to help implement God's will in the world, she needed even "heartier food." However much her illnesses and the intensity of her devotions might have weakened her constitution, she was a healthy animal, spiritually speaking. As she explains elsewhere, even when she is in great pain, she hardly ever gives in to it: "I am not at all like a woman in such matters," she writes, "because I have a robust spirit."

Instead of panting for divine favors, she began wondering what to do for God. It struck her that even though she had lived in a convent for more than twenty years, she hadn't exactly given up her comforts. The Encarnación was a pleasant place, although poor, and in any case, she had spent a good deal of time away. Other nuns had done so too, visiting places "where we could live decently and keep our vows." It was cheaper for the convent to have a nun's expenses met elsewhere. And Teresa's company was so avidly sought that she was always being called away—enough to make her think "the devil must have had something to do with these frequent departures."

Actually, there was nothing inappropriate about her visits, because her convent observed the mitigated rule of the Order of Carmel, which allowed more liberties than the desert hermits who drafted the primitive rule would have condoned. This mitigation had made sense in 1432, when the papal bull was issued; the austerities of the early Carmelites had seemed excessive to those with a more flexible approach to religion. But now, with the Counter-Reformation in full force and (it seemed) with the "Lutherans" at the very gates, strong measures seemed to be called for. Some orders, like the Franciscan Pedro de Alcántara's, had begun reforming themselves already; groups of Discalced, or "barefoot," friars had begun to embrace poverty and abstinence, according to their primitive rules. But no one really expected women to initiate reform. They were too suggestible, too weak-minded, to make such changes unless under the rigorous surveillance of men.

It seemed to Teresa, though, that she—having received so many divine favors and having had a glimpse of hell—should observe her rule more strictly. Pedro de Alcántara lived in a virtual cave: by comparison, her own accommodations were palatial. She now shared her duplex cell, with its beautiful view through a grove of poplars to the church of San Vicente, with her young nieces Leonor and María de Ocampo. (They had moved in after Teresa's little sister Juana had gotten married and moved out.) In fact, Teresa was in her cell one day with these nieces and others—including her cousins Ana and Inés de Tapia and her friend Juana Suárez—when the subject of reform came up. They were all sitting on cushions and mats, in the Moorish way, embroidering, when the conversation lightly turned to the ancient hermits of Carmel. "A certain person said to me and others that even if we couldn't be like those in the Discalced orders, we could still found a convent." Teresa realized that she had, in fact, been thinking along the same lines. She had never really given up childhood dreams of being martyred for the faith, but martyrdom these days could be construed as heroic self-abnegation—still a worthy and romantic goal—which is why it makes sense that her niece María ("a certain person"), who was only seventeen, proposed it.

The prospect of banding together and founding a small, scrupulously devout convent was gently circulating throughout the room when Doña Guiomar arrived, caught the drift, and offered to finance the adventure. But as Teresa had already seen, Yomar tended to be readier with promises than with cash, and she was a little broke at the moment anyway. As Teresa tells it, "I talked over the idea with a companion, that widowed lady, who was having similar thoughts. . . . She began dreaming up ways to obtain the necessary funds. But, as I see clearly now, this wouldn't have gotten us very far." Teresa wasn't too disappointed; it wasn't as if she had made up her mind. But she also couldn't put the idea aside, even though she was, as she points out, "very happy where I was." So she decided to lay the whole matter before God. And as she might have expected, God had a distinct point of view: "One day after Communion, the Lord strongly ordered me to pursue this goal with all my strength, and he promised me great things: that He wouldn't fail to make this foundation, and that it would serve Him very well; that it would be named San José, and that that saint would watch over us at one door and Our Lady at the other, and that Christ would remain with us. He said that the convent would be a star, shining with the brightest light imaginable. . . . He said I should tell my confessor what He had ordered me to do, and that He would ask him not to oppose the project or keep me from realizing it."

Her marching orders couldn't have been clearer. Still, Teresa says she resisted them, knowing from the start what she would be in for. But God spoke to her again, and frequently, pummeling her with "many clear reasons and arguments," until she dropped this latest revelation at her confessor's door.

The weary Baltasar Alvarez was probably thinking, by this time, that he'd gotten a grip on how to deal with Teresa's enthusiasms. However much she had won him over, he could not have been happy with her news. He "didn't dare to tell me I should definitely give up the project" (no man in his right mind would have); he simply told her that it would be impossible to pull it off. Both of them knew that Doña Guiomar was short of funds. And so the Jesuit pointed Teresa toward her superior, the provincial of the Carmelite order, who would be better equipped to discourage her.

What Teresa did next was characteristic of the way she got things done. She wasn't disobedient; she just circumnavigated the request. She and Yomar first wrote to Pedro de Alcántara, explaining their plan to found a small Discalced convent, where nuns would be more strictly enclosed, have no luxuries, and devote all their energies to God. It is hard to imagine the old ascetic objecting, since he had similar projects in the works. In fact, he approved mightily and, based on his own experience, gave the women shrewd advice. He said Teresa should lie low (she was a woman some superiors might want to avoid) while Doña Guiomar approached the provincial. The lady should make the petition to Rome under her own aristocratic name. Someone else should make the actual purchase of the house that would be used for the foundation. Teresa, summoning her troops as usual, wrote to Francisco de Borja and Luis Beltrán, a holy man (later a saint) living in Valencia, who was cautious and slow to respond but finally encouraged her. Then Doña Guiomar, armed with these approvals and her own enthusiasm, went to see the provincial, Angel de Salazar. Salazar pledged his support in principle (which meant he wasn't signing anything yet) and so did Antonio de Heredia, the Carmelite prior in Avila.

Yomar next took Teresa (on the pretext of her being a companion for her daughter, a young nun at the Encarnación) with her to confess at the monastery of Santo Tomás. The Dominican *letrado* Pedro Ibáñez didn't know Teresa except by reputation, and he wasn't inclined to endorse the project. Other Dominicans had warned him not to. But he was a scholar at heart and said he'd study the issues and let the two women know. His only stipulation was that if his answer was negative, they would have to agree to give up their idea. "I said that we would," Teresa writes, and then continues circumspectly, "but even though I said so, and I think that we would have done it, I never wavered for a moment in my conviction that the convent would be founded." By what means, she doesn't say. Meanwhile, Teresa's sister Juana agreed to look for a house, ostensibly for her family, where the monastery of San José could begin to rise.

Ibáñez considered motivations and potential benefits for the church. And after eight days he gave the project his blessing, along with practical advice and assurances that if anyone tried to sabotage it, they would have to answer to him. Ibáñez was very influential, and suddenly the way was clear, even in the minds of Salcedo and Daza, who now saw a positive outlet for Teresa's religiosity.

Predictably, the nuns at the Encarnación disagreed: "I was very much disliked throughout my convent, because I wanted to found a more strictly enclosed house. The nuns said that I was insulting them, and that I could serve God just as well where I was, since others were better nuns than I was; that I had no love for my own house, and that I would have been better off raising money for it than for some other place. Some of them said I should be thrown in jail; but others—though just a few of them—were more or less on my side."

People were just as outraged in the city, where the establishment of yet another destitute convent—and by an unstable woman—seemed a ridiculous idea. Still, the project was on track. A small but adequate house had been found, and Teresa's sister Juana had come down from Alba with her husband, Juan de Ovalle, to buy it when the next blow struck. "When the business had gotten to this point, and was so close to being completed that the deeds were going to be drawn up the next day—that was when the father provincial changed his mind." The pressure on Salazar had been intense. Promptly Baltasar Alvarez wrote Teresa a letter saying that "now I could see, because of what had happened, that it had all been a dream, and that I should correct my mistake by not wanting to leave for any reason, or to speak any more about it, since I had seen what a scandal I'd created. He said other things too, all of them very painful to hear." And she had been expecting him to console her!

As usual in such straits she turned to God, who guaranteed that the foundation would be made but directed her to "keep quiet for now." This was a relief, though the chatter in the city and at the Encarnación continued. She recollected herself and prayed. "Then began the great impulses of love for God that I've mentioned, and stronger raptures, even though I hid them and didn't say a word to anyone about these gains." She didn't have to. Always hot on her trail, "the devil started going from one person to another, letting them know that I had had some revelation about all this. People were very afraid and came to tell me that these were bad times, and that someone might make accusations and I'd have to face the inquisitors."

That, she says, made her laugh: "On that score I was never afraid, because I knew very well that in matters of faith, no one would ever find me challenging even the tiniest ceremony of the Church, and that I would die a thousand deaths for the sake of the Church or for any truth in Holy Scripture. I told them that my soul would be in pretty bad shape if anything about it made me fear the Inquisition, and I said that if I thought there *were* something to worry about, I would go to the inquisitors myself." This is pure Castilian bravado, and it seems to work. Few of Teresa's biographers doubt her lack of fear of the Inquisition—which seems extraordinary, even for a saint.

Pedro Ibáñez, paying close attention as usual, asked Teresa for a full description of the favors she was receiving. And so at the age of forty-five she produced the first of her *Cuentas de conciencia* (*Accounts of Conscience,* also called *Spiritual Testimonies*), a description of her spiritual life that must have told the Dominican all he wanted to know. She explains to him how her intellect becomes useless when she prays, and how her spirit is snatched up so swiftly there is no way she can resist. Sometimes it happens when she is trying to pray and having very little success because of a "great dryness" or because of physical pain: "At other times I'm consumed by a longing for God that I can't control. It seems my life is about to end, and that makes me cry out frantically to God. Sometimes I can't even sit still because these longings make me nauseous—and this pain comes on without my asking for it. . . . It's impossible to recover, because the way to see God is by dying, and I can't take that cure."

Penance helps, but she can't do enough of it, because of her weakened condition. She tries to spend time alone ("solitude consoles me"), but she has to see people. Even relatives seem like strangers. In fact, everyone does except "those who talk about prayer and the soul." Her raptures and visions have improved her by making her determined not to offend God, "for I would die a thousand deaths before doing that." She has learned to obey her confessor (though not perfectly) and to see the virtue in poverty. She has seen such divine beauty that the things she has always loved mean nothing to her: "When I come upon something beautiful, splendid, like water, fields, flowers, scents, music and so on, it seems I don't want to see or hear them; that's what a difference there is between such things and what I've become used to seeing. . . . Beyond a first impulse, I'm unmoved, and consider these things nothing but trash."

She is drawn to spiritual boldness, to people who have gone further than she has in prayer, while timid souls, who try to be cautious in everything, tend to annoy her. On the other hand, she tells Ibáñez, if there is good to be found in someone, she finds it. She has given up her former vanities . . . mostly. (It is an ongoing effort.) Sometimes for days on end she thinks her visions and raptures must have been a dream, and then, "It seems to me I'm loaded with faults, without the nerve to be virtuous, and that the great courage I usually have boils down to this, that I don't think I'd be able to resist the slightest temptation or disparagement from the world. Then I think I'm good for nothing." But a single word from God, a single vision or rapture, and she's at peace with herself again. These favors clear her head, make her tranquil and collected, which makes her sure they came from God. "I can't believe the devil came up with so many ways of winning my soul so that he could then lose it. I don't consider him that stupid." Faith (which, in her case, is often a kind of heightened common sense) assures her that such beneficial effects must have a divine cause. Once prayer has brought her to this conclusion, "even if all the learned men and saints in the world joined together and tortured me in every way imaginable, even if I wanted to believe them, I couldn't think that all this came from the devil—I just couldn't." The devil's effects on a person are different, harmful, and anyone who has been touched beneficially by God knows that very well.

Ibáñez weighed everything she said. Then he presented a *Dictamen* (*Opinion*) of thirty-three points in Teresa's favor to a committee of his peers. Among his assertions: that her experiences brought her closer to God; that she never went looking for them; that she was totally in line with church doctrine; that she was humble and had great *limpieza,* or purity of spirit; that all of her trials, including gossip and illness, were a comfort to her; that she was so strong it was frightening, and that she habitually beat down devils; that she was "free of the affectations and childishness of women"; that she made perfect sense.

Soon after he delivered this document, Ibáñez was transferred from Avila. It could be, as she says, that after considering her case, he became even more devout and went looking for solitude. The politically astute Dominican might also have seen that his defense of the embattled nun could only backfire on his monastery, Santo Tomás. The city was still in an uproar and had suddenly called in Doña Guiomar's sizable debts; bankrolling a new foundation (if it had ever been a possibility) was now out of the question. Not only that, but on Christmas morning of 1560 her regular confessor refused Doña Guiomar absolution until she divorced herself from the scandal. This kind of harassment was no more than the two women might have expected—as Ibáñez certainly had—but they were probably surprised by its meticulous orchestration.

Teresa kept quiet for about five months. She says she was content, though, as always, she pined for a confessor who could understand her. Once when God let her know that her troubles were almost over, she was exultant: she thought He meant that she was about to die. But God was always pragmatic where Teresa was concerned. It turned out He was refer-ring to the arrival of a new Jesuit rector, Gaspar de Salazar. His predeces-sor, Dionisio Vázquez, had kept her on a tight leash, but this Salazar had a flair for spirituality. Teresa grasped this right away—in fact, the minute she entered the confessional. The rector knew how to handle people who had advanced far in prayer by making them "run instead of walking one step at a time." It soon became obvious that she should convince him to back the new foundation, and he did. Baltasar Alvarez (whose faintheartedness Teresa excuses by explaining how Jesuits like to keep a united front) fell into line and said to go ahead—but secretly. So negotiations for the little house resumed. "I was very careful not to be disobedient," Teresa writes. She just didn't tell everyone what she was doing. "I knew that if I told my superiors about it, all would be lost, as it had been before; and this time things might be even worse." So she proceeded alone and with enormous difficulty. Yomar "did what she could," which wasn't much. Funds for the purchase of the house came from two of Teresa's relatives, who would later join her group of nuns. Juana and her husband returned to sign the papers and stayed to make a show of supervising the construction.

It was a slow and painful beginning. As Teresa's biographers Efrén de la Madre de Dios and Otger Steggink graciously put it, Yomar had "all the good will in the world, but no money." She pawned a woolen coverlet and a silk-embroidered cross to help pay the masons. And then, by what seemed like a miracle, two hundred ducats, a large sum, arrived from Teresa's brother Lorenzo de Cepeda in Peru. On reconsideration the house began to look painfully small to Teresa, but God told her not to be so greedy. It would be big enough for the few nuns who would live there. (She had settled on the number thirteen including the prioress.) And it had beautiful views. So things were in good order except where the actual foundation was concerned: there was still the problem of permission. Angel de Salazar hadn't budged—though he had, for the moment, left town.

The brief that had come from Rome, for a convent under the jurisdiction of the Carmelite order, turned out to be void because a crucial clause had been omitted. This was a very narrow opening into which Teresa plunged with all the resources of her faith. That summer she had two visions: the first of Saint Clare, whose order was committed to poverty, as Teresa meant her convent to be. Saint Clare promised her support. The second vision came during the festival of the Assumption, while she was at Mass at Santo Tomás. As Teresa contemplated her sinful, wretched life, she was overcome by a rapture "so powerful that it almost drew me out of myself." She saw herself swathed in a white robe, with the Virgin on her right and San José on her left. These two protectors, her surrogate mother and father, let Teresa know she had been cleansed of her sins: "It seemed to me that our Lady suddenly took my hands in hers, and told me that I gave her great pleasure by serving the glorious San José, that I could count on my plans for the convent being implemented, and that the Lord and the two of them would be very well served there." As if that celestial permission weren't enough, the Virgin hung a gorgeous gold collar with a jeweled cross around Teresa's neck. She emerged from this rapture knowing that she would have to take action in spite of her reservations. She (or rather, some of her advisers) would apply for a new brief, placing the convent under the jurisdiction of the bishop of Avila, Alvaro de Mendoza, instead

St. Thérèse Gets from the Madonna a Necklace, by Flemish painter Gaspar de Crayer (1584–1669), at the Art History Museum in Vienna, Austria

of that of the Carmelite provincial. This idea, too, was a given, as Teresa scrupulously points out: "It upset me not to put the convent under obedience to our Order, but the Lord had told me that that wouldn't be a good idea. He explained why it wouldn't be workable, but told me to apply to Rome in a particular way that He described, and that He would help us out there."

The new briefs weren't sent for until the following winter. Meanwhile, Teresa stayed at Doña Guiomar's, where it was easier these days for her to move about and attend to business than it was at the Encarnación. Construction continued throughout the fall with the usual kinds of setbacks and more. Everyone was nervous. Juana was still blistering from an irate Dominican's sermon that had made innuendos about their project, which was obviously an open secret in town. The young woman kept wishing she could just go home. Yomar panicked when a wall collapsed. Devils had knocked it down, she insisted. It was a sure sign of God's disapproval—an argument that begged to be ignored. Teresa's nephew Gonzalito, Juana's little boy, was found unconscious at the construction site; possibly a stone had hit his head. Witnesses said (and later testified at Teresa's canonization hearings) that he was dead. His aunt carried him inside, closed the door, and cradled him in her arms. Less than an hour later she came out leading him by the hand, as if nothing had happened. Even the masons were awestruck.

But the level of anxiety was high, and Teresa's opponents were marshaling their forces. On Christmas Eve a letter came from Angel de Salazar, and though he didn't say a word about the foundation, he ordered Teresa to leave immediately for Toledo. A wealthy aristocrat named Doña Luisa de la Cerda, the daughter of the duke of Medacineli, had recently lost her husband and was grieving violently. Doña Luisa was in the market for a companion. She could have had any number of earnest Toledan *beatas,* but she was looking for glamour. Salazar could unhesitatingly recommend Doña Teresa de Ahumada, who had an impressive record of consoling bereft widows, and besides, her transposition to Toledo would solve a problem that otherwise might not go away.

Teresa was annoyed at first: she would be leaving behind a very volatile situation. But God insisted, telling her to "ignore the opinions people offered, because few would give me anything but rash suggestions. He said it would be a good idea for me to be away from the convent until the brief arrived, because the devil was cooking up a great plot that was timed to the provincial's arrival." Teresa heard this in a profound rapture, of which the content was (as frequently happened with her) mundane. She was a practical woman; God gave her practical advice.

Chapter 6: *The Conquest of Toledo*

—

Toledo was a pleasant surprise: a lovely old jewel of a city, until recently the capital of Spain (the king had moved his court to Madrid) and still home to a clutch of noble families. The place was bustling with activity: the weaving of velvet and silk brocade, the forging of iron swords, the clatter of carriages along the narrow, winding streets. Teresa was received at Doña Luisa's palace as if she were a visiting dignitary. The widow was immediately soothed by her presence, but Teresa's response to her was more ambiguous. "She loved me very much, and I became fond of her too when I saw how good she was; but almost everything there was a cross to me." People made too much of her, and she felt oppressed by all the creature comforts. Toledans preferred Moorish-style opulence to Castilian austerity, and aristocrats' houses were furnished sumptuously. It is not surprising that Teresa couldn't feel at home. Doña Luisa herself was a very great lady, one of the richest in Spain, and under normal circumstances a woman with Teresa's background would have looked up to her, but God was granting her favors that freed her from any consciousness of rank. She told her hostess as much: "I saw that she was a woman and as subject to passions and weaknesses as I was, and I understood how little nobility mattered, because the more nobility people could claim, the greater were their troubles and trials. I saw how careful these people had to be about behaving in accordance with their rank, which hardly gave them the freedom to live. They can't eat their meals at the right time or in the right order, because everything has to be done according to their rank, and not their physical requirements. Even what they eat often has more to do with their position than with their appetites."

Doña Luisa and her friends were slaves to luxury, in Teresa's judgment—a fate she herself had sidestepped by choosing the strangely liberating confinement of monastic life. She claims that it was during this visit, when she had to settle for the luxurious accommodations that Doña Luisa had provided for her and watch the poor woman pick her way through grueling social occasions, that she "came to hate the very thought of being a great lady"—an emotion that, as a founder, she would translate into policy.

It was in Toledo that she met several people who would figure prominently in her later life. The duchess of Alba would become a loyal if exacting friend; Doña Ana de Mendoza y de la Cerda, the notorious princess of Eboli, would become an enemy. Among Doña Luisa's young female attendants, most of whom were smitten by the nun from Avila, the most persistent was María de Salazar, who regaled Teresa with her inspirational poetry, along with her dream of taking the veil. Teresa rebuffed her. Maybe María reminded her of her younger self, smart and vain and in need of humbling. In any case, the snub didn't work. María de Salazar later joined Teresa's reform and evolved into María de San José, the brilliant and difficult prioress of Seville.

While in chapel one day, Teresa managed to renew an old friendship with García de Toledo, a Dominican who had been vice-rector at Santo Tomás in Avila. How old and how deep this friendship had been isn't known, though biographer Victoria Lincoln pegs García as Teresa's dangerous visitor at the Encarnación. What is clear is that this was a man she loved to talk to. She spotted him at Mass and was "struck with the desire to know the state of his soul, since I wished him to be a great servant of God"—a fairly good indication that he hadn't been before. She got up and sat down three times before she convinced herself (or, as she says, listened to her good, not her wicked, angel) that she could approach him via the confessional. The exchange is teasingly familiar: "I began to ask him about his life, and he began to ask me about mine, because we hadn't seen each other for many years. I started telling him that my life had been full of great spiritual trials, and he pushed me very hard to tell him what these trials were. I told him that they shouldn't be out in the open, and it wasn't for me to talk about them. He replied that since the Dominican father I've spoken about [Pedro Ibáñez] knew about them, and was a very close friend of his, he could easily find out—so I shouldn't hold back."

No confession could have been fonder or more natural, especially as the confessing went both ways. "The truth, it seems to me, is that he couldn't help pushing me any more than I could help confiding in him," she writes in a rush of girlish enthusiasm. She let him in on her private experiences in prayer. She never says what he told her, only that he asked her, next time she prayed, to put in a good word for him. He didn't have to ask. Teresa wept and begged God to raise her friend to a higher spiritual plane (she always wanted the best for her friends), and she kept at it until God gave her a message for his would-be servant. This, she says, made her uneasy ("I always dislike taking messages to third parties"), but she did it with such urgency that García resolved to devote himself to prayer, "though he didn't do it right away": shades of the youthful Saint Augustine asking God to make him chaste—but not yet.

García de Toledo did make spiritual progress; though by the time Teresa wrote about him in her *Vida*—the book she produced at his request—she was still predicting the fulfillment of his potential. ("If he keeps progressing at this pace . . . he will be one of God's most illustrious servants.") She often addresses him directly in the *Vida,* and he may be one reason for the book's warmth and accessibility. In addition to being Teresa's confessor, García was also her pupil and companion on the path to heaven. Once when they were together, she felt his soul burning with love for God and was almost overcome with happiness that he was receiving such favors. "It did me so much good to be with him that he seemed to have left my soul burning with the renewed desire to serve God all over again." Two people suffering the pangs of holy love together can support one another. Since they are "determined to risk a thousand lives for God, they long for chances to do it," she writes with heroic abandon. "They are like soldiers who want to go to war so they can enrich themselves with spoils, because they've grasped that that's the only way it can be done. This work is their profession."

Teresa's chivalric blood was stirred by retrieving this comrade in arms. And the feelings intensified when Fray Pedro de Alcántara arrived in sackcloth at Doña Luisa's elegant doorstep in the spring of 1562 to pay a brief visit. That in itself would have been enough to drive home the difference between spiritual and worldly wealth. Teresa was also pondering the sudden death of the aggressively worldly Martín de Guzmán, her sister María's husband; in a vision Teresa had seen devils wrangling over his corpse and had become concerned about María, whose piety had lapsed over the years. Teresa went to visit her sister to straighten her out. When María died shortly after, her soul was in good order and (according to another of Teresa's visions) passed swiftly through purgatory and home to God.

At Doña Luisa's, the crossroads of sense and spirit, Teresa also met a *beata* called María de Jesús, who had run into familiar problems while trying to found a reformed Carmelite convent in Granada. The *beata* gave Teresa a crash course in holy poverty, as outlined in the ancient Carmelite rule. Teresa hadn't realized that the early monastic foundations had been founded *sin renta*, without any reliable income. For her purposes this would mean soliciting alms from the gentle folk of Avila to establish her convent—not a happy prospect. It would also mean flying in the face of the established norms of monastic life for women. Aristocratic families that placed their daughters in convents fully expected a return on their investment. The families paid a twice-a-year fee, which helped to defray the convents' expenses and to maintain these young women in something like the style to which they had been accustomed. In return the families exacted prayers for the souls of their deceased relatives; special privileges, such as reserved seats in chapel and on-demand home visits from nuns with social credentials and personal skills, like Teresa herself; and even the construction of special family vaults. If a convent were founded in poverty and a nun from an impoverished family were equal in stature to one from the aristocracy, then what *doña* in her right mind would take up the religious life? What family with *honra* would permit her to do so? The symbiotic relationship of religious institutions and the social elite would come to an end.

Clearly the idea of a poor convent was not only romantic; it was revolutionary. As usual, Teresa pulled in advice from all quarters, relying on learned men to guide her. She discussed and argued—that was her forte—and heard a hundred reasons why she shouldn't make her foundation without revenues. All this discussion must have seemed absurd to Fray Pedro, who wrote a letter addressed to "the very magnificent and most pious lady Doña Teresa de Ahumada, may the Lord make you holy," telling her he found it strange that she consulted *letrados* about such a purely spiritual matter. She should have consulted only those who tried to live a spiritual life. But if she wanted to listen to those men, she could found a convent with rich endowments and live in luxury. Otherwise, following Christ's example, she should forget about what made sense and be good and poor.

That settled the matter for Teresa. It was what she had been thinking anyway. From then on, whenever people who had once told her that poverty was a good idea suddenly reconsidered and began to point out its drawbacks, "I told them that, considering how fast they changed their opinions, I preferred to stick to mine." She honed her arguments and presented them to Padre Ibáñez, who "answered me with two sheets of objections and theology." She retorted that she had no interest in reaping the benefits of his theology if it meant she couldn't follow her vocation, or fulfill her vow of poverty, or observe Christ's precepts." Ibáñez mulled this over, then told her to go ahead with her plans—a somewhat academic proposition, considering that Teresa was effectively stuck in Toledo where Angel de Salazar had placed her. But then the provincial rescinded his order. She could stay with Doña Luisa or come home, as she pleased: stay in this gracious old city, where her thorniest problem was deflecting the adoration of noblewomen and servants and trading thoughts with well-disposed Dominican prelates, or return to Avila, where the still irate nuns were bent on humiliating her and the townspeople were bent on blocking the progress of her foundation. To make matters worse, the Encarnación was just then electing its new prioress, and Teresa was afraid she would be chosen—an odd concern, at first glance, considering how embattled she was there. Victoria Lincoln suggests that Teresa had reason to worry, that Angel de Salazar was trying to rig the election on the grounds that power was what Teresa was really after. But life at the Encarnación would never again be what she wanted. She thought that if she stayed away, her chances of not being elected would be that much better. And her health was now as good as it had ever been, though she still suffered her occasional *mal de corazón.* Toledo's climate, which was milder than Avila's, agreed with her. But God commanded her to leave, saying that she had a fine cross awaiting her in Avila, and she assumed that meant her election as prioress. (It didn't; she wasn't elected.) It seems as if she dragged her feet anyway until García de Toledo pushed her to leave, at the same time demanding the promised account of her spiritual progress. Teresa delivered her *Vida* to him, with apologies for having rushed to finish it.

Doña Luisa was hardly sanguine about her adored nun's departure; life would be dispiriting without her. When Teresa determined to leave anyway, the great lady sulked and refused to provide an escort. She was mollified (barely) by the promise of a later visit. Weary and anxious, Teresa finally extricated herself from the silken fetters of the aristocratic life of Toledo, and on a brutally hot day at the end of June—Avila weather—she prepared for the arduous return.

Chapter 7: *Paradise*

—

How did it happen that everything fell into place? The very day that Teresa returned to Avila, the briefs for the foundation (to be made officially by Doña Guiomar de Ulloa and her mother, Doña Aldonza de Guzmán) had at last arrived from Rome. Pedro de Alcántara had also found his way to Avila and, brilliant quarterback that he was, positioned himself to receive the papers when they arrived. The bishop of Avila, under whose authority San José was to be established, was in town. So was Juan de Ovalle, who had escorted Teresa home from Toledo and now came down with an extremely timely case of chills and fever; he would have to delay his return to Alba, setting up his sickbed in the house he had bought undercover for his sister-in-law—who, of course, would have to stay there to look after him.

Whether these were strategic moves or the deft maneuverings of Providence, Teresa returned to find herself in a relatively protected situation. Salcedo and Daza, their friend Gonzalo de Aranda, and Julián de Avila (who was to become the new convent's chaplain) were all firmly in her camp. The brief itself specified that Doña Teresa and the future nuns of San José, as well as the two widows (Doña Guiomar and her mother) who were the convent's patrons, were not to be harassed openly or furtively, directly or indirectly, by superiors, prelates, priors, friars, or any other critics, Carmelite or lay. Still, there were obstacles to overcome. Teresa had Rome's blessing but not that of her provincial, and she was too much of a politician not to care. She would take another crack at Angel de Salazar. And the city of Avila wasn't likely to soften its opposition just because she had the pope's go-ahead. Like their king, most Castilians took papal orders with a grain of salt. Teresa would have to maneuver a cohort of nuns into her unfinished building, but not before Bishop Alvaro de Mendoza had issued a license. Depending on his mood and on the climate of opinion in the city, he could choose to issue it or not.

Don Alvaro chose to avoid the dilemma by taking an unscheduled trip to El Tiemblo, his secluded country house. He had agreed to a new convent, but not one that would be entirely without revenue; that struck him as bad business all around. Luckily, the brief didn't say anything about the convent having to be poor, so he could consider his qualms justified, despite his earlier endorsement of Doña Teresa's plans. Fray Pedro had written a letter from his sickbed (Daza and Aranda had delivered it personally) reminding Don Alvaro of the rationale for the new foundation. Its founder was a great servant of God and would adhere to the ancient rule—this could only make the bishop look good. Besides, though ill, Pedro had worked hard to get Pope Pius IV's permission. He had negotiated the details and had even paid a nice sum, more than 5000 reals, to get the brief written and sent. When a voluntary pauper resorts to such measures, why should a well-heeled bishop hold back?

When Don Alvaro failed to respond, Fray Pedro, who was deteriorating rapidly, arranged for a litter on which his emaciated person could be carried to El Tiemblo. Under the best of circumstances, the holy ascetic was an unnerving sight; at El Tiemblo he must have looked like the wrath of God. The bishop was persuaded. He agreed to go see Doña Teresa—anything to get such an apparition out the door.

The result was predictable. She could always work wonders face to face, and Don Alvaro emerged from their meeting that August day in 1562 her willing prisoner. Just as remarkably, Juan de Ovalle leaped up from his bed of pain, declaring that he saw no further point in being laid up. Teresa was so grateful to Fray Pedro for his intercession that she insisted on cooking him a meal at the Encarnación, "an angel's banquet" according to the nuns who testified they saw Christ himself spoon-feeding the old man.

Next she had to attend to logistics. Having outfitted the little convent with necessities—a secondhand bell, cracked but operational; an altar; beds of rough straw; statues of the Virgin Mary and San José to guard the entrances (as per her vision)—she began to recruit her company of nuns. Her idea was for the convent to have its full complement of thirteen—enough to form a cohesive community, but not so many as to create the kind of chaos she had endured at the Encarnación, which housed more than a hundred souls. For the moment, though, she would only bring four women, and she was lucky to get them. They were no spring chickens; the youngest was twenty-seven-year-old Antonia de Henao, a woman with a somewhat unpleasant flair for self-mortification, whom Fray Pedro had diverted from her plans to enter another convent. At San José, where worldly connections were to be abandoned, she would take on the name Antonia del Espíritu Santo. Gaspar Daza's contribution was forty-one-year-old Ursula de Revilla y Alvarez (Ursula de los Santos), one of his penitents, who had been a woman about town but was now admirably devout. Julián de Avila produced his sister María de Avila, thirty-seven and unmarried. She was sweet and a little slow; people said that talking to her was like talking to an innocent child. And Doña Guiomar passed along a faithful servant, María de la Paz (María de la Cruz), who came from a humble family and, having had enough of genteel surroundings, was looking forward to a humble life.

At the first blush of dawn on August 24, Saint Bartholomew's Day, the old bell rang and the first Mass was celebrated in the convent of San José, which stood like a valiant little fortress on hostile ground. Teresa was there with her cousins from the Encarnación, Doña Inés and Doña Ana de Tapia, neither of whom was free at the time to move to the new convent. Salcedo was there, along with Julián de Avila, Gonzalo de Aranda, Juan de Ovalle and his wife, Teresa's sister Juana, who must have been relieved to see an end to her long charade. Gaspar Daza celebrated Mass, and Teresa gave the habit of the Discalced—coarse brown sackcloth, in contrast to the more refined black serge worn by the sisters of the Encarnación—to her "four poor orphans," who from then on would live according to the ancient rule, hidden from the world (as demanded by their vows of enclosure), and subject to the rigors of monastic life. Since Teresa was still officially housed at the Encarnación, for now these lonely women would have to fend more or less for themselves.

No sooner was the service finished (Teresa thinks a few hours had passed) than the devil made his appearance, prodding her to wonder whether she hadn't been just a little disobedient. After all, she hadn't gotten her provincial's blessing. As she writes, "It certainly did seem to me that he would be a bit displeased at my having put the convent under the ordinary's jurisdiction, without first telling him. On the other hand, I didn't think he'd care very much, considering that he had withheld his approval and I hadn't revised my plans." The devil also made her wonder whether the nuns of San José would really be happy, especially when they didn't have enough food, and whether Teresa herself, with her many health problems, would ever be able to tolerate such harsh conditions. Did she really want to leave that sunny cell at the Encarnación, where she had some good friends? And what if she couldn't stand the nuns at San José? What made her think she could govern them anyway? How did she know the whole thing hadn't been the devil's idea and not her own?

These were serious doubts, but they were relieved by a beam of light from heaven that revealed their diabolic origin. Teresa then saw that her only problem was a lack of courage. She had asked for trials, now she had them. "I promised before the Most Holy Sacrament that I would do everything I could to get permission to enter the new house, and that if I could do it in good conscience, I would make a promise of enclosure." That got rid of the devil and also used up her last reserves of energy. Right after dinner Teresa allowed herself to go to bed.

The next morning would bring a summons to appear before the Encarnación's prioress, Doña María Cimbrón, who may or may not have shared the outrage of her nuns. Even the least privileged of these women took the new convent's austere way of life as a personal affront. If the sisters of San José were so penitent and content with privation, what did that say about the *doñas* of the Encarnación? It seemed to them that Teresa herself was no model of sanctity, yet she presumed to make rules for others—rules that by almost anyone's standards were far too stringent. She had sneaked around her provincial (not to mention her prioress and the secular officials of Avila). She should wear a habit with tongues sewn on it for having provoked so much gossip and scandal, and she should be shut up in the convent's prison cell.

None of that happened. After quickly installing Ursula de los Santos as San José's prioress, Teresa left for the Encarnación, accompanied by Julián de Avila. She seldom went anywhere without a strong second-in-command. After listening to her explanation, the prioress (who happened to be a distant relative) was inclined to be sympathetic, only remanding the truant nun to her cell, where dinner was sent up to her. Next Teresa had to appear before Angel de Salazar and a committee of clerics. Here she was eloquent. She asked for punishment (but also for forgiveness), admitting that she was full of faults; it was certainly amazing—wouldn't they agree?—that God had chosen someone as flawed as she to found this convent of his: "Since I was internally calm and the Lord helped me, I defended myself in such a way that neither the provincial nor the others who were there could find any reason to condemn me. And afterwards, when we were alone, I explained it all to him more frankly, and he was very satisfied, promising that—if the project went ahead—he would give me permission to go there as soon as the hubbub in the city died down."

Angel de Salazar might well have felt comfortable with that promise, considering that the hubbub wasn't likely to die down anytime soon. As Julián de Avila put it, when the bells rang for the first Mass at San José, the townspeople acted as if plague, fire, and an invading army were rushing over them. There were demonstrations in the streets; shops were closed. People said their children would starve—those nuns would take the food right out of their mouths. A water inspector insisted that the convent would overtax the city's precious water supply. The town council called an emergency meeting and announced that on the next day, August 25, they would hold an assembly *(junta)* and hear complaints. Meanwhile, a horde of citizens stormed the convent, hoping to flush the four nuns out. The *corregidor* of Avila, surrounded by his officers, threatened to break down the doors. The nuns said they could not obey him, as they were under orders from the bishop; the officers could invade the premises at the peril of their souls. The men began to hammer away, but the nuns buttressed the doors with thick wooden planks, then settled in to pray. This was a wild and wooly scene, even for *Avila de los Caballeros,* the city of the knights. By hagiographic standards it was yet another sign that from this point on, holy wars would be waged interiorly, with only the armament of faith.

On August 30 the *junta* was convened with requisite fanfare, as an imposing array of nobles and clergy prepared to voice (for the most part) their disapproval of the new foundation. Baltasar Alvarez was present, the records show, but mum as usual. The Dominican *letrado* Domingo Báñez, who had never met Teresa but knew about her from his friend Pedro Ibáñez, was her lone defender. Speaking before the assembled delegates, Báñez pointed out that there was no need to rush to dissolve the convent; the nuns were perhaps unwise to insist on poverty, but they were harmless enough. It was the bishop's business anyway, Báñez reminded the delegates, and should be referred back to him. The Dominican seems to have defused the situation enough so that the council decided to defer action. Meanwhile, God was assuring Teresa that her convent wouldn't be dissolved. Knowing what she knew about his intent and power, how could she think otherwise?

Another *junta* was called, this time with the bishop presiding. Gaspar Daza rode in waving all his oratorical colors, and Teresa's forces began to rally. Clearly the matter would have to be referred to the royal council in Madrid, an expensive and lengthy process that Teresa could hardly afford. But Gonzalo de Aranda, who was adept in legal matters, volunteered his services, while Daza and Salcedo held the fort at Avila. The *corregidor* was not about to admit defeat, and Teresa marveled at "all the trouble the devil was taking about a few poor women." From his deathbed Pedro de Alcántara reminded the founder that so much interference proved the worthiness of the cause. He urged her to battle on.

As the case wound its way through the courts, Teresa had to practice the virtue of patience. Angel de Salazar was not about to let her move to San José before he saw how the winds were blowing. By November, when an official from the royal council arrived to take testimony from the opposing factions, the case seemed far from a resolution. And yet gossip was beginning to abate. Officials were grumbling about the money that had to be paid to the royal investigators from Madrid. The time was ripe for a compromise, and Bishop Mendoza was just the man to propose one. He thought that if Teresa could only give up the idea of poverty and accept endowments, the town might let the foundation stand. Teresa was inclined to agree with him. She was a negotiator at heart, and she was sick of all the turmoil. It seemed to her that she could accept endowments at first, then later, after the convent was firmly established, she could return to her original ideals.

Souls have been lost by means of just such accommodations, and God lost no time in setting her straight. During evening prayers, he gave her a valuable lesson in politics: that once you make a bad deal, you're usually stuck with it. In case that wasn't enough, Fray Pedro, who had died earlier that fall, returned in a vision, looking fit but irritable, to insist that she stop ignoring his advice. Teresa promptly instructed Salcedo, who was now the linchpin of her supporters, that she would not give in. She reports that he was in full accord with her decision. So the case dragged on. Meanwhile, the intransigent Teresan faction sent a petition to Rome, asking that the convent be allowed to exist permanently *sin renta*. Things were still up in the air when Pedro Ibáñez unexpectedly paid a visit. "The Lord brought him there at a very good time for us," Teresa writes, "and it seems that His Majesty did it just for this purpose, because, as [Ibáñez] told me afterwards, he had had no other reason to come, and had only heard about what was going on by accident."

Ibáñez approved and, "impossible though it may seem that he could have done so in so short a time," convinced Salazar to let Teresa come and stay with her poor orphans at San José. Salazar may not have required much convincing at this point; things were settling down considerably in town. He gave her permission and also provided insurance in the persons of four handpicked (though not by Teresa) nuns from the Encarnación. Doña Ana Dávila (Ana de San Juan) was a harsh older woman with impressive social credentials. She would become San José's prioress—a move meant to silence the scandalmongers. The other three nuns were models of probity who would serve as instructors for the novices. Ana Gómez (Ana de los Angeles) made the move to San José somewhat reluctantly but later became one of Teresa's loyal prioresses. María Ordónez (María Isabel) came more freely, though her impact was negligible. Finding a fourth volunteer was difficult, so Salazar and his new prioress settled for young Isabel de la Peña (Isabel de San Pablo), another of Teresa's cousins, who were always in ready supply. With them in all humility, endowed only with a straw pallet, a scourge, a hair shirt, and a threadbare old habit, came Doña Teresa de Ahumada. Leaving behind her shoes and her family pride—from this point on, she too would drop her surname, as well as the title of *doña*—the nun Teresa de Jesús entered the enclosure of San José.

It was a squat, sturdy building, right in the heart of town. There was nothing unique about it, beyond its being so unpretentious and so unwelcome. The curious must have resented that behind the rough stone walls, a small group of women was quietly revising monastic life, and no one could get close enough to see. During the first few months, Ana de San Juan did her best to make the nuns' existence, and Teresa's in particular, as uncomfortable as possible. She seems to have had a penchant for humiliating others. Teresa didn't mind. She was relieved, and frequently ecstatic, to be living in her foundation at last. In March of 1563 Rome granted the petition for San José to be founded in poverty. The nuns and their prioress would have the honor of forgoing a regular income and of receiving nothing but charity. Ana de San Juan promptly arranged to return to the Encarnación, where her title, along with her comfortable serge habit, were waiting for her to slip them on. Isabel's sister María de Cepeda was sent to San José to replace Mother Ana, though not as prioress. After a brief and unsurprising election Teresa took on that office herself.

It wasn't long before her presence brought an infusion of youth to the convent: well-off women in their twenties who found the thought of marriage less enticing than a life of virtuous deprivation. Teresa's cousin, Doña María de Ocampo—the same overeager María who, as a teenager, had pressed her aunt to follow the ancient Carmelite rule—was just twenty and already engaged when she decided to join the sisters of San José. In something of a grand gesture Doña María—who would become María Bautista, one of Teresa's more bullish prioresses—shed her elegant trappings, only arranging for some much needed funds to be channeled into the convent. Doña María Dávila arrived, according to Ribera's account, decked out in silk and gold and attended by a procession of *caballeros*. (She was related to several of Avila's leading families.) But according to legend, María left all her finery, dashing the hopes of would-be suitors, at the door of San José, where she took the name of María de San Jerónimo. She is remembered now for being decent, levelheaded, plainspoken, and loyal to Teresa over decades. The lovely twenty-three-year-old Doña Isabel Ortega, Pedro de Alcántara's protégée, had wanted to come earlier, but her parents wouldn't allow it in view of the shakiness of the enterprise. Now she finally arrived and took on the name Isabel de Santo Domingo. Teresa would later make her a prioress too. Now that she had almost her full complement of nuns (eleven of a possible twelve), Teresa was ready to get to work.

She had had plenty of time to construct a blueprint for life in the new convent. Everything about the place—its rustic cells designed by Pedro de Alcántara, each whitewashed and furnished with a straw bed, a cork mat on the floor, a water pitcher, and a crucifix; its utilitarian kitchen and refectory; its modest chapel—suggested lives conducted with economy and care. Teresa had enough drama in her life without needing to introduce it into her convent. There would be silence, but it was not absolute. The nuns could speak with one another occasionally, especially to convey information. No gossiping or babbling was allowed. Meals would exclude red meat, a luxury, unless a sister's health required it; in any case, poultry could be eaten once a week. A little bread, cheese, or fruit made a typical meal, and a piece of fish or an egg a banquet. When no food was available, the sisters would come to the table anyway, to be nourished by their love for God. Self-flagellation and other mortifications were to be conducted publicly, and with the prioress's permission, to avoid self-indulgent behavior. Recreation was mandatory (it renewed the spirit for prayer) and might include reading incidental poetry, singing religious tunes, and dancing; the prioress liked to play a little drum and a tambourine.

The ancient Carmelites had gone discalced, or barefoot, and the nuns of San José initially followed their example. But this was rocky, windy Castile, and in time the prioress allowed that hemp sandals, called *alpargatas,* could be worn as needed. Every nun worked, taking her turn in the kitchen, and also sewing, spinning, and weaving. Idleness was no more tolerated than bad will. Obedience was a given, and certainly no one knew its difficulty better than Teresa, who liked to test her nuns. The stories about this good-natured (if sometimes drastic) testing are plucked from diverse points of her career at San José. One day in the convent garden, for example, she handed María Bautista a rotting cucumber and asked her to plant it. "Which way?" asked María. "Straight up or horizontally?" Another time Teresa pulled aside Ursula de los Santos, exclaiming that the sister looked very ill. The prioress ordered the perfectly healthy nun to bed, and when others questioned Ursula about her symptoms, she replied that she couldn't say what they might be, but was sure Mother knew. When Teresa visited the bedside, she reiterated her concern and called for a barber, the professional who in those days performed the therapeutic function of bloodletting. The uncomplaining Ursula was bled, to what Teresa always held was the eternal benefit of the convent, which from then on had a special regard for the virtue of obedience.

San José, once the nuns and their prioress had settled in, ran like a well-oiled machine. Each day was segmented into hours of prayer and work. Time was never flexible; it was managed adroitly and, like food, never wasted. Morning prayers began with private devotions at dawn and continued with the saying of the hours of prime, terce, sext, and none. Mass was celebrated at nine and was followed by a meal. Then came work and recreation and some quiet (and preferably instructive) talk. Prayers resumed with vespers at two, and the rest of the day included chapel, pious reading-aloud (though never of Latin books; nuns were not supposed to be scholarly), and meditation. After compline at eight, absolute silence was observed. The nuns returned to their rooms to pray and to brace themselves for the coming day. Such a schedule would seem to leave little time for sinning, but Teresa knew how small an opening the devil could squeeze through. So in her Constitutions—the official plan for conventual life—she delineated minor and major transgressions. A minor one might be giggling, talking too much, making mistakes in chapel, or displaying bad manners; a not-so-minor one might be gratuitous fault-finding or cliquishness; a major one *(gravissima culpa)* might be gossiping with outsiders, scheming for power, refusing to do penance, or attacking the prioress. The higher the degree of malevolence, the graver the offense. Penalties were imposed at a weekly disciplinary chapter. According to legend, Teresa once punished herself for some unrecorded offense by getting outfitted with a halter and a saddle weighted with stones, and entering the refectory on all fours, led by another nun. Those who were at the table, poised to eat, had plenty of food for meditation that day.

Visitors to the convent were received politely but never regaled with conversation. "Solitude is their delight," Teresa writes of her nuns, claiming that they don't like the idea of seeing anyone, even a close relative, unless the meeting will inflame their love for God. The pious Salcedo came by regularly to speak with the prioress about holy matters. She sat behind the grille in the parlor (the curtains were always drawn between nuns and their visitors) and worked at her spinning as Salcedo talked. The contrast with the "salon" at the Encarnación was instructive. Teresa saw her time in San José's parlor as an occasion to advance the interests of the convent—in this case, generating revenue through the manufacture and sale of handwoven cloth—even as she attended to spiritual concerns. The *caballero santo* found this irritating; maybe it reminded him too much of life at home. So he struck a bargain: if she would just stop spinning while they talked, he would pay the convent for the equivalent of an hour's worth of work.

Her brisk efficiency at the spinning wheel may have concealed a touch of impatience. She had a convent to run, and for once she had little inclination to socialize, even for pious ends. She was also concerned about making life tolerable for her nuns: having convinced them to give up ordinary comforts, she felt responsible for their health and well-being, even to the point of defensiveness: "If any nun thinks our Rule is harsh, she should blame her own lack of spirituality, not our observance here—because people who are delicate, not strong but spiritual, hold up very well under it. Those who don't should go to some other convent, where they will find salvation in a way better suited to their own spirituality."

The women of San José, at least the ones who stayed (illness, physical and emotional, drove some away), seemed at ease with privation. They were always busy, and their lives were not uneventful, mostly because of the theatrical nature of their founder. The stories about her raptures and homely miracles are numerous, and it is easy to imagine them being told and retold by the sisters in the course of their domestic routine. One day the prioress was amused to find some of them singing hymns to which they had added some verses about lice. The nuns had just been given permission to wear coarse wool instead of linen next to their skin, but they were afraid that the rough frieze would be infested. Teresa, touched by their earnestness, added some verses of her own ("Should creatures vile invest our frieze / Deliverance bring"), and from that point on, not a single louse was found within the confines of San José. Whether any had been seen before, nobody knows.

Teresa liked to cook, especially since "the Lord," as she famously remarked, "walks among the pots and pans," and she used her turn in the kitchen to whip up gustatory treats. Once when she seemed to be spending an inordinate amount of time at the stove, Isabel de Santo Domingo peeked over the prioress's shoulder and found her transfixed in ecstasy but still clutching the oiled pot. This seemed not to be the ideal moment for a rapture: oil was scarce in the convent, and fire was a constant threat. But here, as everywhere, Teresa's grip was firm. She held fast, the rapture subsided, and eggs were served.

As time went by, Teresa's raptures became so frequent as to be almost commonplace; at least, they were as much a part of convent life as praying in chapel or scrubbing floors. The occasional visitor, like Bishop Alvaro de Mendoza, might be astonished to see the prioress, her hands pressed forward in prayer and her eyes rolled up to heaven, rise a foot or more off the ground. But the nuns of San José viewed such an event as yet another proof of their prioress's sanctity; they expected no less of her. Teresa ordered that any sister who happened to be present during one of these levitations was to grab hold of her habit and try to hold her down. This, of course, was impossible, obedience being no match for celestial magnetism.

· · ·

As she tells it, Teresa's five years at the convent were the most tranquil ones of her life; she often described San José as heaven on earth. But that tranquillity was often disrupted by forces she could not control. For one thing, García de Toledo had sent back the original manuscript of the *Vida* (which has subsequently been lost) with a request that she tone it down in places and add new chapters about the foundation. The convent might serve as evidence, in case some was needed, of its founder's moral and spiritual rectitude. Teresa, who had rushed the *Vida* to García with a plea that he just strike out whatever offended him, must have been as dismayed as any other writer would have been by the news that she had to put pen to paper again. And maybe more so, considering that the Inquisition would be the ultimate judge of her work. So whether it was anxiety or a fresh impetus from God that propelled her, she knelt at the tiny desk (really an outcropping of wall) by the window in her cell and produced not only four new chapters about the foundation, but eleven chapters composing a treatise on prayer and a fillip of four chapters at the end detailing the divine favors she had enjoyed up to 1565, the year the second version of the book was finished.

The chapters in the *Vida* that follow the founding of San José are the work of a woman who has won a long and difficult campaign. She views her struggles as epic, recalling a vision in which

> I saw myself standing alone, praying, in a large field, and in a circle around me were many different kinds of people. They all seemed to be carrying weapons to attack me with: some had lances, others swords, others daggers, and still others, very long rapiers. All in all, I couldn't escape in any direction without risking death, and I was alone, with no one to defend me. As I was feeling this great spiritual distress, and not knowing what to do, I raised my eyes to the sky and saw Christ, who was not in heaven but way above me in the air, holding out His hand towards me, and from there He supported me so that I stopped being afraid of all these people, and they couldn't hurt me even though they wanted to.

Teresa doesn't say when she had this vision, only that it came before the period she calls her persecution. In general terms, she sees her enemies as the forces ranged against the soul, which will "find itself ensnared, or at least these things will try to ensnare it when it's not on its guard." She refers here not only to bad people but also to very good ones—"the ones who scare me the most"—friends and relatives who, thinking they were doing the right thing, pushed her unrelentingly to change her course. At times, Teresa writes, she felt so besieged that it was all she could do to remember the vision and look to God—and then He would always send a proxy to help her out.

The campaign for San José was traumatic for a woman who longed to please and, in her early life at least, usually succeeded. For the first time, she had been ostracized—and by virtually an entire city. She had been ridiculed, humored, berated, and brushed aside. People had made idle promises and then thought better of them. She had had to use every resource at her disposal to keep her enterprise on track, including kowtowing to people of influence. And even though the convent was established, the kowtowing hadn't ended. "The fact is," she explains toward the end of the *Vida:*

> when I came here I had no idea how I could live. It's no joke when someone neglects to treat people much better than they deserve; because as soon as they notice they take offense, and then you have to convince them of your good intentions. . . . The poor soul finds that it is worn out. It understands that it is required to preoccupy itself with God, that it needs to focus on Him so it can escape all sorts of danger. On the other hand, it finds that it mustn't overlook a single point of worldly etiquette, because that might provide occasions of sin to people who think their honor hinges on these niceties. All this simply exhausted me, and I was endlessly apologizing, because as hard as I tried, I could not keep from making mistakes; and as I've said, the world does not take these lightly.

Teresa's complaint would be familiar to the director of any public institution; the irony here is that in order to win support for a bastion of order and privacy, she had had to accept the convoluted rules of nonmonastic life. Spanish society was formal and (as portraits of the time attest) hopelessly stiff-necked. Nothing of a social or political nature could be done without ceremony. "If this etiquette could be learned once and for all," she writes, "that would be fine. But even the titles of address in letters require a university chair, so to speak. . . . Because sometimes part of the page has to be left blank, and sometimes another part, and a person who, before, wasn't even a 'Magnificence' now has to be addressed as 'Illustrious.' "

Critical speculation about Teresa's character often includes the theory that her distaste for titles and formalities, which she incorporated into her foundations, stemmed from her knowledge that as a member of a *converso* family, she wasn't really entitled to them. Some critics see her discussions of *honra* as, in effect, coded messages to others in a similar situation. Certainly her reform, with its emphasis on equality in matters of the spirit, appealed to others with *converso* backgrounds, and her convents welcomed them, unlike most religious institutions of her day. But in tirades like the one just mentioned, her aversion to titles and social etiquette seems more visceral. She had enough trouble trying to keep her own endlessly deviating soul on course to God. Trying to navigate through the world when the maps kept changing drove her wild: "I don't know where all this is going to end, because I'm not even fifty, yet I've seen so many changes that I don't know how to keep functioning. What will people do who have just been born and have long lives ahead of them? I'm really sorry for those spiritual people who for certain holy reasons are obliged to live in the world—they have a terrible cross to bear."

By enclosing herself in San José, Teresa herself escaped the world to some extent. But she was still the subject of gossip because of her raptures, which continued to occur in public, much to her distress. The suspicion that she was an *alumbrada* kept rearing its head ("many people still say bad things about me, and zealously, others are scared to deal with me or to hear my confession, and others say awful things to me"), and at one point an inquisitor named Francisco de Soto did come by—at Teresa's request, she says—to make sure nothing unorthodox was taking place. Apparently, he was satisfied, though shortly after his visit García de Toledo was relieved as her confessor by the scholarly and evenhanded Domingo Báñez.

In her weariness she craved anonymity. Maybe God, who had favored her so often, had done it again by putting her "in this secluded place, so strictly enclosed, where I'm so much like a dead thing that I didn't think anyone would remember me." Yet there were disappointments: "Things haven't turned out exactly the way I hoped, because I'm forced to speak with certain people."

From the vantage point of the late-twentieth century, this hardly reads like a description of life in paradise. But then Teresa's idea of paradise was always a particularly Spanish one. The phrase *la vida es sueño*—life is a dream—gained literal meaning for her as she moved through her monastic day: "It seems to me that I'm always dreaming what I see. I'm not aware of happiness or great misery. If something makes me feel either way, the feeling passes so quickly that I'm astonished, and it leaves behind the sense that it was all a dream. And this is the truth . . . because the Lord has now awakened my soul from that state in which I wasn't mortified or dead to the things of the world, and so was used to having such feelings. His Majesty doesn't want my soul to be blind again." During her five years at San José, Teresa could at least nurture the hope of shutting out the world and living a recollected life. But the world came to her door at last.

Chapter 8: *Cultivating Souls*

—

One of the particular beauties of San José was its garden. It was small, like everything about the place, but it had enough room for a plot where the nuns could plant their flowers and vegetables, and also, as Teresa soon realized, for some modest hermitages where they could retire to pray. This must have brought back memories: Teresa had always had a fondness for hermitages. These were constructed, thanks to funds supplied by admirers of means, with an eye to privacy and simplicity. Very little adorned them except paintings of the stations of the cross, commissioned from a local artist. The tiny retreats, with their stone walls and red tile roofs, were moving and beautiful, according to Julián de Avila. To Teresa, the hermitages offered a welcome respite from the world, which even monastic walls could never quite shut out. But to the watchful critics of San José, they were a threat. A suit filed by Lázaro Dávila, the same water inspector who had accused the convent of depleting the city's fountains, now claimed that the shadows cast by the hermitages would chill the fountains in winter and freeze the water supply. It was a ludicrous objection, but Señor Lázaro was a bureaucrat who could make people listen; perhaps he was still smarting from his earlier defeat. So Teresa had to go to court again, armed with nothing more than a calm demeanor and a plea for reason: the hermitages weren't large enough to cast such mammoth shadows, and anyway, the prayers said in them would drench the city with blessings. In a letter dated December 5, 1563, she wrote to the gentlemen of the city council on behalf of herself and the other sisters: "Seeing that your lordships are annoyed by the buildings, we beg your lordships to go and inspect them. We are ready to sign all contracts, guarantees and agreements that your lawyers may demand as security that no damage will occur at any time." But the gentlemen weren't convinced. In the winter of 1564 the council ordered the garden wall and all the structures within it torn down.

By now Teresa was inured enough to adversity to keep going in spite of it. Even before the hermitages had been destroyed, she was arranging to rebuild them on the other, more secluded side of the convent, on land acquired in Julián de Avila's name. The bishop's sister María de Mendoza, one of Teresa's patronesses and a friend of Doña Luisa's, donated funds for a hermitage dedicated to Saint Augustine, and several more were built. The hermitage dedicated to Our Lady of Nazareth of the Annunciation was Teresa's favorite. It faced west, where she liked her vistas, and as María de San Jerónimo later testified, the prioress kept books there—including the vernacular edition of St. Gregory's *Morals* and the *Life of Christ* by the Carthusian Ludolph of Saxony—and experienced numerous ecstasies. A third hermitage was devoted to Saint Catherine Martyr and a fourth to Christ at the Pillar, where Teresa commissioned a very graphic devotional fresco illustrating one of her visions and known locally today as the *Christ with the Lovely Eyes.*

It doesn't seem surprising, in retrospect, that when García de Toledo asked Teresa to enhance her *Vida* with the story of the foundation of San José, she decided also to write a little treatise on prayer, taking a metaphorical turn in the convent garden. With its picturesque hermitages and its array of vegetables and flowers, the garden at San José must have been an inspiring and soothing place, fertile with sacred possibilities. And so she writes:

> A beginner has to consider that he is starting to make a garden, for the Lord's pleasure, on very barren ground full of terrible weeds. His Majesty pulls these out, and is going to put in viable plants instead. Well then, consider this done when a soul has decided to practice prayer, and has started doing it. With God's help, we have to make these plants grow, as good gardeners do, watering them carefully so that they don't die but begin producing flowers, which give off an appealing scent, to delight this Lord of ours. Then He will come frequently to amuse himself in this garden and take pleasure in these virtues.

You would think the rest of the job would be easy. The master gardener, God, has done the work; the weeds are out, and the good plants are in. But as anyone living in the parched, windswept climate of Castile—and especially a nun who routinely works in the convent garden—must know, cultivating the soul is a very tricky business. It requires vigilance, fortitude, and a climate of spiritual opportunity.

The subject of prayer is complex, and a woman without formal schooling has few didactic tools available to her. Teresa has to apologize for using metaphor, even though "I'd like to avoid it, since I am a woman and am only writing what they tell me to write. But the language of the spirit is so confusing for uneducated people like me that I have to find some other way to express myself." The last thing she wants is for her readers to suspect her of being artful, so she suggests that she must have seen this garden comparison elsewhere but is too fuzzy-minded to recall its source. That said, she is ready to get down to business. The first step, as in any business venture, is to assess the project at hand:

> Now let's see how this garden should be watered, so that we understand what we have to do and how much work it requires, whether the end result is worth the effort, and how long it's going to take. It seems to me that the garden can be watered in four ways: you can draw the water from a well, which as we know firsthand is very labor intensive; or by using a waterwheel and buckets, worked by a crank (I've sometimes drawn it in this way, which is less work than the first, and brings up more water); or you can get it from a stream or spring, which does a much better job of soaking the ground, because the soil retains more moisture and needs watering less often—and that's less work for the gardener; or from a heavy rain, when the Lord is watering it Himself with no help from us. And this last method is far and away better than all the others.

These four ways of watering, Teresa explains, correspond to the four stages of prayer that she has experienced. At least one of her readers, Pedro Ibáñez, who has also made astonishing progress in prayer, should know what she's talking about. "His garden is watered by all four of these methods," and should soon be completely submerged. On the other hand, he might think she's crazy, in which case he should feel free to laugh at her.

Beginners in prayer, she goes on, are the ones who have to pray with their heads—their hearts aren't ready yet—repeatedly dipping their buckets into the well of their own spirituality, "and God grant that there be water in it!" This is hard labor at best, because it requires shutting out distractions, then thinking back on past sins and on the life of Christ. Or the mind might settle on thoughts of death and even of hell. These meditations should produce some tears or, at least, tender, devoted feelings—enough to begin watering the garden. But what if the well is dry? "What should a person do who finds that for many days on end he feels nothing but dryness, antipathy, distaste and so little desire to go draw water that he'd like to give it up altogether" if he weren't so eager to please God and also see some return on his labor? That person, Teresa says, should remind himself that he's lucky even to be working in such a garden for such a loving taskmaster. And besides, these efforts won't be in vain, though the rewards might be slow in coming. "I endured these labors for many years, and when I drew a single drop of water from this sacred well, I thought God was sending me a favor." This is how He tests the people who love Him. First He shows them how useless they are, so that when they receive divine favors, they won't get puffed up with their own importance. It is a strategy that works, believe her.

The problem arises, Teresa says, when people think that favors should come quickly. But favors are beside the point, which is to make a valiant effort. In her own case, there have been extenuating circumstances: "As for a poor little woman like myself, weak and spineless as I am, it seems right that God should move me along with favors, as He now does, so that I'll be able to suffer certain trials that His Majesty has wished me to experience. But when I see servants of God, prominent, learned, intelligent men, worrying so much because He doesn't give them devotion, it annoys me to listen to them."

As she writes, Teresa is in the uncomfortable position of having to advise men who presumably know a lot more than she does. The only way she can do it is to convince them of her weakness and their strength. If God isn't helping them, that's because they don't need help the way she does, and they shouldn't be pleading for it. "They should take it from me that this is a fault. . . . They are not going ahead with freedom of spirit." As usual with Teresa, "freedom of spirit" is the prerequisite for service to God: "His yoke is sweet, and it is important not to drag the soul, as they say, but bring it along gently, so that it will make better progress."

What the beginner in prayer needs is *determinación*. That is the motor driving the soul toward God. All other motive power is extraneous to the soul, a gift from heaven. It is tempting (and like all temptations, this one is diabolic) to try to accelerate to the second stage of prayer by purposely dulling the mind while it is engaged in the prayer of recollection, in hopes that spiritual pleasures will rush in. But this is a big mistake. "Anyone who tries to go from where he is and lift up his spirit so that it can taste pleasures it isn't being granted will have a double loss, in my opinion." The soul that gives up what it has in order to grab at something better loses them both.

The beauty of the prayer of quiet—the second stage of prayer—is that it comes unannounced, gratis. The gardener still has to work (using the device with the waterwheel), but not as hard, and he can sometimes take a rest. Teresa extends her metaphor: "Now the soul begins to be recollected, and this is where it is touched by the supernatural, because it couldn't possibly reach this stage by its own efforts. True, it seemed to get tired sometimes from turning the wheel and working with the understanding, and filling the buckets; but here the water level is higher, and getting it takes much less effort than by drawing it from the well. What I'm saying is that the water is closer because grace is more clearly evident to the soul."

As it senses the presence of God, the soul becomes more and more aware of its own divided nature. Saint Augustine had famously distinguished the soul's three major faculties—memory, intellect, and will—and Spanish theologians were keeping those distinctions alive. "Although it is true that the rational soul is a single, indivisible substance," wrote Alejo Venegas in 1540, "that fact does not prevent it from having . . . different names, just as we see that a certain man is called a father because he has a son, and a son because he has a father or mother. In this fashion the rational soul, being one, is called *memory* insofar as its function is to retain; it is called *intellect,* insofar as its function is comprehending; it is called *will* insofar as its appointed task is to crave and to desire."

Teresa takes it for granted that her reader sees the soul as many-faceted, so she explains that during the second stage of prayer, or second water, all of the faculties work together, though "only the will is occupied in such a way that—even though it doesn't know how—it is taken captive. It simply consents to be God's prisoner." The other faculties might help the will to enjoy this blessing, but they might also distract it, fluttering around "like doves who are dissatisfied with the food the owner of the dovecote gives them, without their having to work for it, and go looking for nourishment elsewhere, but find so little that they come back." The will has to be very canny in dealing with those restless little birds.

Meanwhile, the water of divine favors makes the soul's virtues grow more quickly than ever. The soul "begins losing its desire for earthly things—which is not surprising, because it sees clearly that not one moment of this pleasure can be enjoyed here." Satisfaction, as Teresa knows from her own experience, is always ephemeral. We have it; then suddenly it's gone, and we have no idea how to get it back. But God, the master gardener, readies the soul for lasting satisfaction: "It seems as if He is filling up a void that was hollowed out by our sins."

As she writes, Teresa is filled with compunctions. She can't forget for a minute who her readers are and how they might react to this course of instruction from an untutored nun. So she bows repeatedly to their judgment, as in "This will be looked over by people who will recognize any errors, so I'm not worried; because although I might be making mistakes in regard to theology as well as matters of the spirit, they'll understand and strike out anything I've gotten wrong." Such deference becomes increasingly important as Teresa ventures into territory that is traditionally closed to someone like her. If she can avoid offending the censors, then her writings may survive to help some other soul in need—the book's eventual reader: "If God leads [the soul] along the path of fear—as He led mine—it's a great hardship if there's no one who understands it. But it is very glad to see itself depicted, so that it can understand clearly which road it is on. . . . I've suffered a lot and lost quite a bit of time because I didn't know what to do, and I feel very sorry for souls who find themselves all alone once they get to this point."

Giving a coherent, accurate, unobjectionable account of God's relations with the soul takes time, and time is exactly what Teresa lacks in her daily life. Her only recourse is to God himself, who she thinks ought to help her craft these explanations:

I have to be part of the community and do much more, since the house I am in is just starting out. . . . So I never have peace and quiet for writing, and have to work in snatches. I wish I had more time, because when the Lord inspires me, everything gets said much more easily and in a much better way. Then it is like doing a piece of embroidery with the pattern right in front of you. But if the spirit is lacking, the words make no more sense than if the writing were in Arabic (so to speak), even though a person may have spent many years in prayer. So it seems a very great advantage for me to be in this inspired state when I am writing, because it's clear to me that I'm not the one who is putting all this down.

Nuns who lived and worked with Teresa, some of whom appeared as witnesses at her canonization hearings, remembered that she often wrote with her eyes lifted and her pen skimming along the page, as if moved by a supernatural power. (Francisco de Zurbarán later painted her with her head swiveled so far from her manuscript that even a healthier woman might have suffered severe neck and head pain.) Teresa felt she took dictation from God, and she often claimed to be surprised by what she had written. Whether or not she was a natural, instinctive writer, as some critics have asserted, or one who carefully adjusted her style to suit the needs of diverse audiences, as others have proposed, is still a subject of some debate. In either case, she wrote the way she prayed, rushing ahead or progressing slowly, making detours, doubling back and correcting her course, then continuing on.

She also stopped occasionally to smell the flowers, "to see how the trees begin to bud, then blossom and bear fruit." In one passage she remembers her own beginnings at prayer, when "it used to please me enormously to think of my soul as a garden, and imagine that the Lord was walking in it. I begged Him to increase the fragrance of those little flowers of virtue that were, it seemed, just starting to bloom. . . . I didn't want anything for myself, and invited Him to cut whichever blossoms He wanted, because I already knew that the plants would be better for pruning."

No one reading this would doubt that Teresa enjoyed her own time in the convent garden—and that she had a flair for the sometimes ruthless operations that invigorate a plant or a soul. "I mention 'pruning,'" she writes, "because there are times when the soul doesn't recognize this garden. Everything there seems dry, and there seems to be no way to water it and keep it up—it also seems as if the soul has never contained a drop of virtue. . . . That's just the time for weeding, and pulling out all the sickly plants, no matter how puny they are, by the roots." The gardener, humbled by a bad season, now tries to predispose the garden to health by cutting out the bad growth. But the only thing that will make a crucial difference is the water of grace.

When the prayer of quiet comes, Teresa says, it is so sweet that the soul gets nervous. "It's afraid to move, because this blessing might slip away; sometimes it's even afraid to breathe." But all the soul needs to do is keep calm and make no noise. "What I call noise is scurrying around with the intellect to come up with lots of words and thoughts to use in thanking God for this blessing, and piling up sins and faults to make it obvious that these gifts are undeserved. Everything is in motion, the intellect showing what it can do, and the memory rushing about." And this is, of course, counterproductive. The will has to keep those other faculties in check because "we cannot deal violently with God."

Up to this point Teresa has been writing about spiritual states that are not uncommon. She notes, in fact, that many people never progress past the early stages of prayer. They grow lazy, or lax, or busy and distracted, and before long the devil is making furrows in their rich soil. But the devil's work is always inadequate; it never results in anything good. The soul that can hold on, not letting go of its benefits, may go further in prayer, as Teresa explains: "Let's talk about the third water now, which irrigates this garden—that is, the water flowing from a stream or spring—with much less work, though some is required to channel the water the right way. But now the Lord wants to help the gardener so badly that He almost *becomes* the gardener, and does practically everything." God does the heavy work. The soul is suffused with pleasure—not inert, but not really conscious of all its motions. "The water—that is, the water of grace—has risen up to the soul's throat, and the soul can't move forward, since it doesn't know how to; it can't even go backward." The stricken soul "tastes this agony with the greatest possible delight. This strikes me as nothing other than an almost complete death to earthly pleasures, and the enjoyment of God." All the soul wants is to bask in its glory, but it doesn't know how. "It doesn't know if it should speak or be silent, if it should laugh or cry. It is a glorious confusion, a heavenly madness, in which true wisdom is gained."

Whenever Teresa begins to describe transcendent emotion, she uses conventional oxymoronic language that turns reason upside down, because the kind of understanding she describes goes beyond reason. Her own experience proves the point. Up until the moment of writing she had no idea how to describe this stage of prayer, even though she had attained it often over the course of the last five years or so. But luckily, God came to her rescue, revealing in a flash that even though the soul receiving this third water appeared to be in a state of complete union with God, it was still cognizant of itself—though just barely. Driven to distraction by the heady wonders it has begun to perceive, the soul "wants to let loose with praise and is beside itself with a delicious disquiet. Now the flowers are opening, and starting to release their scent."

With God doing the gardening, things start to happen quickly. Watered liberally, the garden begins to flourish, and one day "what the poor soul couldn't accomplish over about twenty years . . . this heavenly gardener gives it in a moment. Then the fruit grows and ripens, so that the soul can be sustained by the garden, if God wills it." The more nourishment the soul takes in, the stronger and more virtuous it gets. Like a body returning to health, the soul takes its meals and makes them part of itself. The only requirement is a willingness to be fed. It is also important that the soul not try at this point to give its fruit to others, for fear of sapping its strength.

While the will settles in with God, the memory and intellect are free to go about their usual business—say, running a convent, reading, or doing charity work. Or writing: Teresa is experiencing this third water even as she describes it. At first glance it might seem ideal for the soul to lead such a dual existence, at once active and contemplative, Martha and Mary (the biblical opposites) yoked together for holy work. That duality can be a problem, though, "as if we were speaking to the person on one side of us, while someone on the other side were speaking to us, so that we couldn't give our full attention to either one of them."

It is exhausting to live as Teresa does, straddling two worlds. She is convincing when she prays: "Ordain, Lord, that I no longer pay attention to the world, or take me out of it. . . . This soul wants to be free now. Eating is killing it, sleep is tormenting it. . . . It seems to be living unnaturally, because it no longer wants to live in itself, but only in You."

The soul is longing for what it can never achieve by its own efforts—complete and blissful union with God, the fourth water of her metaphor. That is a state in which divine favors come so fast and hard that the soul is flooded with gratitude: "Well, now, speaking of that abundant water from heaven that soaks and saturates the entire garden: if the Lord always sent it when it was needed, the gardener would have an easy time. And if it was never winter but always mild weather, there would never be a lack of fruit and flowers. Obviously, the gardener would be delighted." But that will no more happen regularly in the gardener's soul than it will in the gardens of Castile. Spiritual weather is too volatile; the gardener has to be resourceful, falling back on whatever method works. When God does decide to send his drenching rain, all the gardener needs to do is take it in:

> While searching for God in this way, the soul feels such a sweet and wonderful delight that almost everything fades away—it falls into a kind of swoon. The breathing and all the bodily functions gradually subside, and in such a way that the hands can't even be moved without enormous difficulty. The eyes close inadvertently, and if they do stay open, they see hardly anything. A person starting to read can hardly make out a single letter. . . . He does hear, but doesn't understand what it is he's hearing. . . . When he tries to speak, he can't even form a word, and if he did he wouldn't have the strength to pronounce it. All exterior strength is lost, and the soul's strength increases so that it can more thoroughly enjoy its bliss.

This enraptured state, during which the soul is in union with God, can't last very long, especially at first. Teresa doubts it can last even half an hour, though she admits that time is hard to judge when the senses are out of order. Afterward, the soul feels tender and heroic, as if it could suffer anything for God. People see this, and they're attracted without the soul's having to explain what just happened; the flowers smell irresistibly sweet. How long this effect lasts depends on how prepared the gardener is to sustain it:

> If the ground is well cultivated by trials, persecutions, jabs and infirmities—and not many can get to this point without

them—and if it's well dug up by going about very detached from self-interest, it soaks up so much water that it can hardly ever dry out again. But if it's just hard ground, and as full of thorns as I was at first, and if it still isn't free of occasions for sin, and isn't as grateful as it should be for such a great favor as this is, then the ground will dry up again. If the gardener gets careless, and if the Lord, in his goodness, won't make it rain again, then the garden is as good as lost. It has happened to me more than once.

This is why the soul has to be so ready to start over in prayer, watering the garden by whatever method comes to hand. When Teresa was young and—inexplicably to herself and her advisers—was swept away by a rapture, she wasn't ready for it. She became too proud, and the rainfall stopped. It was devastating to rise so high and then fall so low. But she learned to go back for the bucket, working at prayer again, and to let the tears flow. "For tears get you everything; and one kind of water attracts another."

In her description of the fourth water, Teresa is tackling a subject of enormous interest not only to her initial readers, who are invested in her spiritual welfare, but to the population at large and to the ever alert inquisitors. As E. W. T. Dicken points out in *The Crucible of Love,* his study of Spanish mysticism, a rich vocabulary supported this pervasive interest in ecstatic states. The difference between *arrobamiento* (trance) and *arrebatamiento* (rapture), or between *impetu* (transport) and *vuelo del espiritu* (flight of the spirit), was noteworthy in some quarters. But philosophical distinctions were not Teresa's strong point.

"I wish I knew how to explain, with God's help," she writes, "the difference between union and rapture, or elevation or what they call flight of the spirit or transport—which are all the same. I mean that these are all different names for the same thing, which is also called ecstasy." All Teresa wants to do—all she is really capable of doing—is to tell how ecstasy works and how it feels. She explains that it comes without warning, so swiftly and powerfully that the soul "sees and feels this cloud or mighty eagle lifting it up and bearing it away on its wings." And again, "Often I wanted to resist, and I fought with all my strength, especially when it happened in public—and privately too—because I was afraid of being deceived. Sometimes when I struggled hard I could make some headway, but I was exhausted afterwards, like someone who had been fighting a giant."

Such heroism would make any true Castilian's heart skip a beat. A mighty eagle or a giant would be an adversary worthy of a Don Quixote—or of a nun with a soul too *varonil* to surrender lightly. Teresa's stories of her own experiences in prayer read like the adventures of an epic hero whose bravery is matched only by sheer humility. She tells of two occasions when she experienced levitation:

> Once it happened when we were all in the choir, ready to take Communion, and I was on my knees. This upset me very much, because it seemed so unusual, and would lead to a lot of talk. So I ordered the nuns (this happened recently while I was prioress) to keep it to themselves. At other times, when I had a feeling that the Lord was about to do this again, and once when some noble ladies were there to hear a sermon . . . I got down on the ground and the sisters came to hold me down. All the same, people saw it happen. I begged the Lord not to keep granting me such noticeable favors, because I was sick of being made so much of. It seems that in his goodness, He heard me, because it hasn't happened since. Granted, I didn't ask that long ago.

The idea of this persuasive nun convincing God, who has a flamboyant touch, not to embarrass her publicly is disarming. And it helps Teresa's argument that the favor of rapture does not puff up the soul but makes it more aware of God's power and its own helplessness. It also makes the soul more appreciative of God's love, which is so intense that while drawing the soul heavenward, it draws the body up too, "even though it is mortal and, because of all its offenses, made of such putrid clay." The pain the body feels when this happens is so great, and the soul's longing for God makes it so miserable and deeply weary that it distances itself from the world and enters a kind of desert. "God brings the soul to such a deserted place that, no matter how hard it tries, it can't find anyone on earth to be with. It doesn't even want anyone; it wants to die alone."

But, of course, death is not an option. The soul is in an intermediate state, "as though crucified between heaven and earth." Teresa becomes fearful when she feels this state coming on, because she knows she will live through it, even though "sometimes my pulse almost stops, according to a number of sisters who are sometimes near me and know more than I do. My bones are rigid and my hands so stiff that sometimes I can't clasp them together. As a result, even the next day I feel a pain where my pulse is, and all over my body, as if the bones were still out of joint." As usual, body and soul are fellow sufferers; they can never really be strangers in this life. Eventually (being only human) the tormented soul looks for human company, someone to complain to, even as it embraces its own pain.

After all this suffering, the soul—which Teresa compares to a body after an illness—will grow stronger and healthier than before. "Now the soul sprouts wings so it can fly easily; the fledgling has shed its downy feathers. And now Christ's banner is raised high, and it seems as if the guardian of the fortress climbs up, or is lifted, to the uppermost tower to raise that banner for God." The gardener has now become the keeper of the fortress and wants nothing more than to obey the orders of his Lord. He doesn't want to be master of anything, not even a pear from the garden. It almost goes without saying that a soul enjoying such a sublime vantage point is amazed that it was once blindly enmeshed in the affairs of the world, and that it now "feels sorry for those who are still blind, especially if they are devout people and already receiving favors from God! The soul wants to call out to them and make them see how deceived they are—and sometimes it even does that, bringing a downpour of persecutions onto its own head. People think the person isn't humble and that she wants to teach the very people she should be learning from—especially if she's a woman. They condemn her, and with reason, because they don't know about the loving impulse that moves her soul." At such times, the soul is truly *desengañada* and can't help offering to save other, less fortunate souls from their illusions.

In the wake of such adventures, getting back to ordinary pursuits like eating and sleeping becomes a torture. Life seems farcical, a ridiculous waste of time. The soul feels an urgent need to talk with others who share its desires but finds itself dealing instead with people who doubt that the soul has deserved the favors God has granted it. To those skeptics she can only say that God isn't constrained by merit; He does whatever He wants, "however He wants to, and whether or not the soul is ready. . . . So He doesn't always favor those who have deserved it by taking good care of the garden (though certainly anyone who does and tries to be detached will be rewarded). But sometimes He decides to show His greatness on inferior ground." The soul may be ready or unready, ripe with experience or green with ineptitude. And still—God willing—the garden grows.

Chapter 9: *Strategies*

—

A life of enclosure—the life Teresa secured for herself and others within the walls of San José—was not an escape from the world but a strategic defense against it. The idea of an enclosed convent was to provide a safe place for prayer, where a small group of nuns could learn humility and obedience while keeping worldly considerations—wealth and honor, especially—at bay. These were dangerous times: diabolic temptations that masqueraded as blessings were everywhere. The Inquisition had outlawed certain books in Spain, but heretical ideas still leaped over borders and overcame unguarded minds. Across Europe, many thousands were embracing religious practices that Teresa feared but only vaguely understood. (Nuns living in seclusion were not usually treated to detailed explanations of heresies.) In neighboring France the Huguenots were making inroads, and Philip II, who had succeeded his father, Charles V, as king of Spain and champion of the faith, was backing diplomacy with shows of force; pockets of heretics had even been flushed out of Valladolid and Seville. Without quite knowing the details, Teresa saw that a holy war was on and that her side—God's side—might be losing. Even though she herself was nothing but a wretched woman, *mujer y ruin,* she pleaded with God ("as though I could do something or were something") to let her fight his holy battle against the infidel on the far side of the Pyrenees. She would gladly die a thousand deaths to win back lost souls. But that (as usual) was not an option, so she exploited the resources at hand: a contingent of nuns and an armory of prayer.

In the *Camino de perfección* (*The Way of Perfection*), the book Teresa wrote for the sisters of San José after her confessor Domingo Báñez reserved the *Vida* for loftier minds, she draws up a battle plan. The convent's urgent mission, she explains to her nuns, is to pray for the spiritual advancement of those preachers and theologians in the front lines against the heretics. This is how women can show what they're made of, by putting lesser matters out of their heads. They have to use their poverty as a shield against the distractions of the world. Even if they have nothing to eat (a convent without a regular income may find itself short on provisions), they can't afford to cater to the spiritual whims of visitors who might express their gratitude with a melon or a piece of fish. "Never try to sustain yourselves by means of human strategies," Teresa advises her daughters, "because you will die of hunger—and rightly so. Keep your eyes on your Spouse! It's up to Him to sustain you."

The nuns have to realize that conventional warfare, which the king's forces tried in Europe, will never succeed against heresy. What's needed is a fallback position. During an earthly war, when the enemy swarms over a lord's possessions and he is hemmed in on all sides, he has to pull back to a fortified city (maybe one like Avila of the Knights, with its impermeable ramparts), taking with him his handpicked troops. From that protected position they might be able to strike back at the enemy and win; but even if they can't, they won't be defeated, because—the troops being handpicked—there won't be any traitors among them. And that will also be the case at San José. At worst, the little garrison of nuns might be starved out, but even then they can't be forced to surrender: "to die, yes, but not to be conquered."

In times like these, a nun's obligations are clear. Just because she has renounced the world doesn't mean that she can afford to ignore it. In fact, the opposite is true: it is up to her to guarantee through prayer that guardians of the faith who don't have the luxury of enclosure have the strength to function in the world, "because they are the ones who have to empower the weak, and give courage to the little ones. A fine thing, if soldiers were left without captains! . . . Do you think, my daughters, that it's a snap to deal with the world and live in it, to conduct its business, and, as I've said, socialize within it, while feeling deep inside like strangers and enemies?" Quite the contrary. Much is required, as Teresa knows very well. She thinks that if the sisters pray for their superiors, God will listen, even though the prayers come from women. She expounds on this idea at some length in the unedited first draft of the *Camino,* reminding God that he never devalued women while he lived in the world; in fact, "You found as much love in them, and more faith, than You did in men. . . . Isn't it enough, Lord, that the world shuts us up and disables us so that we can't do a thing worth doing for You in public, and so we don't dare to speak truths that we secretly weep over, without your also refusing to hear such a just petition?"

This is an unusual complaint at a time when women are routinely devalued by everyone, including Teresa herself. Her writings are filled with conventional allusions to female inferiority, especially her own. But here and elsewhere, she betrays her frustration with the limits that have been imposed on spiritually ambitious women by unenlightened men. God, she knows, is a fair judge, "not like the world's judges, who because they're sons of Adam and, in short, all men, there isn't a single female virtue they don't find suspect." Not surprisingly, the manuscript's editor, the politically astute García de Toledo, advised Teresa to omit these unguarded sentences from her final version. The nuns of San José never got to read them.

What they did get to read was an inspirational training manual that taught them how to obey the rules of their order and the commands of their confessors (no small amount of heroic virtue required there, Teresa could tell them), and how to practice detachment, rejecting all of the world's pleasures, including intemperate love of friends and relatives. Love for human beings, unlike love for God, was slavery, something Teresa rejected in all its forms. The nuns learned how to refrain from excessive mortifications, which were really self-serving, and how to achieve true humility while holding high the standard of the faith. She had to start these women off on the right foot: the road ahead would be long and difficult, and their progress in prayer by no means guaranteed. God would watch over them, but they had to deserve his attention. That meant living up to standards usually waived for women. Not much (beyond a spotless reputation) was expected of them in that society, which was why Luis de León could write in *La perfecta casada* that "just as the good and self-respecting woman was not designed by Nature for difficult undertakings, but for a single simple and domestic function, so also she was limited by Nature in her powers of understanding." Teresa may have believed that women's understanding was limited, but she saw no bounds to their heroic virtue. And she knew that God, the perfect husband, would reward their virtuous behavior: "They say that a good wife has to seem sad if her husband is sad, happy if he is happy—even when she's really not. See what slavery you've escaped, sisters! But I'm not kidding you, this is how the

Lord behaves, turning himself into a vassal, because He wants you to be his lady so He can bend himself to your will." It is very important—in fact, all-important—for beginners in prayer to have "a great and very tenacious tenacity" (that is, the quality she values most in herself, her *muy determinada determinación*) "not to stop until they reach the goal, come what may . . . whether they get there or die on the road, even if they think they lack the nerve for the trials ahead . . . which is what often happens when they tell us, 'it's dangerous,' 'this one lost her way here,' 'that one was deceived,' 'the other one, who prayed a lot, fell into error,' 'it's a danger to virtue,' 'it's not for women, they're prone to delusions,' 'they'd better stick to their spinning,' 'such subtleties are unnecessary,' 'the Our Father and the Hail Mary will be enough.' " These are clearly the words of a woman who has had her fill of bad advice.

From the beginning her nuns must be *varoniles,* so they'd better be careful not to indulge in any "womanish" behavior, like calling each other pet names or indulging one another's weaknesses—a tendency toward melancholy, for example. No gossiping or caressing or pinching. Being a woman is unavoidable; being womanish is not: "I wouldn't want you to be womanish in anything, my daughters—I don't want you to seem like women but like strong men. Because if you do what it is in you to do, the Lord will make you so powerful that you will astonish men."

Teresa, of course, had been astonishing men for some time. Piety was one thing, but *fortaleza,* the strength of mind that could make a man a stronghold of virtue, was something else. Women needed protection from the world, the devil, and the impulses of their own unruly flesh. That was why in 1566, just as Teresa was putting her finishing touches on the *Camino,* a papal bull was issued mandating the enclosure of all convents. This directive was highly unpopular among women who—whether unmarriageable, unmanageable, or at loose ends due to widowhood—currently enjoyed the monastic equivalent of a marriage of convenience. To such women, the primitive rule of the Carmelite fathers, which Teresa had tried to adapt for use in the convent of San José, seemed exactly that: primitive.

The Council of Trent (1545–1563) had called for a thorough reform of all the religious orders, and the man charged with whipping the Carmelites into shape was Prior General Giovanni Battista Rossi, known to Spaniards as Rubeo. With the pope's blessing and King Philip's guarded approval (he was determined to limit Rome's authority in Spain), Rubeo set out to promote holy poverty and chastity in religious houses. He was unwelcome in most of them. By the spring of 1567 he had finished a nerve-shattering tour of Andalusia, where the abuses were epidemic, and had moved on to Castile, where he was surprised and relieved to discover a convent that embraced his every goal. The nuns wore habits of coarse cloth and hemp sandals. They kept their faces modestly covered with black veils. They scorned luxuries—something the prior general himself, with his entourage of servants that included a valet, a cook, a secretary, a laundryman, a barber, several assistants, and grooms for his horses, had never thought to do. Rubeo was impressed.

And then he met Teresa, who was lying in wait for him. She understood that he could dismantle the convent if he didn't approve of it or of the roundabout way she had gone about founding it. She also understood that his approval could help her achieve a goal that seemed unrealistic, if not impossible. Given her expansive nature, it is reasonable to assume that even during her early years at San José, she had been thinking about the possibility of founding other convents. But it was only in 1566, after a visit from a Franciscan friar newly returned from the Americas (the territory then known as the Indies), that she began actively longing to save souls. Fray Alonso Maldonado told the nuns at San José about his missionary work, and as Teresa ruefully notes in her chronicle of monastic enterprise called the *Libro de las fundaciones* (*The Book of the Foundations*), this man "wanted the good of souls as much as I did, but he was able to turn that desire into action, which made me very envious." Hearing Maldonado's lament for the "many millions of souls" that were being lost to the devil because they weren't being taught the true faith, she became so upset that she burst into tears and ran into one of her hermitages, "crying out to our Lord, begging Him to show me some way of enlisting souls in his service . . . so that my prayer might be good for something, since so far it wasn't good for anything else." And she got the kind of answer she had learned to live with: "Wait a little, daughter, and you will see great things."

This time it wasn't a very long wait—about six months, according to Teresa's calculations. As soon as she had Rubeo's ear, she gave him an account of her soul and of "almost" her entire life ("though it is very wretched"), and didn't let up until she extracted his formal permission for her to stay at San José with her nuns. By the time he left, he had wholeheartedly approved her idea of founding more Discalced convents, *"cuantos pelos tenía en la cabeza,"* "as many as the hairs on her head." He had given her patent letters allowing her to make foundations anywhere in Castile, though not in Andalusia, where the forces of corruption, led by the provincial of Andalusia and his two unholy brothers, were deeply entrenched. Teresa claims that she never asked the prior general for permission to found more convents, because "a worthless little woman like me knew very well that she couldn't do a thing." So to her it seemed that Rubeo's own strong desire to foster reform was the engine that (powered by God, of course) launched her on what would become her life's work, or part of it: the work of reform was always congruent with the work of prayer.

After Rubeo left, Teresa wrote to him in Valencia and begged for permission to found monasteries for friars too. This was a more daring proposition: Rubeo's recent experiences with Carmelite friars in Andalusia had been a personal and political nightmare. But Teresa knew that her reform would be limited if it didn't include men; women would never be taken as seriously. She had to go for it. And Rubeo did give in, after a lot of hesitation, allowing her to found just two monasteries, again only in Castile, and with the caveat that at any sign of rebellion, he would "declare them to be men led by an evil spirit." He also made his approval contingent on that of both the present and former provincials of the order—that is, on Alonso González, who now held that office, and on the generally skeptical Angel de Salazar. This may have been Rubeo's way of slowing Teresa down, but if so, it didn't work. She set the usual wheels in motion, "and so it was that, thanks to the bishop, who took a personal interest in the project, both [provincials] went along with him."

Medina del Campo, a city not far from Avila, seemed a likely place to begin. Teresa knew people who knew people there, and it happened too that the recently installed rector at Medina was Baltasar Alvarez. She doesn't say if he was glad she was coming, but he knew enough not to get in her way. He even tried to acquire the needed permissions from Medina's ecclesiastic and civil authorities. By all accounts Alvarez's experience with Teresa had improved him, and he had made some progress in prayer. Still, given his track record, it's likely that Julián de Avila and the Carmelite prior Antonio de Heredia (the worldly Andalusian who had been prior of Avila) did the lion's share of the work. As had been the case in Avila, Medina had more monasteries than it knew what to do with, and the last thing it needed was one that had no visible means of support. The Augustinian friars in particular, who had more or less cornered the market on charitable donations, strenuously opposed a new foundation. Again, as in Avila, a *junta* considered Teresa's case; Domingo Báñez was in town and sat in on the proceedings (Alvarez couldn't make it), and this time a man named Luis de Barrientos insisted that Teresa was a fraud, a regular Magdalena de la Cruz. But his denunciations didn't wash with the largely *converso* merchants and bankers of Medina, who welcomed a religious house not restricted (as most were) to postulants with Old Christian blood. And unlike the financially strained businessmen of Avila, they were charmed by the idea of a rustic little convent right in the heart of their bustling city. Rich men could find holy poverty attractive; Teresa was cleared to move ahead.

"Well," she writes in the *Fundaciones,* "now that I had permission, I didn't have a house or a cent to buy one with. And I couldn't get credit for a loan, unless the Lord gave it to me—how could a footloose pilgrim like me get credit?" This description of herself as a pilgrim (a word often used in those days to describe a person who wandered aimlessly from shrine to shrine) was very telling. When she made her journey to Medina, she hadn't traveled very far in the course of her life; but by the time she began writing the *Fundaciones* in 1573, she had been on the road for six years and had chalked up nine foundations, one more difficult to make than the last. She had traveled enormous distances by mule and by covered wagon in snow and blazing heat. She had slipped into cities with her nuns under cover of night and had seen all hell break loose in the morning. And though when she was writing her book, she still had a long way to go (she meant to keep on making foundations until she died), she was very weary and missed the life of enclosure she had known during her years at San José. A papal nuncio later described her as an "unstable, restless" woman. She saw herself as the most unfixed of souls.

The immediate problem of getting a building for a new foundation was solved by Julián de Avila, who arranged for the rental of a house owned by a wealthy *converso* merchant. All Teresa needed now, or so she thought, was a core group of nuns to travel with her to Medina del Campo. Rubeo had stipulated that she could recruit two nuns from the Encarnación, provided they were willing to go. She chose two of her cousins, and the prioress threw in a couple of others whose vocations were seriously open to question; but Teresa wasn't in a position to be choosy. From San José she brought along the enterprising María Bautista and a novice with a modest dowry.

They were all on their way in donkey carts (Julián de Avila accompanied them on horseback), clattering through the hilly countryside near the town of Arévalo, when Father Julián got word that the landlord wouldn't rent them the house—which was right next to the Augustinian monastery—unless the friars approved it. Teresa's first thought was to keep the bad news from her nuns, especially the unwilling recruits from the Encarnación, who "were both from good families and came unwillingly, because what we were doing seemed ridiculous to everyone." So she arranged to drop them off for a time, along with the other two nuns from that convent, at the house of one of her nearby relatives. She was understandably depressed, but Domingo Báñez, who showed up at Arévalo at just the right moment, told her to be strong. Heredia, fresh from a house-hunting trip to Medina, was more materially persuasive. He had canvassed the gentry and found a wealthy lady with a house to spare. Or part of one—most of it had collapsed, but there was still a roofed patio that could be enclosed with tapestries and turned into a little chapel. The main thing was, Teresa could buy the place for next to nothing. In fact, the lady wasn't even asking for a deposit—which should have been a warning sign, had Teresa been looking for one.

So she proceeded with her plans, first detouring to the country estate at nearby Olmedo of her friend María de Mendoza, whose brother the bishop happened to be visiting. Teresa particularly wanted to see him and convince him to support her new foundation. As she already knew, Bishop Alvaro was annoyed at her for leaving Avila. But he came around, as she knew he would. María was predictably full of enthusiasm, only scolding her friend for not having thought of making this second foundation at Valladolid, where the lady herself lived. The Mendozas saw to it that Teresa's donkey cart was swapped for a coach and off she went with the two nuns she could count on, the faithful Julián de Avila going on ahead to troubleshoot.

He was a gentle man with a taste for the picaresque. Writing about their arrival at Medina, he makes it clear that they shook things up:

I went on first to announce our arrival to the Carmelite fathers. There was I, at midnight, thundering at their door until at last they awoke and opened it to me. . . . Then our Mother arrived, and as in such cases she acted with decision, we took with us the vestments and altar furniture required for Mass and without further delay, started on foot—nuns, priests, the prior, and three other friars. We went through the outskirts of the city as it was the hour for driving the bulls through the streets for the bull-fights next day. Laden as we were, we looked like *gitanos* [Gypsies] who had been robbing a church.

If a watchman had seen this sorry band, Julián asserts, they would all have been tossed in prison. But they only ran across some street thugs who "let us pass with the kind of remarks to be expected from them," and at last they reached the house of the owner's steward. By then they were feeling bold, or desperate. In any case, "We gave him such a bad night, what with our haste to rouse him and our eagerness to enter before meeting with any mischance, that at last he woke." He let them into the house. It was still the dead of night (Teresa's preferred time of arrival when making her foundations) and very dark, though not too dark for her to see behind the cloak of Antonio de Heredia's unfathomable optimism. She writes in the *Fundaciones:* "Having arrived at the house, we came into the patio. The walls looked to me like they had nearly caved in, though not as completely as it appeared when the dawn broke. It seemed that the Lord had wished to blind that blessed father to keep him from seeing that the place wasn't fit for the Blessed Sacrament." Plaster was crumbling off the walls; the roof was full of holes; there was dust and mud and rubble everywhere. This was hardly what she meant by "enclosure." It took a night of sweeping and hauling to make the place even slightly presentable. The steward supplied some tapestries and a blue damask bedspread to hang up, but no one could find any nails, so the nuns had to yank some out of the walls. By dawn an altar was up, a bell was in place, and, Julián writes:

> Nothing remained to be done except to make another attack— this time on the *Provisor*'s house to get him to send a notary as witness that the convent was founded with the permission and blessing of our ecclesiastical superior. He sent us a notary

whom we forced to rise from his bed and be present so as to register the act according to the legal formality lest any one should dare to oppose or contest it.

Legality notwithstanding, this was something of a guerilla approach to making a foundation, and it served Teresa well throughout her religious life. Most of the time she worked legitimately and furtively, never underestimating the value of a legal document or of a surprise attack. When the bell rang for Mass, "the people were amazed and stared at one another, speechless with astonishment," as Julián tells it, "then hurried to fetch their friends and neighbors until the space would not hold the crowd." The town was in an uproar; the running of the bulls had probably been less disruptive. But Teresa now had another stronghold, tumbledown as it was.

What she felt, having successfully stormed the city and ended up with such a poor excuse for a convent, was mixed. She was happy that God's business had been done, but upset that the house wasn't fit for habitation. If the worst happened and they couldn't find a place to rent, the sisters would have to return to their convents, which would be embarrassing for them. (Like any other Spaniard, Teresa was sensitive to embarrassment and was always careful to protect her nuns from it.) She was also scared that "those Lutherans," who might be among the foreigners visiting Medina, would vandalize the jerry-built chapel, so she delegated men to watch it throughout the night. But she still couldn't sleep. She worried that the devil might have conducted her here. Julián writes that "in all the journeys I took with the Mother, I never saw her so depressed." She was gratified, though, that the townspeople came in droves to marvel at the little foundation; it was so humble, so picturesque. But it wasn't until a benevolent merchant came by to offer the nuns an upper story of his house while they repaired their own that she felt she could breathe again. Now that they wouldn't have to rough it, she could send for the four nuns she had left in Arévalo. She could evaluate her options and plan her next attack.

Chapter 10: *Alarms and Diversions*

—

Many hearts were cheered by the sight of Teresa's humble little chapel at Medina. Doña Luisa de la Cerda soon sent word that she wanted Teresa to make a foundation at Malagón, her castle-town south of Toledo, where frequent prayers could transport the soul of Arias Pardo, Doña Luisa's poor dead husband, out of purgatory. Besides, she had been one of the first to recognize Teresa's gifts, and yet another wealthy benefactor—Doña Elena de Quiroga, who was financing repairs to the Medina house—was getting the credit. Teresa wasn't quite ready to think about her next convent. First she wanted to get to work on establishing a friary. She had permission from the prior general, but men like Rubeo had been known to change their minds. It was best to act quickly. She decided to consult with Antonio de Heredia, who was so good at expediting these matters (even though his taste in houses was somewhat questionable). She wondered where she would find friars, and Heredia promptly offered to be her first. Teresa was sure he was joking. He was a settled man in his fifties who liked to be well groomed and comfortably housed in his cell, which he fastidiously decorated himself. He didn't seem a candidate for hemp sandals and a prickly straw bed, a point Teresa tried to drive home to him. But Heredia insisted, maybe because he saw a ground-floor opportunity for power among the Discalced, or because he, like everyone else, was smitten with the romance of holy poverty. He had been about to join the austere Carthusians, he said, but she could have him. This was the kind of situation Teresa would encounter often, usually in the form of bored aristocratic women seeking glamour in deprivation. Still, Heredia had offered, and she couldn't refuse. All she could do was ask him to wait. She wasn't ready to make a foundation after all.

She did agree to speak with a young man that Heredia recommended.

This was a twenty-five-year-old Carmelite friar, a student of arts and humanities recently returned from the University of Salamanca, called Juan de Santo Matía. Meeting him must have been a somewhat odd experience. By all accounts he had about him that high seriousness—it might even have been humorlessness—typical of young intellectuals. And he was unusually small, with a large head, broad brow, and burning dark eyes. He came from a *converso* family and might have been of mixed parentage, his mother being a weaver, a profession commonly practiced by Moors. Unlike Heredia, Fray Juan had no problem with austerity. In fact, he insisted on it. Pale, thin to the point of emaciation—as if his passionate nature consumed his very substance—he was eager to shed the few comforts that the mitigated rule allowed him. Obviously he was the kind of friar she needed, so Teresa took pains to convince him not to join the Carthusians, as he had planned, but to wait for her to make her foundation. Fine, answered Juan, provided he didn't have to wait too long.

Teresa, by then an overworked middle-aged nun, as *desengañada* as life could make her, seems to have been amused by her ardent little visitor. Good news, she subsequently reported in a letter, she now had "a friar and a half." Fray Juan, who joined the Discalced as Juan de la Cruz (John of the Cross), would become a poet, a mystic, and a saint. He was already a perfectionist, especially in regard to his own spiritual progress. His reserve can't have been altogether congenial to Teresa, who seemed to prefer outgoing personalities like those of García de Toledo and, later, Jerónimo Gracián, men with great spiritual potential and large human flaws; but she never allowed herself to criticize Juan. After having worked with him for a time, she described him in a letter of introduction to Francisco de Salcedo, as "discreet and suited to our way of life. . . . There's not a friar who doesn't speak well of him, because he leads a very penitential life. . . . It seems that God leads him by the hand, because even though we've had some difficult moments over business (and they were my fault, because I got annoyed with him sometimes), we haven't seen a single imperfection in him." Once when a priest was needed to exorcise a woman's demon, Teresa recommended Juan with enthusiasm. She couldn't have found a purer or more uncompromising spirit for the job. Most tellingly, when in 1571 she returned (under some duress) to the Encarnación as its prioress, she brought him along as vicar and confessor, entrusting to him not only the spiritual direction of the nuns but of herself as well. She must have made an impression on Juan, humanly speaking, because he wrote occasional poems for her nuns' recreation, and once in a while he even allowed himself to dance.

In some ways the two mystics were on the same trajectory, though Juan, with his scholarly finesse and rigor, was more systematic than Teresa about reaching his ultimate destination; he mapped the exact route in his treatise *Subida del Monte Carmelo* (*The Ascent of Mount Carmel*). But his relationship with God was more anguished than hers, and it is the loneliness of his journey that sets him apart, both as a mystic and as a poet. His greatest works were composed in isolation, the native habitat of his soul.

It is tempting to think that Fray Juan and Madre Teresa had intimate discussions about their respective mystical experiences, that Juan allowed himself the luxury of friendship, at least for the time they lived in close proximity to one another. But no substantive records of their conversations exist. Though Teresa wrote hundreds of letters, none to him survive. Legend has it that he used to keep her letters with him in a pouch for consolation, which was why one day he pitched them all into the fire. It would have been just like him to destroy them, along with any other intimations of his flawed humanity.

Having wrapped up her work at Medina, Teresa now had to set priorities. Should she go ahead with the friary, or with Doña Luisa's proposed convent at Malagón? Bishop Alvaro's cheerfully dissipated brother Bernardino had offered her his estate in Valladolid, where (he had suggested lightly) she might pray for his soul. She took that suggestion seriously—this was a man who could have used some prayers—and Valladolid sounded like fertile ground for a foundation. She had also been approached by Doña Ana de Mendoza y de la Cerda, the princess of Eboli, whom she had first met at Doña Luisa's, about making a foundation at Pastrana. The princess, whose husband, Ruy Gómez, was one of the most powerful men in Spain, had a reputation for being as imperious as she was unscrupulous, which made her a less than ideal patron for a convent full of selfless nuns. Teresa saw that Doña Ana was a dangerous woman and one she could never safely avoid.

At this point, she was suddenly (and perhaps fortunately) pulled away to deal with a crisis. The *beata* María de Jesús, who had taught Teresa about the primitive Carmelite rule when the two were introduced at

Toledo, had founded a convent of her own at a town called Alcalá de Henares. But her patron, a friend of María de Mendoza's with close ties to King Philip's court, was upset about what was going on there. In spite of the convent's healthy income (the *beata* had ignored her own precepts about forgoing one), the nuns at Alcalá were taking self-abnegation to new extremes, going without food, with hardly enough clothing to cover themselves, and without shoes even through the bitter Castilian winter. Their penances were exceptionally harsh. It seemed as if María de Jesús had gone primitive with a vengeance, and her nuns were suffering more than even the ancient rule could have warranted. What was more, the convent was deep in debt. A box with three keys (so that it could only be opened in the presence of witnesses) contained its revenues; yet these had mysteriously disappeared.

María de Jesús was a woman of conviction. Years before, having been widowed with a young child, she had decided to embrace the religious life. She had dressed herself in sackcloth and set off for Rome to beg permission to make foundations. Her little boy had come running after her, but, as an admirer tells it, "without displaying womanly weakness or motherly affection," she sent him to an aunt and never looked back. However, as Victoria Lincoln remarks dryly, "she liked girls." She had some very young ones in her convent—the youngest was fourteen—and a subprioress called Polonia who dressed as a friar. It was a strange situation at best. Teresa's mission was to correct the excesses and to solve the mystery of the missing funds. Whether she did so or not isn't known. She doesn't say a word about the trip in her writings, leaving the impression that it was fruitless. But it must have driven home to her the paradox that extreme religiosity can be destructive. This may be why, in the *Fundaciones,* she follows the account of the foundation at Medina with a chapter full of advice to prioresses on how to get a grip on themselves and gain a better understanding of their nuns, "which will benefit their souls more, even if they enjoy it less." The devil may well be lurking among them, but "I don't think he does as much damage as our imagination and bad temperament, especially when there is evidence of melancholy, since women are naturally weak, and the self-love that governs us is very subtle." In any case, a nudge from Domingo Báñez and word that Don Bernardino de Mendoza had died without absolution, making the need for a foundation on his property very urgent, enabled Teresa to move on.

There was no bypassing Doña Luisa, whose demand for her favorite's services was unremitting. She sent a coach to bring Teresa back to Toledo so that she could get going on the proposed foundation at Malagón. Doña Luisa was used to getting what she wanted, and it went without saying that her needs must be met and soon. But Teresa balked. The castle-town was too far from Toledo to draw on its resources, so the convent would need an endowment, which she had determined never to accept. And she guessed, correctly, that Doña Luisa would be an irritating presence at Malagón, which she intended not just as a monument to her poor dead husband's soul, but to her own piety and power. She would want to have a say about which postulants were accepted, and Teresa vastly preferred to trust her own instincts. Doña Luisa thought that twenty nuns, not thirteen, would be an appropriate number for Malagón (one of them would be María de Salazar, the ambitious young woman from Doña Luisa's household whom Teresa had discouraged years before and who would profess as María de San José), and that they should bring in lay sisters to do the heavy work. The nuns would educate the village children, and their confessor, another favorite of Doña Luisa's named Bernardino de Carleval, would say daily Masses for Don Pardo's soul.

This was not the kind of foundation that Teresa had in mind, and she was gearing up to say no when Báñez intercepted her: she had no business, he said, refusing to found a convent with an income just because that was her preference. God would be served in any case. So she agreed, first making sure that the income would be enough to keep the nuns going. If they were not to be self-sufficient, they should at least be well maintained. And she made the best of a bad situation after being assured by God that the new foundation met his criteria. She reportedly experienced two raptures there—once being literally swept off her feet during Mass, as the host was miraculously transported to her lips, and once seeing a vision of Christ bleeding not from his wounds but from the sins of the world, about which she was learning more, it seemed, by the day.

While staying at Malagón, she entrusted Doña Luisa with a copy of the *Vida* to pass along to the saintly Juan de Avila, an Andalusian reformer whose practiced eye would detect any errors. Báñez had advised against this, as Juan de Avila was not in the Inquisition's best graces; but Carleval had assured her that by sending Juan the manuscript, she would be doing God's will. (There was more to this advice than Teresa could have suspected: Carleval sneaked a long look at the manuscript while visiting the master and adapted its lessons for his own use. Years later, after Carleval had acquired a following as a self-styled messiah, the Inquisition condemned him as a heretic, citing the *Vida* as one of his most pernicious influences.)

As she always did when an opportunity presented itself, Teresa took the advice that suited her best. And this time she paid a price. Doña Luisa was not as punctilious about doing favors as she was about receiving them. She held on to the manuscript for an unconscionably long time, in spite of Teresa's remonstrances, which she repeats in letter after letter. "I can't fathom why your ladyship didn't send my manuscript to Master Avila right away," she writes from Malagón in May of 1568. "For the love of God, stop delaying and let a messenger take it now (I hear he lives no more than a day's journey from you). . . . I believe the evil one is troubled, thinking that saint might read it, I don't know why. . . . I beg your Ladyship, then, to send it at once and to do what I begged you to do in Toledo. This is more important than you think." By the end of the month Teresa had made her way to Toledo, but by then Doña Luisa had gone to Andalusia, taking the book with her. Teresa writes a very politic letter, commiserating with Doña Luisa on her illness (which has all the earmarks of depression) and reminding her of Teresa's own, which has been severe. In her letters she typically offers a detailed inventory of her illnesses, then passes them off as inconsequential, leaving the impression that she is stoic about her suffering—which her admirers confirm. She's been in very bad health lately, she writes to her thoughtless patron, but it "would have been worse, if your ladyship hadn't ordered such comforts for me here. I needed them, because, what with the blazing heat on the road, the pain I suffered when your ladyship was at Malagón increased so much that when I got to Toledo, the doctors had to bleed me twice. I couldn't move in bed, because of the pain in my head and shoulders, so the next day I was purged. . . . I will leave here considerably weakened (I lost a lot of blood) but I do feel better." If this doesn't soften up the lady, maybe an optimistic report on the new convent will. Teresa assures Doña Luisa that the sisters are "highly contented" and that arrangements have been made for a woman to come and teach the little village girls needlework and Christian doctrine. The nuns' needs, practical and spiritual, are also being met. "In fact, I'm completely satisfied, and you will be too." Moving on to less comforting matters, she lets her patron know that she is borrowing a saddle for her journey home to Avila. As before, Doña Luisa has objected to her departure and neglected to provide a coach. And again Teresa urges her to send the *Vida* on "by your own messenger, and sealed," because new dangers have arisen. Domingo Báñez has asked her to send him the manuscript, which even if she had it, she would be loath to do "because—as I told you—it would harm me terribly if they knew about it." The Inquisition wants a look. She is stalling as best she can, but toward the end of June, writing from Avila, she begins to sound more desperate: "Your ladyship must keep in mind that I entrusted my 'soul' to you. Send it back safely, as soon as you can, though not without a letter from that saint letting us know what he thinks of it, as you and I arranged. I'm nervous that . . . Fray Domingo will arrive and catch me in the act—they say he's coming here this summer. For the love of our Lord, send me the manuscript as soon as that saint has seen it. You'll have time to read it when I return to Toledo."

No wonder Teresa suffered from headaches and worse. She had, in effect, hijacked her own manuscript, which officially belonged not to her but to the church. Her friend and former confessor García de Toledo, who had ordered the book to be written in the first place, had fallen out of favor and been demoted to the rank of novice master, a very humble position for a man of his stature, as Teresa writes to Bishop Alvaro de Mendoza in early July. She tries to construe the demotion in its most positive light, explaining to the bishop that this lowly job was given to García "only so that his spirit and virtues might benefit the Order through the souls he trains." No other explanation could reconcile Teresa's persistent optimism about García's spiritual progress with his apparent fall from grace.

With her own fate hanging in the balance, and her friend Don Bernardino's soul languishing in purgatory until she could found his convent (a locution told her he was suffering), she must have been a bundle of nerves. And, as usual, when she felt this way, she got back on the road. She decided to make the foundation at Valladolid, but first she had to take a side trip to Duruelo, a farming village with barely twenty permanent inhabitants some thirty miles from Avila, where a local gentleman had offered her a house. She thought she could establish a friary there. Since she had two prospective friars in the wings, it made sense to get the process started as soon as possible. So Teresa recruited a nun from San José and the stalwart Padre Julián, and set out on what should have been a short and productive expedition.

As it turned out, Duruelo was almost impossible to find: it barely existed. Teresa and her companions kept going in circles under a hot Castilian sun, asking directions of innkeepers and others who had never heard of the place. Finally, at the end of the long day, the travelers pulled up at what might euphemistically be called a house. It was really a decrepit shack kept for the occasional use of a farm administrator. Teresa hadn't been expecting much—she had already learned what kind of real estate people of means were willing to give away—but even she was alarmed by what she saw. The house was very dirty, having been used for storing grain, and it had become a campground for migrant workers who were in Duruelo for the harvest. It had a patio, one room, a kitchen, and a loft, all in serious disrepair. The nun who had accompanied Teresa, "although much better than I am, and very fond of penance," thought there wasn't a soul who could live in such a place. Possibly she hadn't yet met Juan de la Cruz, whose idea of adequate housing was minimalist, to say the least. Picturing Antonio de Heredia at Duruelo required more imagination and much faith. But he surprised Teresa when she described the place to him by proclaiming that he would live in a pigsty for the privilege of being a Discalced friar. So she told him to start gathering necessities for the friary, which he did with enthusiasm. She remarks in the *Fundaciones* that he later "came to Valladolid to speak with me and very happily told me what he had collected, which wasn't much. He had stocked up only on clocks— five of them—which struck me as very funny. He told me they were for keeping the hours strictly; he didn't want any carelessness. I don't think he even had anything yet to sleep on." While Heredia was scurrying about in search of clocks, Teresa went about getting permissions from the current and ex-provincial, as Rubeo had directed. These came fairly easily, since Alonso González was, as she writes in the *Fundaciones*, "elderly, good natured, and without malice"; and Angel de Salazar "needed a favor from Doña María de Mendoza." The Duruelo foundation, however primitive, was as good as made.

In the early days of August she gathered some nuns from Medina, others from Avila, and made her way to Valladolid. She took Juan de la Cruz along with her so that she could instruct him in the rules of the order. (She never took so much trouble, or expected so much, from Fray Antonio.) She had reason to be sanguine about this foundation, since Don Alvaro and Doña María de Mendoza were keen on seeing it made in the city that was their family's stronghold. Family loyalty was the cog on which more than one Castilian enterprise turned. But anti-Mendoza factions would raise complications, and it turned out to be best, as always, to proceed covertly. Teresa thought that the house itself would present no problems, but again she was wrong. The building was big and beautiful, as advertised by Don Bernardino, and it did have a very pretty garden with a vineyard. But it was remote from the city, so the nuns would have a hard time seeking alms. Worse, the property lay in a river valley where there was a constant threat of malaria. Some Carmelite friars to whom Don Bernardino had given the house six years earlier had succumbed to it, and Teresa was justifiably alarmed. But it was impossible to reconsider the move. As always in Spanish society, etiquette reigned even in matters of life and death—as could well be the case here. So she comforted herself with the thought that taking the house would position the group to search for another and then they could quietly relocate. Meanwhile, she followed her usual procedure of secretly hiring workmen and having them rig up a chapel while she got together a few essentials and arranged for the first Mass to be said there. It all happened very quickly, and as the Mass was being said, Teresa was surprised by a vision of Don Bernardino, his face aglow, happily ascending from purgatory. Given the way he had lived, "caught up in worldly matters," and how suddenly he had died, she hadn't expected to see him on an express route to salvation. But God "repays our mean little actions with eternal life and glory, and makes them seem great, even though they're worth so little."

Just about everybody got sick from the pestilential air in the river valley, and Doña María de Mendoza had to come to the rescue (as she had for those unfortunate friars), moving the nuns into her palace until she could locate another house for their foundation. Teresa became very ill, and her friend "half killed me with kindness," as the founder later wrote in a letter to her brother Lorenzo. Still, she was determined to do business, and there was plenty to do. She was relieved that Doña Luisa had finally passed the *Vida* on to Juan de Avila. ("You could not have managed the matter better," Teresa wrote to her, "so I have forgotten my rage with you about it.") That danger, at least, was past. Now she could direct her energies toward her monastic foundations. She had never stopped thinking about friaries; Fray Juan, who was in Valladolid with her to learn about the reform, was probably a constant reminder. He must have been chomping at the bit as summer lapsed into fall and they remained at Valladolid. As Teresa acknowledged in her letter to Salcedo, Juan was no silent partner. He had a great deal to say about convent management and especially about finances. Teresa later wished she had taken some of her time with him to learn theology instead of quibbling about money. In any case, by the end of September, Teresa had packed Juan off to Duruelo, making sure he stopped first at Avila to make connections that would help him later on. She assured Salcedo that Juan was worthy of his attention: "Even though he is a little fellow, I know he is tall in the sight of God."

She spent the rest of the year at Doña María's, and by February the lady had turned up another house for the foundation right in town. The move was made with great fanfare, the nuns and various dignitaries moving in procession through the city streets as Don Alvaro and his sister beamed with satisfaction and the populace cheered. For Teresa, this success was heartening. She was feeling healthier now and eager to leave.

Through a former confessor in Toledo, the Jesuit Pablo Hernández, Teresa had had an offer from a wealthy and ailing *converso* merchant named Martín Ramírez to bequeath money for a foundation at Toledo. This was too good to pass up, but it could present problems with respect to Doña Luisa, who was not likely to want to share Teresa with another patron, much less a *converso* aspiring to social distinction via pious benevolence. But Teresa would need her support, since the king's approval was required for any new foundations in Toledo, and Ramírez's family lacked Doña Luisa's royal connections. The best way to disarm her would be to include her; so Teresa wrote to her friend: "What does your ladyship think of the way His Majesty arranges matters so as to ease my mind? Blessed be His name, because He has been pleased to effect this through people who are such servants of God, I think He'll be well-served by them. Out of love for His Majesty, I beg your ladyship to try to get the license." She told Doña Luisa that though she herself was at Valladolid, her heart was in Toledo, and she hoped to be with her patron soon, "for the Lord doesn't seem to want us to be separated." She worried about Doña Luisa's health and assured the lady that all the nuns at Valladolid were praying for her and banking indulgences for her in heaven.

Doña Luisa's response was silence. She simply closed the doors to her aristocratic heart. Though she allowed Teresa and her two nuns (one was Isabel de Santo Domíngo, who would be the new convent's prioress) to stay at the palace during the negotiations for the convent, she herself remained inaccessible. Teresa got the same treatment from Toledo's other grandees. For once the aristocracy and the civic authorities were in full agreement. As if this weren't discouraging enough, Martín Ramírez was now dead, and she had to deal with his brother Alonso Alvarez (Ramírez) and his brother's son-in-law Diego Ortiz, who, in the way of greedy executors, blocked her plans as effectively as they could. She tried to be optimistic, admitting in a letter to Alonso (the more affable of the two) that experience had taught her how "the devil can't stand these houses and so he's always persecuting us. But God can do anything, and the devil goes off clasping his head in his hands."

For the moment, though, the devil was up to his old tricks. All of Toledo seemed to be against her; the city was in a militant frame of mind anyway, its *caballeros* bent on suppressing a Moorish rebellion in Granada and, by extension, any upstarts of impure blood who posed a threat to the status quo. This was not a very good time for *conversos*. If Martín Ramírez wanted a safe house for his soul, the reasoning went, he should have founded one somewhere else. Teresa didn't share these views, though she may have wavered a bit. Rubeo, always eager for new foundations, wrote to encourage her, sermonizing that "men who fear God, afraid of being caught in the snare of riches, give the greatest part of their gains to the Church. . . . You, Reverend Mother Teresa, must not be surprised that the noble and devout *caballero* Martín Ramírez, wanting to be united with Jesus Christ and his holy Mother in paradise, has given away a part of his goods to this end."

"Noble" may have been a stretch by current standards, but Teresa did think Martín Ramírez merited a chance at heaven. Unluckily, Diego Ortiz, "a theologian and a very good man," according to her gloss, was impossible to work with. He picked apart the Constitutions for her convents and argued with her on every point. Eventually she gave up on him and the money he was so loath to part with—proof that she was courageous, or shrewd, or perhaps both. Without the Ramírez bequest, she would have no capital whatsoever with which to found her convent. But she could hardly be unaware that by cutting herself loose from this ambitious mercantile family, she might seem less of a threat to the social order.

Given Teresa's impatience with bad business practices and her disdain for *honra,* as her world understood it, it seems safe to assume that she was fed up with Ortiz's manipulations. But given her conviction that God's work must be done, she may have severed the Ramírez connection with some degree of relief.

Under normal circumstances, she would have sought permission for her foundation from the archbishop of Toledo, the Dominican Bartolomé de Carranza. He was an open-minded prelate and an intimate of the king's. But he had made an enemy of Inquisitor General Valdés, who had had him imprisoned on suspicion of heresy, so Teresa had to direct her petition to his stand-in, the ecclesiastical governor. She had no reason to hope that this man, Don Gómez Tello Girón, would break with the city council and the principal families of the city to allow her to found a convent of impoverished nuns. He didn't even want to meet with her, but she cornered him in church, armed with nothing but her *muy determinada determinación* and her personal magnetism. These turned out to be quite enough: "When I saw him I told him it was hard that there were women who wanted to live austerely and perfectly, closed off from the world, and that those who felt none of this, but only wanted their luxuries, wished to keep the others from doing so much for our Lord. I said this and quite a bit more, with the great determination God gave me, and moved the governor so deeply that before I left, he gave me the license." Teresa's arguments must have been powerful, especially when she laced them with gentle threats. If the foundation failed only because of him, she reportedly asked Tello Girón, did he think he could justify his actions when the time came for him to stand before God? Tello Girón caved in, with the stipulation that the convent was to have no patrons or income (so much for the social aspirations of poor Martín Ramírez), a condition she could now meet.

She needed a house, though there was no way she could pay for one, and not surprisingly, there wasn't a building for sale or for rent (at least to the nun from Avila) in the entire city. A *converso* merchant—one of many in Toledo—offered to help her find one, but he suddenly took sick. A helpful Franciscan friar told her he knew someone who could solve her problem, but the person who showed up was a down-at-heels, twenty-two-year-old student named Antonio de Andrada, who looked like the last person in the world the nuns could depend on. When he approached Teresa in church and offered his services, "I thanked him and was quite amused, and my companions were more so. . . . He was hardly dressed for a meeting with Discalced nuns." Teresa might have dispensed with conventional notions of *honra,* but propriety was something else. Still, her other resources were exhausted, and even though the nuns made fun of her, she decided to give Andrada his chance. He lit out like a meteor and by the next day had come up with a house for them to look at. Teresa was amazed, as usual, by God's ingenuity: "For almost three months—or at least more than two, I can't remember—some very rich people had searched all over Toledo for a house and couldn't come up with one, as if there weren't any in the city—and then along came this young fellow who wasn't rich but poor, and because the Lord willed it, he found one right off the bat."

It was a good house, too, and Andrada somehow made sure it became vacant instantly. He told Teresa she should move her belongings in, and she said that would be a breeze. She had nothing but two straw pallets, a blanket, and a couple of religious pictures that she'd bought with the little money she had left. The sterling Andrada, who was apparently indifferent to the fact that the nuns were as poor as he was, went off to get the house ready, while Teresa borrowed some money from the ailing merchant for a month's rent and some necessities for saying Mass. *A boca de noche,* as night fell, they slipped into the house very quietly, though the noise made by Andrada and his mason roused two elderly ladies next door who shrieked that they were being robbed. Teresa hushed them with some money borrowed from Doña Luisa's butler. Or, as she puts it, "As soon as they saw what we were doing, the Lord calmed them down."

Others were harder to appease. Andrada had neglected to mention to the house's owner that it was about to become a convent. She was irate, though less so when told that the renters would buy the place if it suited their purposes. (Perhaps these women were not as destitute as they looked.) The city council was furious. Teresa's account of their reaction is a textbook example of how to bend the rules and minimize repercussions:

> When the councilmen saw that the monastery had been founded—which they never would have wanted to license—they went wild and told a gentleman of the church (whom I had secretly let in on our business) what they planned to do to us. Because the ecclesiastical governor had gone on a trip after giving me the license, he wasn't available, so they had to tell this

person how flabbergasted they were at the gall of a worthless little woman, who founded a monastery against their wishes! He pretended he had no idea what they were talking about, and calmed them as well as he could, by telling them that she had done the same thing in other places, and always with proper authorization.

The council ordered that no more Masses be said until she produced the documents authorizing her foundation. "I answered very meekly that I would obey their orders, even though I wasn't obliged to obey them in any way." And she sent them enough paperwork to convince them just how obedient she planned to be.

Doña Luisa, freed from her compunctions by Teresa's break with the Ramírez heirs, had showed up at the first Mass to pray devoutly in the little chapel with her friends and servants. Still, she kept a certain distance from the new convent, which had to make do with virtually nothing, "not even a stick for grilling a sardine." The place was cold, and the three nuns had only one blanket and their rough woolen mantles to keep them warm. But as it always did, help began to come: some kindling here, some gifts of food there. Even Alonso Alvarez felt stirrings of regret and provided a few necessities, including furniture. Only Doña Luisa held out. "It will seem impossible," Teresa writes with all the discretion she can muster, "since we had stayed in the house of that woman who was so fond of me, that we had to enter in such a destitute way. I don't know the reason, unless it was that God wanted us to appreciate firsthand the virtue of poverty. I never asked her for anything—I hate to be a burden—and maybe she wasn't aware of our predicament. All the more reason why I owe her such thanks for what she has already done for me."

Poverty did have its attractions. Teresa had recognized this when, on her way to Toledo, she stopped off at Duruelo to see how Fray Juan de la Cruz and his unlikely companion Fray Antonio de Jesús (Heredia) were getting along. Fray Juan had arrived there first to get the house in order, much to Fray Antonio's chagrin; he had wanted to be the first Discalced Carmelite friar. He took pains to show Teresa and the merchants she had brought with her from Medina how humble he had become—she found him sweeping the porch steps. The friars lived at Duruelo under the most primitive conditions. In their tiny cells, decorated with crosses and skulls, stones were used for pillows; hay lined the floors for warmth, but some-times it was so cold and drafty in winter that the friars (who insisted on going barefoot) rose from their prayers dusted with snow. To the Medina merchants this must have been a charming sight ("they did nothing but weep," reports the founder), one they would be sure to advertise back home. To the farmers of Duruelo, a place where nothing much ever hap-pened, this friary materializing among them, with its colorful occupants, must have seemed like a miracle. They lapped up sermons like free wine, and felt blessed. Even though the miracle of Duruelo was short-lived—it wasn't long before Antonio's well-connected friends found a softer berth for the friars at a town called Mancera de Abajo—its impact was lasting.

Teresa writes about how moved she was by the holiness of the place. A rough but powerful image of Christ that the artistic Fray Juan had drawn on paper and pinned to a wooden cross "inspired more devotion than if it had been something very expertly carved." She was always impressed when men, who had the power to do anything, chose to live humbly and ascetically. By founding this house, she felt she had really accomplished something. Duruelo was "a much greater favor than God had granted me in founding houses of nuns."

The sisters of Toledo were more than resigned to their poverty: they were elated by it, even a little giddy. They couldn't wait to demonstrate their piety to the founder, who at this point was busy overseeing construction at the new convent and was a little impatient with such displays. She tells a story in the *Fundaciones* about a nun who approached a prioress (but it was really Teresa herself) while she was looking at a pond in the garden. Maybe the nun got on her nerves, because Teresa wondered aloud what would happen if she asked the sister why she didn't jump in. "This was no sooner said than the nun was in the water and got so drenched that she had to change her clothes." Another nun had trouble waiting for confession and started talking to Teresa; the holy mother snapped that this was hardly the way to recollect herself; she could just "go stick her head in the nearby well and ponder her sins there." The nun rushed toward the well and was only saved by some others holding her back. Blind obedience had its drawbacks.

Teresa was exhausted from overwork, but the new convent was up and running. It occurred to her one day, as she was beginning a meal in the refectory, that she could finally take a rest. She felt so relieved and happy that she could hardly force herself to eat. But what really killed her appetite was the news that a messenger from the princess of Eboli was waiting in the parlor and urgently needed to speak with her. The princess, he said, demanded that Teresa come right away to Pastrana. A coach was waiting at the door. Obviously Doña Ana de Mendoza y de la Cerda had heard enough admiring reports of austere little convents, and even a monastery out in the sticks, and was not about to wait any longer for the founder to work her, the wife of Ruy Gómez, into her schedule.

Teresa, of course, had other ideas. She had to stay in Toledo, she told the messenger, until this convent could manage without her; some of the nuns had only just arrived. Besides, "since the monastery had been founded so recently, and despite opposition, it would have been dangerous to leave." He should rest, the sisters would give him a meal, and then he could bring Teresa's letter of explanation back to the princess. But he couldn't do that, the man said: Doña Ana had already left for Pastrana. She and the prince would be waiting there. He didn't dare return with an empty coach.

Teresa went to the chapel to pray for guidance. Usually, when a situation like this arose, she had a pretty good idea what God's reaction would be. It wasn't that she expected Him to second her own thoughts. It was that, like a trusted, longtime servant, she felt she knew what the master had in mind. All she really wanted this time was practical advice about how to decline the princess's invitation without raising her hackles. This was of great strategic importance, "because the friars were just starting out, and above all because it made sense to stay in the good graces of Ruy Gómez, who had so much influence with the king and with everyone. I don't remember if I was thinking all that, but I'm sure I didn't want to offend Ruy Gómez." To her surprise God ordered her to go to Pastrana. He said He had reasons that went beyond that one foundation. This sounded very odd to Teresa, and she decided to double-check it with her confessor. If this was really God's will (and she hoped, for a change, that it wasn't), He would let the confessor know.

At the time, her confessor was Vicente Barrón, who had counseled her father and her so sternly in the past. She didn't tell him anything about the locution, but Barrón, who was good at sniffing out danger, judged that she should go to Pastrana. So in May of 1569, a little more than a year after her arrival at Toledo, she let obedience convey her where it would.

Chapter 11: *The Terror*

—

The princess of Eboli is Teresa's nemesis, the dark lady of the story. Doña Ana de Mendoza y de la Cerda, like Teresa de Jesús, has descended through history via images, but they are always the same, unambiguous. One anonymous portrait reveals everything: a delicate, feline face beneath a plumed hat, set at a jaunty angle; a black eye patch in place of her right eye (lost in childhood or, some said, at a joust), her left eye coldly assessing the painter, or the world, beneath a brow as sleekly curved as a hunter's bow; a straight nose, and delicately contoured lips, inviting or mocking—it's impossible to tell which. From her small ears, flat against her sleek black hair, dangle teardrop pearl earrings. Her neck is not long, but it is armored with a triple strand of pearls, beneath which plunges the lace-edged neckline of her dress. Between the thumb and forefinger of her right hand (just where Teresa grasps her quill pen), the princess holds a rose. If it has thorns, they are invisible to the painter's eye.

At the time she summoned Teresa to Pastrana, the princess was twenty-nine years old. The founder was fifty-four. Although their paths in life crossed occasionally—Doña Ana was related to both Doña María and Doña Luisa, and so was a scion of two of Spain's most aristocratic families—their itineraries couldn't have been more different. As Teresa moved resolutely through her world, founding convents as outposts of the heaven she hoped to reach in time, Doña Ana zigzagged from palace to court to country estate, seducing courtiers (her much older husband, Ruy Gómez, the king's childhood friend and trusted adviser, was often away), frightening servants with her fits of rage and exhausting friends with her incessant demands for attention. She did have spurts of generosity, which she later regretted. She was known for her beauty (her one eye, sycophants said, was a sun that enlightened the world), for her smoldering resentments, and for the habit of lashing out with her fists as well as with her tongue. She was either insane, people whispered, or completely wicked. Her husband was by nature and by profession a diplomat (the king relied on him to keep the peace, though he turned to Gómez's rival, the duke of Alba, in matters of war) and kept out of the line of fire. His wife did her matrimonial duty, as she construed it, giving birth in quick succession to eleven children, whom she deftly ignored. She had been married to Ruy Gómez at the age of twelve, but she was not about to squander her youth on his (if, in fact, they were his) progeny.

She wanted not only wealth and power but also eternal glory. Her cousins María and Luisa were on the verge of achieving it with the help of Mother Teresa de Jesús, by founding convents of pious nuns. Doña Ana was pious herself when the spirit moved her, and she had great plans for her convent. She was already fixing up a house and deciding how it would be organized. Teresa, who at God's command was bringing along a copy of her Rule and her Constitutions to Pastrana, was full of misgivings as she stepped into the waiting coach with a friar and two companion nuns. But even she had no idea what chaos the next few months would bring.

The group stopped off at Madrid (a convenient way for the princess to advertise her newest acquisition to the court), where they were welcomed by Princess Juana, the king's sister, and Doña Leonor de Mascareñas, who had been his governess and was the patron of the troubled convent at Alcalá. Teresa had stayed with Doña Leonor in the past, liked her, and respected her piety. Princess Juana was a gentle soul who had had some bad luck—she had been widowed at the age of nineteen—and found consolation in religion. These two were always a pleasure to meet. Unfortunately, Teresa was also greeted at Madrid by throngs of noblewomen, some very devout and some just curious, who had come at Doña Ana's urging in hopes of seeing the famous nun swept away by a rapture. After a tiring journey this kind of foolishness must have strained Teresa's patience, but she didn't show it. She simply bored her eager visitors with pointless conversation ("what fine streets there are here in Madrid!") until they drifted away, disenchanted and confused.

She did enjoy the company of two visiting hermits: one an Italian with a checkered past named Mariano Azzaro (who would become Ambrosio Mariano de San Benito); the other, also Italian, named Giovanni (called Juan) Narduch, an odd little man she describes as "simple." The two had been at loose ends in Seville when they met Ruy Gómez, who had been sent there to monitor the Moorish uprising at Granada. The prince, a decent man, had invited the hermits to live at Pastrana, which the princess had dotted picturesquely with hermitages. But they had detoured to Madrid, where Juan was taking lessons in painting, courtesy of Doña Leonor. In the past he had had some unusual experiences, including being picked up and transported by supernatural hands. But those experiences must have stopped: there is no sign of otherworldly intervention in the painting he did of Teresa seven years later, after he had joined the Discalced and adopted the name Juan de la Miseria.

Teresa was taken with (or, perhaps more accurately, by) Mariano, and she was moved by his sad companion. She wanted to found a second friary; Pastrana could be the place to do it. That might even be God's primary motive in sending her there. Mariano and Juan agreed, after some becoming hesitation, to be her friars, and she immediately wrote to the two provincials whose permission she would need, as well as to Don Alvaro, who could convince them to grant it. Then, taking with her a young protégé of Doña Leonor's who wanted to be a Carmelite, she continued on her way to Pastrana, where the lord knew what she would find.

At their glamorous palace in the main square of town, close by the modest homes and churches of their villagers, the prince and princess greeted her warmly. Then Doña Ana surprised Teresa with the news that the house for the nuns was very far from ready; the women would have to stay in the palace until construction was completed. Even then Teresa could see that the building being outfitted for them was much too small, but the princess had decided that squeezing into cramped quarters would be a useful discipline for the nuns—a point with which Teresa disagreed. She knew that breathing space was essential to recollection and that a small group of women, however holy, could get on one another's nerves. That was why she insisted on admitting only postulants who could function well within a given group. Doña Ana, who had her own ideas about who should be admitted, produced a disgruntled Augustinian who wanted to switch orders. Teresa quickly wrote to Báñez and got his go-ahead to reject the woman.

Doña Ana could not defy him, but she could and did make Teresa's days a torment by going back and forth about the convent's revenues. The foundation, she said, should be made in poverty. Under normal circumstances,

Teresa would have jumped at the chance. But the princess's motives were too obvious to ignore: if the villagers didn't sustain the nuns with alms, then she might dole out some funds—or she might not. This meant, of course, given how frightened the villagers were of her, that the convent's fortunes would be completely dependent on her whims. She had other requirements too, or, as Teresa puts it, "The princess asked me to do things that were inappropriate to our way of religious life, so rather than agree to them, I determined to leave there without making the foundation."

Ruy Gómez talked her out of it. He got the princess to yield some points, and Teresa others—the carrot at the end of the stick being the friary, which meant so much to her. That promised to be a real success because the prince was willing to fund it (stealthily) from his own pocket, and also because it would have attributes that Teresa prized highly: a garden and a view. The hermitages that had been reserved for Mariano and his friend, along with others who would join them later on, sat high up on a hillside. Nothing much grew there; but since, among his other talents, Mariano was skilled at geometry and hydraulics (the king had utilized him for many projects, including the construction of a canal), the new friar would design an irrigation system that would enable the others to create terraced gardens and orchards. Nature was, as at San José of Avila and every other convent where she could carve out a piece of virgin land, the one luxury that Teresa allowed. The hermitages themselves were perfectly austere, just as at Duruelo, inspiring awe among the villagers. Mariano boasted too much humility to be ordained a priest, so one was sent for from Medina, along with a request for more nuns. Isabel de Santo Domingo, Toledo's prioress and a woman of rare abilities, was summoned to be prioress at Pastrana, where she would be Teresa's eyes and ears. The priest who arrived from Medina, inexplicably recommended by Antonio de Heredia, was called Baltasar de Jesús. He was, in fact, one of the notorious Nieto brothers, that gang of Andalusians who had been flushed out by Rubeo. Teresa wouldn't have known any details about Nieto; her superior had kept that travesty to himself. So she welcomed the new priest and considered that, all in all, her work at Pastrana could be judged a success. She never dreamed how much trouble it would bring.

She had one personal disaster. The princess, who knew how to extract information and was always apprised of what went on in Doña Luisa's household, had heard about a book Teresa had written, full of instructive marvels. She begged to be allowed to read it. Teresa tried to put her off, but soon the princess was venting her frustration in ways that terrorized the community, and the prince himself was cajoling Teresa and swearing that he and his wife would keep the book's secrets safe between them. Again she had to choose between antagonizing powerful patrons—one of whom, the princess, was already seething at Teresa's intransigence—and parting with the book that she called her "soul." She made the most pragmatic and, in this case, the most destructive choice.

Deep within the palace, as in a sinister fairy tale, the princess of Eboli sat with a book in her hands, surrounded by tittering servants. Her shapely lips turned up just a bit at the corners; her sleek eyebrow, above her one piercing good eye, arched even more than usual; one jeweled finger pointed like a dagger at a piquant phrase. Before long, details about the *Vida* were circulating throughout the household, and from there they naturally made their way to Madrid to all the listening ears at court.

Teresa never mentions that incident in her *Fundaciones,* but she closes the chapter on that period of her life with a description of what happened at Pastrana four years later, after the death of Ruy Gómez. The princess was stricken, as only she could be, when she learned that he had died in Madrid. She plucked Mariano from his nest at the friary so he could escort the cadaver back home for burial—in fact, she ordered him to strip off his habit so that she could wear it to display her grief—then climbed into a donkey cart (for the purposes of "recollection") and steered the funeral cortege toward Pastrana. Nieto ran ahead to inform the nuns that the princess ("led by the devil," as Teresa writes, "or maybe because the Lord allowed it, only His Majesty knows why") was on her way there to become a nun. When Isabel de Santo Domingo heard this, she exclaimed, "The princess a nun! That's the end of this convent!"

From that point on, life at Pastrana became untenable. The princess demanded that two of her traveling companions be given the habit too; then she settled into her own approximation of monastic life. "Our novice the princess," wrote Antonio de Jesús to Doña María Enríquez, the duchess of Alba, "is five months pregnant, and is ordering everyone around as if she were prioress; she wants the nuns to address her on their knees. Tell our Mother, if she doesn't already know." Teresa had, of course, heard all the stories: about the princess's extravagant public displays of grief and about the endless flow of obsequious visitors into the tiny convent. She had heard from Isabel de Santo Domingo how Doña Ana refused to obey her, proclaiming that she had only obeyed one person on earth, the noble Ruy Gómez, and would never obey anyone else. "The princess of Eboli as a nun," Teresa later remarked in a letter to Domingo Báñez, "was enough to make you weep." Even after the king heard about the debacle and ordered Doña Ana to return home on the pretext that she was neglecting her children, she continued to plague the sisters by withholding funds and creating as many obstacles to recollection as she could think of. "The princess came to dislike the prioress and the rest of the nuns," Teresa wrote, and the feeling was mutual.

Báñez, Fernández, and Salazar (among others) all agreed that the convent would have to be relocated. Isabel de Santo Domingo, *muy determinada* herself, wrote to an influential relative (Isabel was a Bracamonte by birth) in the town of Segovia who agreed to provide a house for a foundation there, and Teresa began arranging for a covert retreat. She secured the house, applied for her permissions, then called in a rescue party headed by Father Julián and a gentleman from Alba named Antonio Gaitán, who would function as Teresa's aide-de-camp on many future foundations. They made their way back to Pastrana, where the nuns were packed and ready. Isabel the prioress had kept an inventory of everything the princess had given to the convent; all these things were left behind on that happy night when the nuns of Pastrana quietly climbed onto a fleet of donkey carts and rolled away.

Doña Ana's reaction, when she heard the news, has never been recorded, but it is almost too easy to imagine her storming about the palace, flailing at the terrified servants and vowing revenge. She had not only been disobeyed, she had been publicly humiliated. She would have to endure the cloying sympathy of Doña María and Doña Luisa, and the undisguised scorn of her mortal enemy, the duchess of Alba. As later events proved, it would not have been out of character for the princess to even the score against Teresa with the help of hired assassins. But such drastic revenge was hardly necessary. Doña Ana simply denounced the *Vida* to the Inquisition, and waited with hope in her heart.

. . .

Detail of an anonymous seventeenth-century painting showing Teresa with the prince and princess of Eboli (standing, center, the princess with an eye patch) at the profession of Pastrana's first two friars, Mariano Azzaro and Juan Narduch (Juan de la Miseria)

Given one portrait of a determined, middle-aged nun on a divine mission and another of an unscrupulous young princess on a quest for power—and sometimes revenge—it seems obvious which one was the sinner and which the saint. But while the two women lived, the distinctions were not always so clear. Some people thought the princess of Eboli was brilliant and dashing. She could have been a Borgia or a Medea: her passions were that intense. She was scandalous, but so was Teresa, the woman who left her convent to roam about the countryside wheeling and dealing like a man, putting ideas into the heads of nuns who were better off ignorant, wreaking havoc in the lives of prelates and municipal officers, invading cities in the dead of night. The papal nuncio Felipe Sega scorned her as a *femina inquieta, andariega, desobediente y contumaz*—"an unstable, restless, disobedient, and contumacious female"—not a bad description, if one were needed, of the princess herself. It's true that both women had a reputation for subterfuge. But while Teresa's manipulations were finally taken as evidence of her sanctity, Doña Ana's brought her only infamy. In November of 1592, ten years after Teresa had died at Alba in the odor of sanctity, surrounded by adoring nuns, the princess of Eboli, who had been convicted as the mastermind of a vicious and deadly court intrigue, died a closely guarded prisoner in her suite of rooms at Pastrana at the age of fifty-two.

Chapter 12: *The Other Side of the River*

—

Teresa returned to Toledo in July of 1569, after just two months at Pastrana, with two more foundations under her belt and the sense that the situation was more or less under control. She knew that Isabel de Santo Domingo would run the convent with a firm and gentle hand. And with her Bracamonte background, she would know as well as anyone how to deal with volatile aristocrats like the princess of Eboli, who, for the moment, was feeling content. Doña Ana had created a sensation in Pastrana by celebrating the foundation of her convent with enormous hoopla—bells pealing and villagers dancing with excitement as the procession of nuns, nobles, and village dignitaries moved slowly through the streets toward the sumptuously appointed chapel. Small as it was, the house seemed well and safely established. The friary, too, seemed secure; as far as Teresa knew (for once, she knew less than others), Mariano and Nieto were men who wanted nothing more than a simple community and some quiet moments with God.

She reentered Toledo as even more of a celebrity than she had been in the past. Another great—and difficult—lady had sponsored a foundation, and Teresa's reform movement was gaining momentum. On the other hand, gossip about her book had galvanized her detractors, whose numbers were on the rise. One of them, a priest, greeted her as she stepped down from the Eboli coach, asking her if she was the "saint" who had been bamboozling everyone—and riding in a coach! Teresa thanked him for alerting her to her sins, and from then on, whenever humanly possible, she traveled by covered wagon or by mule.

She also fielded a visit from inquisitor Soto, who seems to have wanted nothing more than a friendly talk. It isn't clear what brought him to her doorstep, but it does seem as if the Inquisition kept a paternal eye on Teresa, at least until the complaints against her could no longer be handled discreetly. All in all, she was glad to be back in Toledo, where the weather was mild and where she was often in good health. This time she felt especially strong and ready to iron out any remaining problems with the relatively new foundation. As she writes to her brother Lorenzo, who is about to return from Peru with his family and has asked her to make some transactions for him in Spain, her work as a founder has turned her into "such a bargainer and businesswoman" that she can easily manage his affairs. And she thanks him for his financial help, which has kept her from having to extract it from wealthy friends. "I like to be independent with these gentlemen," she confides to Lorenzo, "so that I can speak my mind to them." She'll spread the money around, she tells him, to whichever of her convents needs it; personally, she can't wait to get rid of it. It's strange that money repels her, yet she continually attracts it. People insist on trusting her with very large sums, "so, now that I find money and business distasteful, God wishes me to be occupied with nothing else, which is no small cross."

She did try to talk God out of putting so much stock in her business skills. "One time I was thinking about how much more purely a person lives when divorced from business matters," she writes in one of her *Cuentas de conciencia*, "and how, when I'm caught up in them, I progress badly and commit many errors. Then I understood God to say: 'Don't expect any letup, daughter. Just try to do the right thing, be detached in everything, and keep your eyes on me, so that what you do will be in harmony with what I did.'"

It was one of the many ironies of her existence: she was a humble nun who had renounced the world for God, but to satisfy God, she had to spend her time on worldly affairs. This being the case, she made up her mind to be a capable businesswoman, even when God suffused her consciousness with love.

Alonso Alvarez wanted to resume negotiations, and that posed a problem. She had promised Tello Girón, Toledo's ecclesiastical governor, that she would make her foundation without any (that is, without *converso*) patronage, which had relieved the anxieties of the city's power elite. But as time went by, that accommodation bothered her more and more. "At the time I was negotiating the foundation with Alonso Alvarez," she explains in the *Fundaciones,* "a lot of people thought it was a bad idea—and they told me so—because it seemed to them that the family were not illustrious and noble, even though they were good enough in their own way, as I've said before." Her elegant friends assured her that in a city as prosperous as Toledo, she'd have no trouble keeping her convent afloat without having to resort to such patrons. Luckily, she didn't believe them. "I didn't put much stock in this because, glory be to God, I've always valued virtue more than lineage. But so much had been said to the ecclesiastical governor that he gave me the license on the condition that I make the foundation as I had done elsewhere."

Alonso Alvarez and Diego Ortiz persisted and were now making some very handsome offers, hard to refuse. She based her decision on a technicality. Since the convent had been founded already, they didn't have to be involved at all with the actual foundation; she could make them patrons of the chapel instead. No one had (strictly speaking) forbidden that. The only trouble was that someone else, very rich and important, wanted the patronage of that chapel too. Only God could referee such a contest, and He did it succinctly: "He told me how little He cared about lineage and social position, and scolded me harshly for having listened to those people, whose concerns were meaningless to those who had already scorned the world." Once she had made her decision, Teresa never regretted it, because (assurances notwithstanding) no one else ever came forward to help, whereas her ostracized patrons not only enabled her to send north for additional nuns but eventually helped her to get a much nicer house, "one of the nicest in Toledo."

The time would come, about a year later, when the Ramírez heirs would make irrational demands on the nuns, like requiring them to sing extra Masses in the chapel the heirs had funded. Teresa would fight, then seem to relent after receiving an angry letter from Ortiz. In her reply she would thank Ortiz ("your grace is so kind and generous to write to me that, even if your last letter had been much more scathing, I would have been very amply rewarded and felt a renewed obligation to serve you") and praise his skill at argument. ("I've been set straight [*desengañada*] because your grace is so good at making a case for what you want . . . that what I say will have little impact"). Luckily for both of them, she writes, the apostolic visitor will have the last word on the matter: "Your grace will enjoy talking with him; I think he will come this summer without fail, and can authoritatively execute all your commands, as I will ask him to do." Ortiz, no stranger to friendly blackmail, must have smiled at that.

Having breached the defenses of Toledo, Teresa was ready to move on to Salamanca, on the banks of the river Tormes. The home of Spain's most prestigious university, Salamanca was, like so many academic environments, then and now, a battlefield for contentious intellects. There was hardly a bishop, a lawyer, or, for that matter, an inquisitor of the day who hadn't tested his mettle there. Teresa's future editor, the Hebraic scholar and humanist Luis de León, was a celebrated lecturer at Salamanca, antagonizing so many less brilliant thinkers that they ultimately denounced him to the Inquisition. He languished in a dungeon for five years until his trial, at which he defended himself so well that he was allowed to return to the classroom, beginning his lecture famously with the words "As we were saying yesterday. . . ." Of the Dominicans who prowled those hallowed halls, the most powerful and dangerous was Bartolomé de Medina, a conservative theologian who was also suspicious of Jesuits, especially when they had "impure blood." Salamanca was well stocked with Jesuits and others with *converso* backgrounds, including the Augustinian Luis de León and Martín Gutiérrez, the rector of the new Jesuit college who had invited Teresa to bring her reform movement to the city.

Teresa must have worried, as she always did, about opposition to her plans, though all she says in the *Fundaciones* is that she was nervous about founding in such a poor city. (If not exactly poor, Salamanca did lack a nucleus of generous merchants.) Still, the offer was too good to refuse. After all, it came from Gutiérrez, an idealist and a scholar—a combination Teresa never could resist. This was a man she could trust and even confide in; among other confidences, she would hand him the book she called her "soul." She also had the backing of the bishop, Alvaro de Mendoza's brother Pedro. But if she was looking for a tranquil, supportive environment in which to settle a convent of poor nuns, this city of cutthroat intellectuals and their restless and often rowdy students could hardly be it.

The journey to Salamanca was long and difficult, as so many of them were—though this one at least supplied an incident for the saint's legend. Teresa's covered wagon and the mules that carried her escorts were making their way toward Salamanca through the hills of the Sierra de Avila when they reached the Arevalillo River. It was swollen from the autumn rains, and everyone was sure that the wagons couldn't make it across—except Teresa, who scolded the others for having so little faith. She showed them where to cross, a clear and shining path at a point where the churning river appeared perfectly serene. To everyone's amazement but hers, the wagon forded the river easily, and yet when one of the men turned to look back at the crossing, it was as murky and dangerous as before. The conquest of the Arevalillo has often surfaced as proof of Teresa's devotion and of her can-do temperament. But unfortunately, as smooth as this particular crossing was, it wasn't typical. More often Teresa had to cope with every kind of hardship on her journeys, which left her debilitated. She preferred not to complain, at least not publicly. As she explains in her narrative of the *Fundaciones:* "I am not recording here the terrible hardships suffered on the road—cold, heat, snow (one time the snow didn't let up all day), sometimes getting lost and sometimes coming down with dire illnesses and fevers—because, thanks to God, I'm usually in bad health; but it's always been clear to me that He gave me strength. It happened at times that while working on a foundation I'd have so much illness and pain that I'd get very anxious."

Or it could have been the other way around: maybe the anxiety produced the illness and pain. In any case, she didn't hesitate to complain to God, asking "how He could require me to do what I was incapable of doing." But eventually, she says, she always forgot about herself and returned to the work at hand.

She was nervous when she arrived at Salamanca, and predictably ill. She tried to convince herself that this foundation would be easy, considering how quickly she had gotten her permissions and a house to rent. She even arrived in daylight for a change, but still made sure to move in surreptitiously and make her foundation before anyone quite realized what was happening. She had brought only one other nun with her. That way, if some unexpected situation arose (and when hadn't it?), she wouldn't be sidetracked by the need to provide for the sisters. As it turned out, the house that she was supposed to rent (procured by a relative of her brother-in-law Juan de Ovalle's) was still occupied—the students who lived there had refused to vacate, even though their school terms were up. By the time they were finally kicked out, it was night and she was facing her usual daunting clean-up operation. The students, she observes ingenuously, "seemed not to have a gift for cleanliness"; so Teresa and her companion, María del Sacramento, had to spend the night in what must have been a typical undergraduate dormitory—a shock to anyone, not least to a couple of middle-aged nuns. The jittery María, "a nun who was older than I was, and a great servant of God," couldn't sleep, but kept wandering through the cavernous house and thinking she spotted malevolent students in every corner. She calmed down a little after Teresa got her back into their room and locked the door, and—perhaps because she was embarrassed—she attributed her panic to concerns about the founder herself. What would happen to Teresa if she, María, suddenly dropped dead? To which Teresa replied, "Sister, if that happens I'll figure out what to do. Now let me get some sleep."

Sister María's fears notwithstanding, they both survived the night and by morning were faced with the reality of a house that was filthy, in disrepair, and not at all fit to say a Mass in. Teresa reports that the nuns she had commandeered from Medina, Valladolid, Toledo, and Avila didn't seem to mind their shabby and unhealthy lodgings—right near an open sewer—which may have been the closest they could come to the austere conditions that the friars of Duruelo (now transposed to Mancera) had so willingly endured. The nuns would make do here until another house finally became available, and even then their troubles wouldn't end. Teresa always said that the Salamanca nuns suffered more than those in any of her other foundations.

For a while, at least, they had to suffer alone. The unexpected midwinter visit, just a couple of months into her stay at Salamanca, of her sister Juana and her husband, Juan de Ovalle, meant that the founder was being summoned to nearby Alba de Tormes, a place that was fraught, for her, with political implications. It stood to reason that the duchess of Alba, like so many of her peers, would want Teresa to make a foundation in her castle city. But the bellicose duke (her husband) and the peaceable Ruy Gómez were arch rivals, each pressing his own agenda on the king, who sometimes favored one of them and sometimes the other, while the duchess and the princess of Eboli were open rivals at court. Dealing with Doña Ana was difficult enough without provoking her by founding a Discalced convent at Alba. Conveniently, though, the duke was quashing rebellions in Flanders, and the duchess was out of town, so the approach to Teresa was made not by them, but by their estate administrator, Francisco Velázquez, and his wife, Teresa de Laíz.

As the story has come down through legend, this woman, and not the duchess, was the driving force behind the Alba foundation. Teresa de Laíz, according to the *Fundaciones*, wanted desperately to have children, for which she prayed continually. Then she had a vision that turned out to be very fortunate for the Discalced. She thought she was in a house with a patio, and when she looked out, she saw a well. "And there she saw a lush green meadow filled with white flowers, beautiful beyond description. Near the well, Saint Andrew appeared to her in the form of a very venerable and attractive person—which delighted her no end—and he said to her: 'These are different children than the ones you've been hoping for.' "

By this, Teresa de Laíz, a habitually devout woman, understood that she should found a convent. Shortly afterward her husband was offered a position by the duke of Alba and a house to go with it. This offer threw the wife into a depression because she didn't want to move to Alba (where the two had lived unhappily before), and then, when she saw her new home, she hated it. She went to bed sulking, but when she walked out to the patio the next morning, faith came to the rescue. Before her were the well, the meadow, everything but the white flowers (and the wise old saint). This had to be the spot where she was to found her convent! Others, not surprisingly, disagreed. As Teresa de Jesús tells it, "Since the project saddened the devil, he wanted to put obstacles in its way, so he made [her advisers] think that they were making very sound arguments." The unsubtle Teresa de Laíz couldn't help but agree with these men. So instead of founding a convent, she and her husband decided to shore up their family legacy by transferring some land to her nephew and his niece, who were about to be married. By this time, though, the decision was out of their hands, "since our Lord had ordained something else." The nephew died suddenly, and the convent began to sound like a good idea after all.

It didn't necessarily sound good to Teresa de Jesús, who, with Pastrana still fresh in her mind, was more put off than ever by the idea of an endowed convent—the only kind that the castle city of Alba could sustain.

But as usual, Domingo Báñez was on the scene (he happened to be lecturing at Salamanca), pressing her to go ahead: her nuns could be as poor and virtuous with an income, he insisted, as without one. This was a replay of the argument over Malagón, and again Báñez prevailed. But his intervention may have been much more complex, as biographer Lincoln speculates. The duchess wanted a convent but had heard conflicting reports about Teresa de Jesús. She (and her embattled husband) couldn't chance a dubious connection, especially at a time when the king himself was scrutinizing the monastic life of Spain and pitting his own ideas about reform against the pope's. But if the convent was founded under the patronage of Teresa de Laíz, with Alba's money channeled through Francisco Velázquez (who handled his accounts anyway), the duchess could hedge her bets. Lincoln believes that Báñez talked Teresa into this unorthodox arrangement and handled the negotiations himself. In any case, a meeting was arranged with Teresa de Laíz, who was not adept at business. She couldn't even sign her name; Juan de Ovalle had to do it for her. Teresa de Jesús came away from the meeting with an agreement that would provide her nuns with food, clothing, medical care, and anything else they might need, but she also left with serious doubts. "In the course of founding many monasteries in poverty, without an income, my courage and confidence never fail me," she writes. "I'm always sure that God will not let them down. In founding monasteries with an income, but a small one, everything fails me, and it seems better that they not be founded."

In the course of all this aggravation, there was a crisis at Medina del Campo that she had to attend to personally. A niece of Simón Ruiz's, the merchant who had boosted the convent into being, was a novice there and wanted to give her enormous dowry to the convent. Her family insisted on some return on all that money: the patronage of a chapel would do. The wealthy novice, as well as the other nuns and their prioress, Inés de Tapia (Teresa's cousin), hated the idea. So did Teresa herself: she knew how noisy and distracting the Ramírez family chapel at Toledo was for the nuns there. But Angel de Salazar, who was again provincial of Castile, thought the family had a point, and he determined to drive it home by getting a more pliant prioress, Doña Teresa de Quesada—one of those fussy nuns from the Encarnación whom Teresa had brought with her to Medina—voted in at the convent's upcoming election. In no time Teresa de Jesús was on her way to Medina, where she held immediate elections, with expected results, and reinstalled Inés as prioress. When Angel de Salazar heard about this preemptive strike, he was furious. Rushing to Medina, he voided the election and appointed Doña Teresa de Quesada prioress. Then, declaring Teresa de Jesús excommunicated, he ordered her to leave the house.

She was stricken, emotionally and physically. By the time they carried her out to the waiting wagon, she was suffering from partial paralysis and every other ailment her weakened system could improvise. This was how she traveled through the winter landscape, stopping over at Avila to recover as best she could. When she got back on the road, she took with her a remarkable twenty-four-year-old novice called Ana de Jesús, who was reputed to be as devout as she was noble and beautiful. She was also intelligent and politically shrewd. En route to Alba, the founder stopped at Mancera and arranged for Juan de la Cruz to come along with her. She needed his help now, and he needed to know about Angel de Salazar's hostility, which could so easily extend to him.

Teresa was understandably distraught, and she complained to God about the trouble that seemed to be coming at her from every direction. God replied, perhaps a bit testily: "You're always asking for trials, and then you refuse them. I arrange these things according to what I know of your will, and not in order to comply with your weak, sensual nature."

So she continued to forge ahead. The excommunication had shaken her, but Báñez assured her it would be overturned, as it later was. Right now she needed to wrap up the negotiations at Alba, which Báñez (who was good friends with the duchess) could facilitate from behind the scenes. He did, and in February 1571 the Alba foundation was made. The duchess even materialized for the procession to the convent. Juan de la Cruz then returned to Mancera, and Teresa headed back to Salamanca. On the way she stopped at the palace of the duchess's close friends, the count and countess of Monterrey, where she accomplished a miracle, restoring their dying daughter to life just by putting her own cool hand on the young woman's cheek. The event must have lifted Teresa's spirits too—it had been a very depressing winter.

In Salamanca, she tended to her poor sick nuns, who had weathered the cold in their hopeless mess of a convent and now begged her to find them another house. She tried. But houses were always scarce in Salamanca, and she began to feel increasingly anxious. She needed someone to talk to who would understand. In the past she had always turned to *letrados* like Báñez, who would give her sound advice. But as much as she admired these men, she hadn't usually viewed them as soul mates. García de Toledo had been an exception: he had stirred the soldierly blood in her veins and fired up her love for God. With all his imperfections, spiritually speaking, he had made her want to draw him toward the heights she knew he could attain. Another man who stirred her this way was Martín Gutiérrez, the Jesuit who had invited her to found in Salamanca and who was, in the romantic language of her biographers Efrén de la Madre de Dios and Otger Steggink, "one of those 'channels' that her feminine heart had to find in order to pour her secrets into it." He was forty-six, nine years younger than Teresa, with a warm and engaging manner. His intelligence was unique: he was known for being able to memorize a passage from Aquinas after having glanced at it just once or twice. Teresa felt that he understood her, and this freed her to tell him everything. They reportedly had long, ardent, pious conversations in the confessional, overheard (no one is quite sure how) by a young friar named Bartolomé Pérez Núñez, who testified at Teresa's beatification hearings. She showed Gutiérrez her *Vida;* he loaned her the manuscript of Luis de León's brilliant vernacular translation of the biblical Song of Songs.

At some point, Gutiérrez's conversations with Teresa began to be less frequent, as he became more and more caught up with other concerns—or perhaps, given Teresa's notoriety and the unstable position of the Jesuits in the university community, simply more cautious. In April of 1571, after she had been in Salamanca for about six months, she addressed to him a letter that is now included in her *Cuentas de conciencia,* in which she confides to him that on the night of Easter Sunday, when all the sisters were together, she began to feel terribly lonely. As she listened to the others sing about the hardships of a life far from God, her hands suddenly grew numb and she experienced a violent rapture that transfixed her soul. The pain was intolerable. She felt once again as if her body were being torn apart, and her fingers felt disjointed as she tried to write about it. The next morning she felt the same anguish, then had another rapture in which she knew that Christ was offering back her spirit to God.

This favor should have quelled her loneliness, but she still felt the need for another living soul who could understand her. She writes:

> Since your reverence went away so quickly yesterday, and I can see how your many concerns keep you from being able to comfort me, even when I need it—because I understand that those concerns are more pressing—I remained sad and troubled for a while. Being alone, which I mentioned earlier, intensified this feeling. And since I don't consider myself attached to any creature on earth, I started having scruples, and worrying that I was beginning to lose this freedom. That happened last night. And today our Lord answered me, and told me not to be surprised, because just as mortal beings want companionship so that they can talk about their sensual pleasures, so the soul—when there is someone who can understand it—wants to communicate its delights and pains, and becomes sad when there is no one like that around.

She also wrote to Gutiérrez about how on Palm Sunday after Communion, she suddenly became so immobile that she couldn't swallow the host, but how "when I more or less came to, my mouth seemed to be filled with blood, my face and all of me seemed to be covered with it, as if the Lord had just then finished spilling it. It felt warm, and excessively sweet." Teresa had always taken Communion avidly, and here she conflates the experience of that morning with another she had had a few days before. She was experiencing her awful loneliness, the sense of being separated from God, and had been so sick that she had missed dinner. Later, as she was trying to force herself to eat some bread (when she didn't eat, she became too weak from her frequent vomiting), Christ was suddenly feeding her: "It seemed to me that He broke the bread, and as He was about to put it in my mouth He said to me, 'Eat, daughter, and deal with your pain as best you can. It troubles me that you suffer, but this is appropriate for you right now.'"

Whether or not she was fully detached from human love, as she intended to be, Teresa always needed to make some close connection. She was not a solitary traveler, and talking about prayer with someone who approached it the way she did was one of her greatest pleasures. She did have conversations, not only with angels but with men; but these conversations often lapsed when the men neglected to visit or keep up their end of the correspondence. More often than not, her letters betray a longing that she struggled hard to manage and comprehend. Gutiérrez must have known, as very few other people could have, how hungry for genuine human closeness—however narrowly she defined it—Teresa de Jesús really was.

Chapter 13: *Dueling Saints*

—

While Teresa was preoccupied with her struggling foundations in Salamanca, Alba, and Medina, Mariano de San Benito and Baltasar de Jesús (Nieto) were busy networking in Pastrana. They had ingratiated themselves with Ruy Gómez, who, at their urging, had opened up a Carmelite college at nearby Alcalá de Henares. The idea (unknown to Rubeo, who authorized the creation of the college) was to provide a ready supply of friars for the new Discalced monasteries that Nieto and Mariano planned to found. These would reflect well on the prince of Eboli, who needed to prove his value to the king's reform. The monastery at Pastrana was already a credit to the prince because of the remarkable austerities practiced by its friars. Mariano's clever construct of linked hermitages on the terraced hillside also had great appeal, and would-be friars—especially members of Calced orders—were flocking to Pastrana in record numbers. That success could be replicated throughout Castile and even in Andalusia, where Nieto, despite his ouster years earlier by Rubeo, still had tremendous influence thanks to changes that King Philip himself had set in motion.

The king, worried about the "Lutheran" menace, had secured a papal brief in 1566 putting the Spanish bishops in charge of the visitation (that is, ecclesiastic inspection) of monasteries, with a view toward giving the stubbornly independent monarch more control of monastic reform. As luck would have it, the bishops' delegates had hit it off with the scurrilous Carmelite friars of Andalusia, reinstating them in their offices and revoking their excommunication by Rubeo. The prior general had been furious and had asked the pope to issue a counterbrief, taking the visitation out of the hands of the bishops. He had eventually gotten his counterbrief, but it hadn't restored his own authority. The visitation of the Carmelite monasteries had been placed in the hands of two Dominicans, Pedro Fernández for Castile and Francisco de Vargas (an old friend of Nieto's) for Andalusia. The hamstrung Rubeo had then ordered his provincials to resist undue interference by the Dominican visitors, and had issued a letter forbidding any more Calced friars—specifically those Andalusians who had given him so much trouble in the past—from joining the Discalced. He had cited by name two of the three nefarious Nieto brothers, though not (out of courtesy to Ruy Gómez) Baltasar.

It is hard to imagine how much it must have galled Rubeo that the reform he had made his own particular crusade was being usurped by others, among them the man he had exiled from Andalusia, who was now ensconced as prior at the most ostentatiously holy friary in Castile. On some level Rubeo must also have been irked with Teresa de Jesús for prodding him into sanctioning Discalced friaries in the first place. Nuns could be controlled; friars had agendas of their own.

Teresa, for her part, was trying to make sense of the rumors she had heard about Pastrana, especially about extreme penitential practices there. She didn't know Nieto's history and had no reason not to trust Mariano: maybe the two were simply overeager and needed reining in. Antonio de Jesús had paid a visit to Pastrana and reported back that things were going beautifully—but she had had reason to doubt his judgment before. She learned the truth after Juan de la Cruz was sent to Pastrana and revealed it to be the nightmare it was. Nieto had appointed a novice master named Angel de San Gabriel, who had been subjecting his novices to what Juan could only describe as "the penances of beasts." The young men were all emaciated—they had been systematically starved. Their feet were swollen and torn from walking barefoot on the hard rocky soil, and their skin was purple from exposure to the icy Castilian winds. These novices were being scourged mercilessly, sometimes in front of a dampened woodpile, on the theory that if they were holy enough, fire would come down from heaven to ignite the wood. One young man who had been ordered to keep his eyes perpetually closed had died of self-inflicted injuries, humbly requesting to be allowed to look at the world one last time.

Juan, who subscribed to Teresa's more moderate views on penance, corrected the abuses with Nieto's and Mariano's blessings. He brought in a reasonable novice master and instructed the friars in the virtues of self-restraint. But as soon as he left the premises, Angel de San Gabriel, who had always been working in tandem with the prior, resumed his sadistic practices, and Nieto and Mariano turned back to the project at hand: making Pastrana the flagship for their self-styled reform. They were lucky enough to find a figurehead, a woman who made the nun from Avila look tame. This was Doña Catalina de Cardona, an Italian ascetic who, as the illegitimate daughter of a nobleman, had spent her childhood tucked away in a monastery. When she reached adulthood, she attached herself to the princess of Salerno, after whose death she moved on to Toledo, where she met Mariano and was absorbed into the entourage of the princess of Eboli. A glutton for mortification, Doña Catalina, who dressed as a Franciscan friar, was a peculiar sight in the ornate palace at Pastrana. Her physical suffering made her look ancient, though she was actually younger than Teresa; her holiness seemed carved into her skin. Eventually, when the princess had had enough of her, the prince supplied Catalina with a cave of her own in the wilderness of La Roda, where she lived on roots and berries and an occasional piece of bread. "One wonders if she had a calendar," remarks Teresa's French biographer Marcelle Auclair, "for she was reputed to eat only on Sundays, Tuesdays and Thursdays." Her penances were unremitting. She was said to whip herself with a heavy chain for hours at a time, and what was more, devils in the form of wild dogs and snakes tore at her flesh. All this inspired awe among the local peasants, who venerated La Cardona as a saint.

Mariano and Nieto were thrilled. Mariano even reported that—atypically for him—he had an ecstasy in her presence in which he had a vision of dead martyrs. (Teresa believed him. As she remarks, "He is not a man who would tell about something he hadn't seen.") Catalina offered an opportunity for high drama that could do nothing but good for Pastrana's reputation. The two entrepreneurs convinced her to become a Carmelite, got her a new friar's habit, and whisked her off to court at Madrid, where she begged for alms. While there, she ran into the papal nuncio, who tried to talk her into entering a convent. "I am not going to live among affected, sentimental, sugary nuns whose imagination makes our natural weaknesses worse," she reportedly snapped at him. He decided to let her be. She left the city loaded with trunks full of silver and gold, not to mention jewelry harvested from the fingers and necks of smitten courtiers, then set off to see the king at the Escorial, where he often went to sift through matters of state and conscience. La Cardona was exactly to King Philip's taste: her gaunt appearance, her unflinching penances (she traveled with a horsewhip), her strict but familiar way with him. Fluttering around her like a host of angels were Nieto, Mariano, even Juan de la Miseria, all ready to sound the trumpets of the king's reform.

After their return, pilgrims came in droves to see Catalina in her cave at La Roda: she had to be lifted high above the crowds to bless them all. She could hardly move without someone snatching at her hair or clothing, so that Mariano had to build his saint a secret underground tunnel to the chapel. With the treasure she had amassed at Madrid and the king's enthusiastic permission, he and Nieto helped her to found a monastery at La Roda, which became something of a shrine. Another monastery had sprung up at Altamira, and more were already in the works. By 1573 there would even be one at Granada in Andalusia, Nieto's old stomping ground. The reform of the friars was taking on a life of its own.

If this flurry of activity troubled Teresa, she didn't acknowledge it. For the moment, she could take comfort (she thought) in the knowledge that the abuses at Pastrana had been corrected and that the friars, if somewhat precipitous, were still acting in good faith. As to Catalina de Cardona, Teresa's opinion seemed more than favorable. In the *Fundaciones* she tells of good reports from her nuns at Toledo, who were bowled over by the odor of sanctity that suffused even Catalina's habit and got stronger the closer they got to her. This seemed remarkable because "given how she dressed, there should have been a bad smell." Teresa (always particular about personal cleanliness) portrays herself as far inferior to the hermit, whose austerities made her own sins look even worse. "There's no comparison. . . . I've received much greater and more diverse favors from the Lord, and the fact that I haven't yet landed in hell for my sins is the greatest one. The desire to imitate her, if I could, has consoled me, though not much—because I've spent my life desiring but not doing."

Imitating Catalina was, of course, out of the question for Teresa, who had other obligations. In one of her *Cuentas de conciencia* she recalls that once, "when I was thinking about the terrific penance performed by Doña Catalina de Cardona, and how I could have done more of it myself (the Lord had sometimes made me want to) if I hadn't been obeying my confessors, I wondered if it wouldn't be better to stop obeying them about this from now on. The Lord said to me, 'No, daughter, that's wrongheaded.

You're following a good, safe path. Do you see all the penance she performs? I prize your obedience more.'"

For a woman like Teresa, life in a hermit's cave was never an option. While Catalina de Cardona fought off snarling devils and nibbled on roots, Teresa de Jesús had to settle for fighting off sneering prelates and dining on day-old bread—and once in a while, even a bit of meat. The truth is that when she was hard at work on the business of founding convents or refining her art of prayer, she didn't mind a taste of luxury. "I could be bribed with a sardine," she once admitted in a letter. She never pretended to be a saint.

Chapter 14: *An Autumn Rebellion*

—

"I've learned through experience (leaving aside what I've read in a number of places) how much good it does a soul not to stray from obedience," Teresa writes in the prologue to the *Fundaciones*. "I see that this is how a person advances in virtue and acquires humility. This is how a person is protected from the suspicion that we mortals have (and rightly) that we might wander off the road to heaven."

Obedience was a problem that Teresa wrestled with all her life. As much as she wanted to obey the orders that God so frequently and succinctly conveyed to her, she was committed to working within the boundaries set by the church, which weren't always clearly defined. She had to be quick on her feet to determine exactly what obedience demanded, even as she realigned her own *determinación* with God's plan for her—a tricky adjustment. Just as the devil could invade a person's prayers and redirect them toward hell, he could distract a person from obedience through appeals to those naughty faculties, the intellect and the will. And just as a journey through the craggy Sierra de Avila became more dangerous when the guide was unreliable or inept, so the journey from earth to heaven had its pitfalls, especially when a confessor or other superior hadn't taken direction from God. Even the most tractable daughter of the church had to keep her wits about her.

Teresa's obedience was about to be tested in a way she could never have anticipated. She was at San José de Avila in the summer of 1571, when she learned that Pedro Fernández, the Dominican who was the apostolic visitor for Castile, was on his way over to meet her. He was on a mission to discover the truth behind the stories he had heard about the headstrong nun from Avila. He had patiently listened to Angel de Salazar's version of their skirmish at Medina; then he had interviewed the nuns there, who were committed to Teresa de Jesús and were scrupulously ignoring her replacement, Doña Teresa de Quesada. He had spoken to the Salamanca nuns, too, and to Domingo Báñez, who, sensing an opportunity, had suggested that Fernández air his doubts with Teresa herself.

She responded brilliantly, as always, displaying her usual blend of self-deprecation and quiet assurance. The visitor came away smitten with her humility and good sense. In fact, he was so impressed with her that he decided to send her to the Encarnación, which badly needed a prioress with her spiritual and administrative expertise.

The hidden reason for this strange—and from Teresa's vantage point, extremely undesirable—turn of events was that Angel de Salazar had had a brainstorm. Seeing how Doña Teresa de Quesada had been frozen out by the nuns at Medina, he had considered setting her up as the Encarnación's prioress. But then it occurred to him that if he stuck the Avilan nuns with Teresa de Jesús, the reformer who had publicly humiliated them nine years before, they would be even more outraged. The upstart would get what was coming to her. What Salazar told Fernández was that Teresa was just the woman to rescue the convent, which was in serious trouble. Food was scarcer than ever, and some nuns had moved back home out of necessity. At the same time, a lot of lay boarders, women who wanted to change their style of living or get away from a violent husband or an oppressive father, had taken up residence in the convent, so that it was even more crowded and chaotic than it had been in the past. Teresa must have been startled to hear that Father Angel was now in favor of sending her back to this Babylon, as she now thought of it, and she must have been suspicious. After what happened at Medina, she was never able to trust him. Still, obedience dictated that she agree to be installed as prioress of a group of women who hated everything she stood for.

Fernández tried to make the move more palatable. He told her to go first to Medina, to take her time and straighten things out there. She could send the unlucky Doña Teresa de Quesada back to the Encarnación where she belonged and let the nuns of Medina elect the prioress of their choice. (Not surprisingly, they elected Teresa de Jesús.) He told her that she wouldn't have to stay at the Encarnación past her three-year term of office, and to prove it, he let her officially renounce the mitigated rule of Carmel, signing a document at San José that promised she would observe the primitive rule for the rest of her life. And he made her a member of the Salamanca convent, which was one way of comforting the unsettled nuns and, at the same time, alerting hostile forces in the city that she wasn't leaving the foundation to its fate. In early October, after spending a couple of months reorganizing the convent at Medina, she headed back to the institution where, in her own judgment, she had squandered too much of her religious life.

It was one of those returns that must have sent more chills down her spine than the autumn wind could have accounted for. In a locution God had promised that she was doing the right thing—a lot could be accomplished in these unreformed convents—but that didn't make her approach any less dangerous. She decided to attack the problem head-on. From her unofficial headquarters at San José, even before she had been officially installed as prioress of the Encarnación, she ordered the removal of all the lay boarders. It was a classic power play, and it brought matters to a head. Once the interlopers had left, very unwillingly, some of the nuns who had abandoned the convent returned, but others were outraged. A rebellion began, fanned by the Carmelite friars, who had always considered Teresa a threat, and by relatives of the nuns and ousted boarders. They all resented Angel de Salazar (a development he hadn't anticipated) as much as they resented the woman they assumed must be his lieutenant. The nuns and friars were sure Teresa had come back to the Encarnación under false pretenses and was really planning to reform them all—which was the last thing they wanted, having been insulted by her reform in the first place. The nuns worked themselves into such a frenzy that they conscripted a number of *hidalgos* to guard the doors of the convent: it was a siege mentality.

The cool-headed Pedro Fernández saw no reason to change his plans. He simply ordered Angel de Salazar to accompany Teresa on her procession to the convent—an order that must have strained the provincial's own capacity for obedience. One day in mid-October she put on her ceremonial white cape, picked up a statuette of her protector, San José, which she always carried with her to make foundations, and walked with Father Angel, several friars, and a couple of magistrates (brought along to keep the peace) to the convent just outside the city, where the angry sisters and their henchmen were ready for them. When the procession came into view, the shouting began, growing louder as Salazar's men tried to muscle their way inside, and the angry nuns, hurling insults, used their bodies to block the entrance. Teresa waited some distance from the door, as still as the rock she was sitting on, her white cape pooled around her feet. As soon as the friars had broken through, the provincial led her inside, and the nuns' screams grew so strident that (a witness reported) people could hear them all the way inside the city walls.

The violence peaked after Angel de Salazar sat Teresa in the prioress's chair and read the patent authorizing her appointment. Some of the nuns fainted; others screamed obscenities and demanded a vote. The exasperated provincial shouted back to them, "So, you don't want Mother Teresa de Jesús?" And out of the blue a small brave voice called out, "Yes, we want her and we love her!" Another nun, and then a few more, seconded the motion, and as these partisans started to move toward her, the others tackled them and knocked the crucifix to the ground. That stunned most of the women into silence, and Teresa seized the moment. She had watched the commotion quietly, looking (as witnesses remembered) very serene. But now she began to make soothing overtures, telling the nuns she understood that they were blameless, that a legion of devils had invaded the room. (And who could have doubted it?) It seemed clear that the battle was won. That night she went to sleep in the prioress's cell in a house that was new and strange to her, though she had lived there for more than twenty-five years.

The next afternoon the nuns of the Encarnación filed into the chapel for the first chapter meeting with their new prioress. A little die-hard group of rebels who now called themselves *las valerosas,* the valiant ones, came in ready to make trouble. The tension in the room was palpable. Then Teresa made her entrance in her white cape, but she didn't seem to notice anything wrong. In fact, she seemed very distracted, and instead of taking the seat reserved for the prioress, she drifted over to the one she had used during the years when she had been just another nun. *Las valerosas* were caught off guard. They didn't know what to think, especially when they glanced at the prioress's stall and saw that it was occupied by a statue of Our Lady of Mercy; the keys to the convent were dangling from her hand. Next to her, in the seat meant for the subprioress, stood the statuette of San José.

Teresa waited for the stragglers to arrive, then walked over to the prioress's stall and stood by the statue's feet. She knew how to work a room. "Ladies," she addressed them, "my mothers and my sisters, obedience sent me to this house to serve you as well as I can, and beyond that, to learn and be taught by you." But as they could clearly see, she said, pointing to Our Lady of Mercy, their real prioress was there before them, and she was the one who would govern. Teresa would simply reorganize convent life in a way that the nuns would find congenial, though she herself would continue to obey the rules of the Discalced.

Even *las valerosas* were disarmed. It took some time for her to win them over completely, but here, as elsewhere, Teresa's talent for pleasing people served her well. As she wrote to María de Mendoza the following spring, "We should thank our Lord for the way He has changed them. The harshest ones are now the most contented and friendliest toward me." Now she had to resolve the convent's financial crisis. Over the winter she had solicited money from her friends and even from her financially strapped younger sister Juana, who never ceased to disappoint. Teresa had better luck with the duchess of Alba, who made a substantial monetary donation to the convent, so that the nuns finally had enough to eat. Teresa straightened out the administrative mess that she had inherited and did her best to control what seemed to be an endless flow of visitors. She didn't ban male admirers altogether, but she did try to dampen their ardor. One young gallant, who couldn't take no for an answer, kept pestering her to let him see the nuns, until she told him that if he didn't back off, she would arrange for the king to have his head cut off. And that was the last she saw of him.

Such efforts had their cost. Writing to Doña Luisa in November, she thanked her for her comforting letter: "And I'm telling you, I needed some comforting." It was hard, after living in her own small convents, to get used to such a busy, noisy place. The nuns were cooperating with her efforts to rein them in. ("Old habits die hard, as they say, but they're taking it well.") Still, there were a hundred and thirty of them, and managing so many souls required tremendous tact. All in all, though, "I'm not too uneasy in this Babylon, thanks to God. I just get tired."

By Christmas she was running fevers almost continuously and had to be bled three times and purged. Then her quartan ague returned, and she got chills every night at around two a.m. Her throat hurt; her face ached; she had a severe pain in her side. "Any one of these ailments would have been enough to kill me if God had been pleased to desire it," she told María de

Mendoza in a letter, "but apparently He's not about to do me that favor." He did others, though. In place of the statue of Our Lady of Mercy the Virgin Mary once appeared, surrounded by angels. On Easter a white dove spent the afternoon perching on Teresa's shoulder and fluttering over her head as she tried to fend off an ecstasy.

It was a peculiar time for her. She was surrounded by people night and day, and she had never been more alone. Domingo Báñez had been transferred to a desirable position in Valladolid; Martín Gutiérrez was still in Salamanca but was unreliable about answering her letters. And she had no confessor. She wouldn't have turned to the Carmelite friars, even if they hadn't been so hostile: they couldn't measure up to her standards. She realized that whatever progress she was making with the nuns at the Encarnación was being systematically undermined by these men, who knew little about spirituality and less about the goals of her reform, and so she began to look for someone who could work with her. Juan de la Cruz, the obvious choice, had been made rector at Alcalá, where he was training future Carmelite friars to take a reasonable approach to prayer (one way of neutralizing the lessons they might later learn at Pastrana). But Juan could be transferred if she made a convincing case for bringing him to Avila. She sent her advance guard, Julián de Avila, to Pedro Fernández at Salamanca with a carefully reasoned petition. The apostolic visitor agreed, provided that the Calced friars continued to confess those nuns who still wanted them, and he arranged for the papal nuncio, Nicholas Ormaneto, to supply the official approvals.

Bringing in Juan de la Cruz was an inspiration. He was the soul of gentleness with the nuns. He never pressured them, but they were entranced by his holy composure. One story has it that when a nun asked him whether he was *discalced* or *calced*—that is, literally, barefoot or not—he pulled the edge of his wool habit down so that it covered his feet, then, smiling, said to her, "I'm *calced,* my daughter." The woman was charmed. He had a similar effect on a pretty, tomboyish young nun who was known for being so mischievous that her nickname was "Robert the Devil." She wanted to confess to Juan but was afraid of his reputation for saintliness. When she finally approached him, he saw how scared she was and assured her that he wasn't a saint by any means: if he were one, she'd have even less reason to be afraid of him, because saints were too human to be scandalized—even though human nature did make them weep more than most people did.

He was somewhat tougher on the prioress herself. He wanted her to be more wary of her visions and raptures; she was too easily uplifted, in his opinion. He thought she should work on self-mortification. "When *la madre* confesses," he told her nuns one day when he knew she was within earshot, "she reveals her sins very prettily." Teresa tried to tone herself down, but it seldom worked. Once when she was taking Communion, Juan, knowing that she especially loved the way a large wafer filled her mouth, broke it and gave her half. She realized that he was doing this for her good, to mortify her, but she had an ecstasy all the same. She heard God say, "Don't be afraid, my daughter, no one can separate you from me." Then He took her hand in his and said, "Look at this iron nail, it's a sign that from here on in you are my wife; until now you didn't deserve to be. From now on, see my honor not only as belonging to your Creator, King, or God; see it as my true wife does: my honor is yours, and yours is mine."

For the rest of the day she felt blissfully disoriented by this transaction, which is recognized by the church as her spiritual marriage, the permanent union of her soul with God. She had described just such a union in her *Meditaciones sobre los Cantares* (*Meditations on the Song of Songs*), which advanced the idea of spiritual marriage as the consolidation of a passionate friendship. Teresa had written that when the soul (the bride in the biblical text) was approached by God, its future bridegroom, it would feel "as though the sweetest ointment—powerfully fragrant—was poured into the marrow of the bones." The soul would feel an overwhelming happiness, a "divine intoxication," at being so close to its beloved—a feeling that would deepen as God united it with himself. He would nourish it as a mother nourishes an infant ("the soul feels suspended in those divine arms"), and it emerges from this heady sleep "as if stunned and dazed, and with a holy madness," but stronger than ever, newly armed to fight God's battles in the world.

Juan watched her carefully, and when she came to, he advised her to think critically about what had happened. She noted his reservations, but she also trusted her own time-tested means of verification. The event had left her feeling peaceful, strong, and sure of her situation, as she always did when a favor came straight from God. Juan, whose own religious emotion was too intense for words (one reason his poetry is so transcendent), would try to teach her moderation, at least as far as mystical experience was concerned. Teresa would try to learn from him. But in the end, she had to submit to God's imperatives, which, luckily for her, agreed with those of her immoderate heart.

Chapter 15: *The Priests' Tale*

—

Life at the Encarnación was as tranquil as it could be. Given the problems Teresa had faced, even controlled chaos seemed like a miraculous accomplishment. Juan de la Cruz, in his role as confessor, was able to draw his firm line in the sand between inappropriate emotion and genuine religious experience. His quiet perseverance was exceeded only by his psychological astuteness: sent to the convent at Medina to oust a devil from a nun, he diagnosed her not with diabolic possession but with melancholy (in this case, expressed via a nervous breakdown), talked her through it, and returned home. Teresa, who never could get over the disparity between his size and his intellectual capacity, called him her "little Seneca."

When Pedro Fernández came to the Encarnación to see how things were going, he was amazed and gratified. She had accomplished so much more than he had imagined possible. It made him think that he could do as much with the friars if he removed some officials (the prior, the sacristan, the porter who manned the gates) and replaced them with others culled from the ranks of the Discalced. This was not the way to generate goodwill. Fernández also ordered a small house to be built for Juan de la Cruz and his assistant, Germán de San Matías, making them independent of the friary. These changes, which seemed so constructive to the apostolic visitor, were devastating to the status quo. So an old animosity that had been fanned by Teresa's installation as prioress became a burning resentment, and the anger of the Calced toward the Discalced spread beyond anyone's control.

All Fernández could see was the holy mother's local success, and for the moment that was enough for him. But it wasn't enough for her. She began to work on him, pointing out that her other convents needed her too. Pastrana was having trouble coping with the princess's ambivalent patronage, and Salamanca was surviving on little more than prayer. If she was going to save these tenuous foundations and shore up the fortunes of the others, she had to find a way to return to them. Fernández sympathized, but he knew that the odds were against her. The pope had mandated the enclosure of nuns, and permission for her to travel would be hard to come by. Teresa would most likely remain a prisoner at the Encarnación, at least until the end of her term as prioress.

Her deliverer turned out to be the duchess of Alba, who claimed that she urgently needed to see the founder. The reason for this urgency may well have been both personal and political. The duke of Alba had just been recalled from the Netherlands, where he had been dealing with rebellion in his usual way, by executing heretics. Partly as a result of the duke's brutality, King Philip was more unpopular than ever in those regions and had now decided to try Ruy Gómez's gentler persuasions instead. This was bad news for the duke; his rival now had the advantage with the king. What might help even the score would be a more public connection between the house of Alba and the successful reformer of Avila.

Fernández wrote the duchess a letter explaining that Teresa couldn't be spared; the convent had only just begun to settle down, and the nuns couldn't do without her. He was sure the duchess would understand. So Doña María Enríquez, whose instincts were rarely altruistic, turned to the king, who was only too happy to flex his muscles with the pope, and soon Teresa was on her way to Alba. As a witness reports, the duchess greeted her with an overwhelming display of affection—a signal change from her cautious behavior at the time of the Alba foundation. It seems that in her enthusiasm she even forgot to serve dinner and made Teresa (whose patience was never more in evidence) sit up with her half the night talking about "matters of the soul."

While seeing the duchess through this crisis, Teresa took care of other business, resolving an annoying legal dispute for the Alba convent brought on by her brother-in-law Juan de Ovalle, who refused to grant the convent a right-of-way through some land he owned. There was no time to reform his stingy nature; she simply threatened to cut off funds that Juana was receiving from their brother Lorenzo. Using whatever spare time she had, Teresa made the changes to her *Camino de perfección* that Báñez had indicated, in hopes that this book, at least, would see the light of publication.

After her trip to Alba, she returned to the Encarnación but left again after a month or two. Once the prison walls had been breached, they could no longer contain her. In the summer of 1573, in response to gentle but unyielding pressure from Ana de Jesús, Fernández okayed a trip to Salamanca so that the founder could straighten out the nuns' living arrangements. That journey, as reported by Julián de Avila with his customary flourishes, turned out to be a comedy of errors. The group of travelers—Teresa and Julián, Antonio de Jesús, and a nun called Doña Quiteria with her attendant from the Encarnación—set out on mules in the early evening to avoid the blazing late July sun. Almost immediately the aging Fray Antonio, who was accident-prone, tumbled off his mule, but "God willed that he should not be injured either by this or his many other accidents while on business connected with the Order." Later on, Julián writes, the nun's assistant "fell headlong from her saddle: I thought she must be killed, but God preserved her, for she was unhurt." And so the little group ventured on at a pace that must have irked Teresa, who liked to move expeditiously through the world.

It was very late and very dark when the mule that carried Ana de Jesús' substantial dowry—earmarked for the purchase of the convent's future home—wandered off, and the travelers had to spend the night trying to find it, with no success. By the time they reached the inn, it was after midnight, and poor Julián, who was hungry, had to abstain from eating dinner so that he'd be able to say Mass the next morning. It turned out that he couldn't do that either, because the local hermitage lacked everything he would need for the service. By the time he gave up on trying to rustle up the necessary items, he had missed breakfast too. He was worn out, as were the rest of them. The only one who had had a decent night's sleep was the wandering mule, found grazing by the side of the road with its precious burden intact.

The next disaster was even more unnerving: "We were traveling through a night as black as pitch and had divided into two parties. He who accompanied the holy Mother (I omit his name for the sake of his reputation) left her with Doña Quiteria . . . in a little village street, asking them to wait until the rest came up so that we might make one party. He went off to search for the others, but when they arrived he could not discover where he had left the Mother and Doña Quiteria."

How the man could lose them was more than anyone could fathom. The night was black, and the chronicler's mood was blacker. No amount of searching turned up the missing women. At last they did show up, having pried a country bumpkin out of bed and paid him to guide them back to the others. Everyone had a good laugh, which ended when they finally arrived at an inn that was so crowded with sleeping muleteers that there was no place to walk without stepping on one. Inns in those days were almost always oppressive, filthy, overpriced, and with no amenities. It wasn't even possible to eat in one unless the travelers brought raw food along with them and asked the innkeepers to cook it. Beds, when provided, were usually full of bugs. "The one good point the inns possessed," writes Julián, "was that we longed to leave them."

Accommodations weren't much better in the city, where the sisters had reached an agreement with a local businessman named Pedro de la Vanda ("a gentleman well born, not very rich, and flatulent," as Teresa describes him) to buy a house he owned; but of course, there were complications. It seems he wasn't exactly authorized to sell it. The property was entailed to his wife, and a license from the king was required to formalize the sale. But since Teresa did have an agreement and the nuns were in such a desperate state, she decided to move ahead quickly, even though her friends advised her not to. It wasn't as if they were offering a viable alternative, or, as Teresa put it, "A person in dire straits does not welcome advice that is no help whatsoever."

The nuns moved into the house; it is not clear that the owner knew. But experience had taught Teresa the value of being physically ensconced in a place. All she needed was the barest hint of acquiescence, and she was at the door with her straw pallets and one or two other necessities. The house was in disrepair, so some hurried construction was done, but when she arrived in the pouring rain, she found that although the chapel was in good shape, the roof was leaking. She was so aggravated that "I said to our Lord—really, I was on the verge of complaining—that He should either stop ordering me to take on these projects, or help me get them done." A companion calmed her down, promising that God would help, and in fact, the weather did clear up just in time for the first Mass.

The next day Pedro de la Vanda came by and instantly began to make trouble. "He was so furious that I didn't know what to do with him," Teresa writes. "And the devil arranged that he couldn't be reasoned with." From her point of view, the devil had been unusually busy in Salamanca. Years after the foundation was made, she was still in negotiations with this querulous man. Her letters reflect their tussles over every little detail of construction, and Teresa's frustration that "God seems to want to keep me at Salamanca, because nobody in the house except me understands anything about work or business matters." In the course of founding (which often included rebuilding) numerous monastic houses, she had become a very efficient general contractor, and yet this particular building was still close to uninhabitable. She could only trust "that God is served very well in it since the devil hates it so much."

If the scholars of Salamanca agreed about anything, it was about the nun from Avila. These men, particularly the Dominicans, were adamant that nuns be strictly enclosed—with no exceptions. Bartolomé de Medina, the most fanatic of them all, took his shots at Teresa from the lectern: she was one of those *mujercillas* who went here and everywhere when they should have been in their convents praying and spinning. Medina was a particularly dangerous enemy because of his widespread influence, as well as his close ties to the Inquisition. That was why his fellow Dominicans Báñez and Fernández made a point over the years of talking her up whenever they got the chance. She herself recognized the need for cordial, if not always friendly, relations with Medina, who was the duchess of Alba's confessor (and more often than not the arbiter of her opinions). At one point, Teresa writes to Báñez, "I'm doing all right with Father Medina. I think if I had some good long talks with him, he'd soon come around." These efforts eventually did pay off, and Medina comes down through history as a hard-won friend. The mention of his name, among those of other supporters, on documents she submitted to the Inquisition proved invaluable. But there apparently wasn't much genuine closeness between them; she was always wondering what he thought of her. Her anxiety must have been high when she instructed one of her prioresses to forward a letter to him and to "pay no attention if he isn't very friendly—he's not obliged to be. Never mind what he says about me: why don't you tell me what it is?"

She did manage to make a conquest of another of her Salamanca critics, the Jesuit Jerónimo de Ripalda. Having heard her confession and read her *Vida*, Ripalda did, in fact, reassess her religious practices and motives and was surprised not to find them suspect after all. Then he ordered her to extract some useful lessons from her experiences as a founder, picking up where the *Vida* left off by writing the book that became the *Fundaciones*.

It was a depressing assignment. She was feeling tired and unwell and had too much on her mind. Reliving the making of eight foundations, each of which had drained her energy and tested her faith, ingenuity, and political skill, was not something she would have volunteered to do. She wasn't even sure she *could* do it, weak and worthless as she knew she was. She was also worried that someone might think she wanted to take credit for her monastic work, when it was really all accomplished in spite of her by God himself.

She had written her *Vida* to justify her spiritual life to her advisers and perhaps to the inquisitors who would eventually scrutinize her life and work. Beyond that, she had little interest in reviewing her past and claimed that she could hardly even recall the details. "Since I have a bad memory," she writes in the *Fundaciones,* "I believe that a lot of important things will be left out, and that others—which could be left out—will get in. In the end, the work will be in keeping with my lack of talent and refinement, and also the lack of peace and quiet for writing." This is a disclaimer that covers a lot of ground because Teresa, like any politician, has to omit a lot in order to tell the truth. It is often in the spaces, the gaps, the events left out or only alluded to, that the story of her active life as a founder is told.

Martín Gutiérrez, for example, hardly figures at all in the *Fundaciones,* where she devotes many pages to people who figured prominently in her life, including her future confessor Jerónimo Gracián. Victoria Lincoln finds the omission of Gutiérrez telling. She thinks the relationship between the Carmelite nun and the Jesuit rector bordered on the scandalous. Efrén de la Madre de Dios and Otger Steggink, who are among the few biographers with much to say about Gutiérrez, never speculate on the propriety of the relationship between him and Teresa, only about its intensity and tragic resolution. Returning from a trip to Rome, he came overland through France and was captured by Huguenots, who tortured him until he died. Gutiérrez's loss devastated Teresa: it was one of the great tragedies of her life. She rebuked herself for caring so deeply about one of God's servants that she couldn't be comforted, even though he had lived a holy life and died a martyr's death. The fact was that she had nobody else to turn to.

·   ·   ·

Teresa was glad when she heard that Baltasar Alvarez, her former confessor, had been appointed rector at Salamanca, but she was much less pleased when she heard that Juan Suárez, Martín Gutiérrez's companion on the trip to Rome, had been made the Jesuit provincial for Castile. Suárez openly detested Teresa and scorned men who wasted time trafficking with women that Suárez considered no better than *alumbradas*. His unshakable prejudice made him savage the reputation of Alvarez, the very man who had raised money to ransom him and Gutiérrez from the Huguenots (too late to save Gutiérrez, a failure that made Alvarez physically ill for months). Suárez would later inform the Jesuit general that Alvarez was visiting Teresa's nuns too often and talking with them about dubious subjects like silent prayer. As a result, Alvarez was ordered to stay away from the convent in the future or be "gently and efficiently removed." Suárez was not a man that Teresa could educate to her way of thinking, and the sword he laid between her and her longtime Jesuit advisers remained in place.

As embattled as she was on many fronts, Teresa was deluged with invitations to found more Discalced convents; there was no dearth of pious aristocrats in Spain eager for the prestige of patronage. As far as she was concerned, the decision as to where to found was relatively simple. In a locution God pointed her toward Segovia, the city to which Isabel de Santo Domingo, Pastrana's prioress, was desperate to escape with her nuns. So Teresa made the necessary arrangements, securing the Segovia house, finalizing her plan of attack, and setting off with her rescue brigade to liberate the long-suffering sisters of Pastrana.

On the way there, she stopped off at Alba to see the duchess, who was in an agitated mood. The impetus this time was a scandal involving the seduction of María de Mendoza's young niece by María Enríque's son. The king and the bishop of Avila had been brought into the controversy and, outraged by the young man's depraved indifference, had thrown the roue in prison. Teresa now had her hands full soothing the duchess, even as she fired off a politic letter to Bishop Alvaro and long-distance kisses to María de Mendoza. Doña María Enríque was so grateful for Teresa's efforts that she sent her the extravagant gift of a trout. Without missing a beat, Teresa expressed the fish to Salamanca with a letter for Bartolomé de Medina. Make sure he gets it, she told the prioress, "and then we'll see if he drops me a line or two."

Teresa also arranged to have Medina copy the *Vida* for the duchess, who was gratified by the news that the ignorant Doña Ana had failed to understand it. The duchess came to the manuscript fairly late; it had gone through numerous hands. For a book that only a few confessors had been authorized to see, it had a remarkably brisk circulation. Even without the princess's denunciation, it was inevitable that the manuscript would fall into the hands of the Inquisition. The only question was when.

The foundation at Segovia was meant to be a quick hit: in by night, established by morning. The problem was—and Julián de Avila says his heart sank when he heard this—Teresa had received only verbal, not written, permission from the bishop of Segovia to go ahead. On his word she had assembled a group of nuns to make the trip from Avila, along with Julián, Juan de la Cruz, and Antonio Gaitán. When they arrived at Segovia, they took immediate possession of the house, and by morning Julián himself had said the first Mass. Unfortunately, the bishop was out of town, and his deputy, a man notorious for his bad disposition, was furious when he learned what had happened. After the nuns had retreated to their enclosure, the *provisor* stormed into the chapel (Julián noted this from his hiding place behind a staircase) and began shouting at Juan de la Cruz, who must have firmly deflected him. The *provisor* threatened that he would have Juan thrown in jail. The gentle Padre Julián muses that he too would have risked imprisonment if caught: "In fact, having shut up so many nuns in the cloister, it would only have been fair if I had been enclosed for once myself." Then again, he reasons, the nuns were always locked up willingly, so they must not mind imprisonment the way *he* would.

The *provisor* did his best to unmake the foundation, but he was no match for Teresa. Having presented her case (and Isabel de Santo Domingo's Bracamonte connections) to the local authorities, she soon had the permissions she needed. She then began mapping her approach to Pastrana; unlike the *provisor*, she knew precisely how to take a foundation down. Late one April night she pulled up her carts where they couldn't be seen and went on foot to the convent, where the inmates were poised and waiting. They must have been very nervous: defying a woman of Doña Ana's stature—and temperament—was no light undertaking. Julián remarks that "flight needed as much courage in this case as attack at other times."

It was another journey full of mishaps—the worst being when the carts got stuck in the middle of a river. As Julián tells it, "The muleteers cried to the mules and the sisters must have cried to God," because one wagon finally got across, which freed up mules to pull the others. It was a close call, as the priest (who had gotten across on his horse and was watching in safety from the opposite bank) could testify. At last the little caravan rolled into Segovia, and "Antonio Gaitán and I went home, counting our labours well spent in so good a cause and resolved to go wherever the Mother chose to take us."

As Teresa was wrestling with mules and patrons and prelates, Mariano and Nieto were basking in the Andalusian sun. With the blessing of Vargas (the apostolic visitor), Nieto had founded a Discalced friary in Granada, and by the time he went home, he had two more friaries under his belt—a development that enraged the Calced friars of Andalusia. Because Vargas had applied directly to the pope for permission to bring the Discalced to that province (on the grounds that the friars of the Mitigation were so corrupt), Rubeo, who had forbidden any expansion, was never consulted—although the rumors he heard made him wild. Nieto, who knew when to lie low, passed the torch to Mariano, who went back to Andalusia to pick up where his colleague had left off.

Mariano took along a traveling companion from the Pastrana foundation, an idealistic priest—formerly a student at Alcalá—called Jerónimo Gracián de la Madre de Diós, or Gracián. The two stopped first at Toledo to get advice from Antonio de Jesús (who knew Andalusia and had ambitions of his own), then made their way to Granada, where Vargas enthusiastically welcomed them. Given Mariano's checkered history and the growing dissention over the reform, Vargas had the idea of making Gracián the apostolic visitor to both the Calced and the Discalced in Andalusia. It was an appointment that Gracián was not experienced enough to refuse.

At first things went well enough; he won the confidence of the Sevillian friars through a clever bit of diplomacy, giving them back the friary of San Juan del Puerto, which had been handed over previously to the Discalced. But then he set up the Discalced friars in a gorgeous monastery called Los Remedios, dramatically positioned by Seville's majestic river, the Guadalquivir. This display of power enraged the Calced, who successfully petitioned the pope to revoke the upstart Gracián's authority. Vargas protested, and soon the king was complaining to the pope, the pope was reconsidering, and the papal nuncio Ormaneto was reinstating Gracián as the apostolic visitor. It was the first of Gracián's many skirmishes with the friars; he would hardly have a moment's peace from then on.

Teresa had a vague sense of what was going on in Andalusia. She was sporadically in touch with Mariano and had also been exchanging letters with Gracián, whom she had not yet met. The newly established Discalced friaries worried her. Unlike her convents, they had no constitutions of their own—or at least they didn't use the ones Rubeo had sketched out for them—and were so badly managed that "they could have fallen apart at any moment." She had even sent an emissary with a letter to the king to explain how devoted the Discalced were to his reform, to beg for his support, and to assure him that "the more this order progresses, the more will be your Majesty's gain." She certainly prayed that this would be the case. By midspring, as reports of Gracián's successes filtered back to her, she began to feel giddily optimistic about the Andalusian foundations, though she also felt a twinge of concern. In a letter to María Bautista, now prioress of the convent at Valladolid, Teresa writes: "Oh, if you could see the brouhaha that's going on—secretly, of course—on behalf of the Discalced! It's something to praise God for—and it was all started by those fathers who went to Andalusia, Gracián and Mariano. My pleasure's quite a bit muted by the pain this is bound to give our father general, who I'm so fond of, but on the other hand, I can see that inaction would have spelled disaster."

It must have been tempting to forget that Rubeo had expressly forbidden the expansion of the Discalced friars into Andalusia. Gracián was perfectly capable of such an oversight but not Teresa. She always distinguished among the claims of her numerous superiors. She resolved the issue in her own mind by reasoning that these foundations hadn't been made in defiance of Rubeo's authority but in obedience to someone else's, and not by her. In fact, the news she received about the Andalusian houses was often late and partial, at best.

Rubeo wrote to her several times during the fall and winter of 1574, demanding a full account of what was going on with the friars. According to her biographers, she didn't receive those letters until the following summer, and by then there was no talking to him. Though she had warned Gracián to inform the prior general about his activities in Andalusia, he had casually stopped doing so, and by the time Rubeo learned about all the Discalced houses being founded without his permission, he had lost whatever patience he once possessed. From then on, the man who had championed her reform became her adversary. With all her persuasive skills, Teresa could never win him back.

By this time Gracián and Teresa were in close touch. He urged Teresa to make her next foundation at a town called Beas de Segura on the border of Castile and Andalusia, where two pious sisters had offered her a house and financial support. One of the sisters, Catalina Godínez, had regaled the founder with the legend of her own conversion, which if not exactly miraculous was certainly astonishing. Catalina had been (by her own account) a beautiful girl, and her parents were plotting an auspicious marriage for her when she decided, instead, to starve and mutilate herself for God, until no man would look at her. Her parents still wouldn't let her enter a convent, so she tried to achieve spiritual perfection at home. When she realized, for example, that she had been imperious with the household servants, she waited until late at night when they were asleep, then tiptoed into their quarters and kissed their feet. She wore her father's *cilicio* next to her skin and prayed in solitary places, where the devil made fun of her. She claimed to suffer from countless diseases—including cancer, gout, sciatica, and an inflammation of the liver that burned a hole right through her nightclothes. "If the doctors and others in the house hadn't told me this was true," Teresa writes, "I'm so wretched, it would not have been out of character for me to think that some of this had been exaggerated."

Catalina began to recover (more or less) after her parents' deaths, when she vowed to finance a convent—the only way she could get into one because a woman with her infirmities wasn't considered an acceptable candidate. She was a familiar type: what Teresa usually described as a *mujercilla*. But she was also financially independent, and that gave her a certain amount of credibility. She was even holy in her way, though she lacked the qualities that Teresa's favorite nuns had in abundance: unobtrusive piety and good sense. The founder was much more partial to an adolescent girl named Casilda de Padilla, who, though engaged to her aged uncle, had run off repeatedly to the Valladolid convent, enraging her parents and risking her considerable fortune. Casilda, quiet and devout, was in Teresa's opinion born to be a nun. Catalina Godínez would have to work hard to become one—but that was very often the case.

The more Teresa thought about founding in Beas, the better she liked the idea. It was admittedly a stretch for her. She had never ventured so far from home or so close to the forbidden territory of Andalusia. Like a child venturing past the boundaries her parents had set for her, she took one step and then another until finally she was at the very edge of her legitimate world. Beas's situation was, in fact, ambiguous; she had to do some probing to find out if it really was within the boundaries of Castile. Gracián assured her that it was. What he didn't tell her was that this border town, while technically (that is, for administrative purposes) Castilian, actually belonged to the ecclesiastical province of Andalusia.

Pedro Fernández, who would have liked to see Teresa cool her heels for a while in any case, did his best to discourage her. He had always behaved as considerately as possible toward Rubeo, and he wasn't looking for trouble. But he thought he had an easy out: permission would have to be sought from an entity called the Knights of Santiago that governed the town of Beas and was famously uncooperative. Much to his surprise, the Knights approved the foundation, and Teresa happily prepared to go ahead with it.

Domingo Báñez, scenting danger, advised her to hold off. So did her bossy niece María Bautista, who had become friendly with Báñez at Valladolid but lacked his diplomatic skills. "I think I can make out the words you crossed out," Teresa writes to her in answer to what must have been a profoundly annoying letter. "You can rest assured that Beas is not in Andalusia, but five miles this side of it. I know that I'm not allowed to found convents in Andalusia." She crisply thanks her prioress for her concern and informs her that the foundation will go ahead as planned. "It will happen this winter, because that is how God arranged it—I don't know how I could get through another winter in this frigid part of the country."

Teresa returned to Avila in late September, 1574, to finish up her term at the Encarnación. Then, instead of going straight to Beas, she stayed for a few months at San José, possibly because of what was going on at nearby Córdoba, where the Inquisition had hauled in Doña Luisa de la Cerda's former confessor Bernardino de Carleval as an *alumbrado*. Carleval had acquired a large cult following since that time in Malagón when he had encouraged Teresa to send the *Vida* to Juan de Avila (against Báñez's orders) and had sneaked a look at it himself. When he cited the book as one of his primary inspirations, the Inquisition at Córdoba impounded it. This was the second time the *Vida* had come under scrutiny. Officials at Pastrana had examined it too, thanks to the princess of Eboli, but had let the matter drop. The Córdoban authorities sagely tossed this political hot potato into the lap of the tribunal at Madrid, where Teresa had powerful protectors, including the king. She was safe for the time being, though the Inquisition kept the *Vida* out of circulation from that point on. Carleval, shielded by nothing more than his charismatic personality, went to the stake at Córdoba.

Teresa should have been happy during those months at San José. But she was consumed by a feeling of emptiness—what she called a "dryness and darkness of soul." In December she wrote to Báñez: "As I see it, my father, there can be no peace of mind for me in this world. I don't have what I want, and I don't want what I have. My problem is, I can't be comforted by my confessors, as I could before—a confessor has to be more to me now. Something that barely resembles a soul can't bring out its deepest desires." She tried to come to terms with her malaise, writing to Antonio Gaitán, who was now back home at Alba and struggling with prayer, "You need to understand that just as in this world there are variations in weather, so it is in the interior world—there's no getting around it. So don't be upset, because it isn't your fault." If only she could have convinced herself.

In February 1575 she headed toward the Andalusian border. She took her usual lieutenants, Julián de Avila and Gaitán; a group of nuns that included Ana de Jesús (as prioress); María de San José, the ambitious young woman from Doña Luisa's palace; and Isabel de San Jerónimo, the nun that Juan de la Cruz had cured of melancholy. She also brought along a priest called Gregorio Nacianceno, who had decided to join the Discalced. One extant story has them wending their way through La Mancha—Don Quixote's field of dreams—getting lost in the Sierra Morena and teetering on the edge of a chasm. Teresa told them to pray, and then they all heard a disembodied voice directing them to back up a certain distance and change direction, which got them out of danger. It was enough to bring even the surly muleteers to their knees in gratitude.

Julián de Avila tells very little about this journey, but makes more of the triumphant procession to the new foundation. The nuns and their companions were flanked by knights on cleverly prancing horses, he recalls, and ushered into the church by the entire populace of the town. According to Julián, Teresa was glad to be in Beas, a balmy oasis that must have been a refreshing contrast to her native Avila. And her happiness peaked a few months later, when she finally met the man who would become her protégé and confessor, Jerónimo Gracián.

The two of them understood one another from the start. She was twice his age (he was close to thirty), but she had no sense of that discrepancy or of her own much broader experience in politics and prayer. He was everything she liked—scholarly, diplomatic, passionately religious (as a boy, he used to address an image of the Virgin as *mi enamorada*, my love), affable, eloquent, and urbane. In person he was far from threatening: a soft, plump man who displayed some affectation in his speech and writing that Teresa found very attractive. "He has such a pleasing way about him," she writes, "that for the most part he is loved by everyone who has dealings with him—that's a grace the Lord gives." She had written almost identical words about herself as a young woman. "He is so tender and agreeable that no one can find anything wrong with him." This was true for the moment, at least. Teresa saw Gracián as an almost perfect religious, with none of the vices she condemned in herself. She was impressed by the way he had submitted to the outrageous demands of the novice master at Pastrana, an inexperienced friar with "no learning and very little talent or wisdom in governing," and thought that God must have been impressed too—that was why He had given Gracián "the greatest enlightenment concerning matters of obedience, so that he could teach it to those beneath him."

Obedience, as it happened, turned out not to be Gracián's strong suit, but he had other talents. He had seduced Mariano and Nieto with his diplomatic skills and court connections. He won Teresa's affection by means of spiritual intimacy, flattering her by revealing so much about himself that she felt she had to make excuses for him: "It may seem impertinent that he confided so many details about his soul. Maybe the Lord wanted it to happen so that I'd write about it here, and He could be praised through his creatures—but I know that he never said so much to his confessor, or to anyone else." Given Gracián's volubility, he must have come close at times. He was a man who liked to have and communicate secrets, a man after Teresa's own heart.

She enjoyed every minute she spent with him in Beas; it was probably the most uninterruptedly happy period of her life. "Since I was going through such a hard time then, it seemed to me when I saw him that God was showing me all the benefits he would bring to us, and I spent my days feeling so thoroughly consoled and contented that I even amazed myself," she writes. Gracián, for his part, was delighted to have finally met her. Unlike Mariano, he had every intention of including her in the Andalusian reform and told her that he knew just where she should make her next foundation: in Seville. This didn't seem like such a brilliant idea to her, given Rubeo's explicit orders. Anyway, she had decided to found in Caravaca and had recruited a prime group of nuns—she was only waiting for the permissions to arrive. But Gracián thought the nuns would be wasted in remote Caravaca. The place for them was Seville, where they would be well looked after by some prosperous benefactors he had already lined up.

Teresa overcame her hesitations. After all (as she had now learned) she had already founded in Andalusia, and—welcome news!—Gracián had been made apostolic visitor to the province, so he was officially her superior there. She really had no choice but to obey his orders. This, she perceived, was a grace the Lord had given her: to think that her superiors were always right.

He became her confessor. She had been making do for a long time, confessing to brilliant men who couldn't really understand her and to understanding men who were confused by what she was telling them. Suddenly here was someone whose thoughts and emotions seemed calibrated to her own. Even so, she couldn't have predicted what was about to happen between the two of them. In one of her *Cuentas de conciencia*, written during that time in Beas, she tells the story:

> In 1575, during the month of April, while I was at the Beas foundation, Jerónimo de la Madre de Dios, Gracián, happened to come there. . . . One day while I was having a meal (and not in the least recollected) my soul began to be suspended and recollected, so that I thought a rapture was sweeping over me. And a vision appeared suddenly, as they usually do, like a lightning

flash. It seemed to me that our Lord Jesus Christ was beside me, in the form His Majesty most often takes when He appears to me, and this very same Gracián was on his right side. The Lord took Gracián's right hand, and placed it in mine, and told me that He wanted me to accept this person as his surrogate for the rest of my life, and that it was fitting for the two of us to bring our wills into perfect harmony.

Teresa was sure this vision came from God; the devil couldn't possibly come up with anything that felt so right. She couldn't wait to tell her sisters in Castile about Gracián. In a letter to Inés de Jesús, her prioress at Medina, she writes:

> Oh my mother, how I wished you were with me during these past days! I want you to know, they've seemed like the high point of my life—and I'm not exaggerating. For more than twenty days father master Gracián has been here, and I tell you, as much as I've worked with him, I still haven't fully understood the valiant nature of this man. In my eyes, he's perfect. We couldn't have asked God for anyone better equipped to help us. What your reverence and the rest of you need to do now is to ask His Majesty to make Gracián our superior. Then I'd be able to take a rest from governing these houses, because such perfection, with so much gentleness, is something I've never seen before.

Some of these prioresses took a lot of convincing, but Teresa was fully loaded with praise for Gracián. "I'm telling you, he's a saint, and not at all impulsive, but very circumspect," she shot back in answer to one of María Bautista's snide remarks. "It's like dealing with an angel, which is what he is and always has been." Teresa imagined how wonderful it would be if Gracián could govern the Discalced in Castile as well as in Andalusia, and then she got an idea. She, Teresa de Jesús, could take a vow of obedience to Gracián. It might not seem like she was giving up much at first, but the truth was that she would be giving up something she had always prized: her freedom. "On the one hand," she writes, "it seemed like nothing to me, since I had already decided to do this. On the other hand, it seemed very hard, when I considered how you don't reveal your soul's deepest secrets to superiors, and how they keep changing anyway, so that if you don't hit it off with one, another comes along. This vow would leave me with no freedom, in action or contemplation, for the rest of my life. So I was inclined, and pretty much convinced, not to take it."

An anonymous sixteenth-century portrait of Teresa's superior and confidant, Gracián de la Madre de Dios

As usual, the fine points of obedience were a headache for her. At last she made the decision to proceed with her vow, even though "I don't think I ever did anything . . . that made me resist more, except when I left my father's house to become a nun." She knelt down and promised God that from then on she would do everything master Gracián told her to do—except in inconsequential matters or in cases where his orders were directly contradicted by God himself or by her superiors. "Blessed be He, who created someone so pleasing to me that I could dare to do this."

In May of 1575, around the time that Teresa was writing her jubilant letter to the Medina prioress, Rubeo was presiding over a Carmelite chapter general in Piacenza, Italy, which he had called to address the crisis in Spain. None of the Discalced were there. Rubeo displayed the papal brief that he had received the year before, ending the terms of the apostolic visitors. (The king, resenting this foray into his territory by the pope, subsequently reinstated them.) Everyone present agreed that any superiors who had been appointed without due recourse to Carmelite authorities should be immediately kicked out of office, and that any religious houses they had founded in Andalusia should be evacuated in no more than three days. From this point on, no friar was ever to go barefoot or to identify himself as "Discalced"; instead, he should call himself a "Contemplative" or "Primitive," to distinguish himself from the friars of the Observance. Other directives emanated from Piacenza too. Contemplative nuns who left their convents were to be excommunicated, and the nun Teresa de Jesús was to go back to Castile and shut herself up in any convent she pleased.

Teresa, as it happened, wasn't in any position to hear of these new restrictions. She was on her way to Seville.

Chapter 16: *A Season in Seville*

—

It was mid-May, and Teresa headed south with her handpicked group of nuns and their escorts to a province remote in every sense from their native Castile. Christ had wept (according to legend) while passing through the windswept plains of Avila, and his petrified tears had turned into rocks—though as Francis Parkinson Keyes once observed, that quintessential Castilian landscape is more accurately a place where tears are not shed, but are dried. Andalusia, on the other hand, was soft, drowsy, sensuous. Africa had long been a presence there, not only geographically (the tip of southern Spain is only a hair's breadth from Morocco) but also culturally. The intricate flourishes of Moorish architecture, poetry, and philosophy remained long after the *reconquista* and gave the cities of Granada, Córdoba, and Seville their exotic ambience. Diverse populations once blended easily in Andalusia, where, as Jan Morris writes in *Spain,* "the air is heavy with jasmine and orange blossom . . . there are prickly pears at the roadside . . . and often there hangs upon the evening the sad but florid strain of *cante jondo*—the 'deep song,' part Oriental, part Gregorian, part Moorish, part Jewish, that the gypsies have made the theme music of the south."

The story of the journey to Seville, as Teresa tells it in the *Fundaciones,* is much more entertaining than anything else in the book—partly because she wrote these chapters at the request of Gracián, who brought out the best in her, and partly because she was seeing the city through alien eyes. However hardened she thought she was to extremes of heat and cold, this was her first experience of an Andalusian summer: "Even though we weren't traveling during siesta, I tell you, Sisters, after that hot sun beat down on the wagons, climbing inside them was like going to purgatory. By sometimes meditating about hell, and sometimes about how this suffering was all for God, those sisters kept right on going, contented and full of joy."

The analogy was apt. The nuns had to cope not only with excruciating heat but with other torments. Julián describes how the food they brought with them went bad after only one day of traveling, and how some men at a filthy inn began attacking one another with knives and curses. "In fact, their bad language was fouler than the mud." Teresa tells how she came down with a high fever, made worse by the relentless sun, which was inescapable. Even the water the nuns splashed in her face gave her no relief: it too was hot. Her room at the inn had a bad roof and no window, and when the door was opened, the sun barreled in ("not like the sun in Castile, but much more annoying"). The bed was high in one part and low in another, and trying to rest on it was "like lying on pointy stones." She thought she'd be better off stretched out in an open field than trying to recuperate in that room. "What must it be like for those poor souls in hell," she wondered, "where nothing can ever change! Even going from torment to torment brings a certain amount of relief."

As if pursued by a horde of devils, the barge that was transporting the nuns and their wagon across the Guadalquivir broke loose from its tow-rope and went racing down the river. "We were all praying," Teresa writes. "The others were all screaming." Luckily, the barge grounded itself on a shoal, and men from a nearby castle came to the rescue. The shaken travelers continued on, then made a stop at Córdoba, where they tried to enter a church inconspicuously, but with no luck: a group of women with black veils over their faces, white mantles over their shoulders, and hemp sandals on their feet were not a typical sight in that city. Everyone knew immediately who they were, and according to Teresa, there was such commotion ("you would think that a herd of bulls had entered the church") that it shocked the fever right out of her. Slipping away from Córdoba, the group took its siesta under a bridge.

As far as she knew, Mariano had befriended the archbishop of Seville, Don Cristóbal de Rojas y Sandovál, who would have the licenses ready when the nuns arrived. She knew something was wrong as soon as she took a look at Mariano. "Not wanting to upset me, he was holding something back, but he didn't have any explanation—which was how I figured out what was the matter, that the license hadn't been granted." It turned out that the archbishop was famous for his opposition to monasteries founded in poverty. But knowing what a tremendous asset Teresa's convent would prove to be for the city, Mariano had been sure—and Gracián had agreed with him—that the prelate would quickly change his mind when he met the founder. Just to be on the safe side, Mariano had neglected to mention the proposed foundation at all.

So Teresa arrived in Seville and found that she had . . . nothing, except a very inferior house that Mariano had procured for her in the center-city neighborhood of the Calle de Armas. The house was damp and unpleasant, and had nothing in it but some hard wicker pallets that could be used for beds, a few thin, straw mattresses, a frying pan, a table, some plates, a candlestick or two, and a pail for drawing water—almost all of which were quickly reappropriated by neighbors who had loaned them out. It was such an absurd situation that the sisters had to laugh. There was very little else they could do. They had no money, no friends, and no way of founding a convent without written permission. The perfectly congenial archbishop made it known that as much as he lauded Teresa's reform, he had never licensed a Discalced convent in the city and wasn't about to start. Seville had more than forty monastic institutions and needed no more. Anyway, even if she could contrive to establish her nuns there, they would need an income—a suggestion that Teresa refused to entertain. Seville was a bustling transatlantic port where ships sailed in weighted with gold and silver from the Indies—how could her foundation not thrive on alms alone?

The Calced friars were, of course, ready for battle, so Teresa trucked out what little ammunition she could lay her hands on: the patents for founding reformed convents that Rubeo had given her years before. The friars who came roaring into her presence were subdued by these somewhat antique documents, probably because they were in Latin and none of them could decipher it. The irony was that they assumed Don Cristóbal had betrayed them by giving the foundation his blessing, even though at that point he had no intention of doing so.

He finally did, though, after a flurry of letters from Gracián, currently in Madrid, who realized that he had helped put the holy mother in a tenuous position (and not for the last time). Mariano made some appeals to the archbishop too, but it was Teresa's heart-to-heart talk with Don Cristóbal that seems to have made the difference. From then on, he was her strong supporter, for all the good that did her: the people of Seville turned out to be the meanest and stingiest she ever knew: "I don't know if it's because of the climate—I always heard that devils were freer to tempt people there. . . . They certainly went after me, because I've never felt more timid and cowardly in my life. I didn't recognize myself."

Teresa was appalled at the local women who wanted (or thought they wanted) to join her reform. The typical candidate was dressed to the nines and—to judge from her *tapado de medio ojo,* the veil revealing one heavily made-up eye—was only flirting with religion. Teresa was glad she had a core group of virtuous nuns, but she worried about having brought them to this sinful southern city infested with foreign thieves and adventurers after Peruvian gold, where "they use lies as currency—it's enough to make a person faint!" Her anxiety about the move to Andalusia, as well as word that Gracián, Mariano, and Antonio de Jesús had been excommunicated for disobedience (Gracián had decided to ignore the rulings of the Piacenza chapter) made her write Rubeo a long, belated letter, larded with compliments and excuses. In this letter dated June 18, she reports that she has only just received his letters from the previous October and January and that she has written twice to him to let him know about the Beas and Seville foundations, as well as about one that didn't pan out, but still might, for Caravaca. This kind of business letter, like nonstop conversation, means to drown objections in a torrent of words: "Your lordship should know, I asked everyone about Beas to make sure it wasn't in Andalusia, since I had no interest in going there and don't like the people. It turns out Beas is not in Andalusia, but is a province of Andalusia—I learned this more than a month after the convent was founded, and the nuns were already established there, so it seemed to me that I shouldn't abandon it."

This is a clumsy excuse by anyone's standards, especially hers. She does her best to apologize for her colleagues. ("I really think they are your loyal sons and hope not to aggravate you, though I can't absolve them of blame—but it does seem that they're beginning to grasp that it would have been better to follow another path so as not to annoy your lordship.") She praises Gracián, who is "like an angel, and had he been on his own things would have turned out very differently. . . . He only came here because Fray Baltasar ordered him to." Teresa could hardly have known how dropping Nieto's name would raise the hackles of his old enemy Rubeo. She continues with a plea for Mariano, "a virtuous man, very penitent and well known for his talent. Your lordship can be sure that he was moved purely by his zeal for God and the good of the order—but as I say, he has overdone it, and been indiscreet. I don't think he has a bit of ambition in him; it's just that the devil—as your lordship likes to say—gets into the act, and Mariano says things before he understands what they mean." Mariano's dearest wish, she insists, is to throw himself at the father general's feet—just as soon as he gets the chance.

Teresa's letter to Rubeo isn't one for the hagiographers. She's heavy-handed with compliments and shameless about flaunting her connections. Rubeo has to hear about how the papal nuncio objects to the excommunications of the Discalced fathers and about how Fernández and Vargas, Don Cristóbal, even King Philip himself admire the new houses in Andalusia. Finally (the coup de grace), Rubeo must "remember that you are a servant of the Virgin, and that she will be offended if you abandon those who are trying, by the sweat of their brow, to augment her order."

While waiting for a reply from Rubeo (which never came), Teresa fired off a letter to King Philip, urging him to make the Discalced a separate province governed by Gracián, who was clearly an emissary from God. But events were careening beyond her control. Gracián, newly empowered by the nuncio Ormaneto as the apostolic visitor not only to the Discalced of Castile and Andalusia but to the Calced of Andalusia too, was on his way back to Seville to launch his own crusade against the friars, whose excesses he was ready to curb with force if necessary. In some sense, history was about to repeat itself: if Gracián had confided in Rubeo early on, the general might have seen in him a shadow of his younger, more arrogant and idealistic self.

Teresa never had any doubts about Gracián: to her, he seemed so pure as to be almost unearthly, as evidenced by visions in which he appeared as her mind's eye always saw him. Once, while she was feeling too distracted to pray and wishing that God had relegated her to a desert instead of the pandemonium of Seville, "my spirit found within itself a very delightful forest and garden," so Edenic that it made her think of the Song of Songs. And then, just as she was repeating a verse to herself, she saw Gracián. Like the beloved in the Canticle, he was comely, though, as she reports in all seriousness, "certainly not in any way black." He wore a garland of what looked like precious stones, "and many maidens went before him with branches in their hands, and they were all singing songs of praise to God."

There was no other man around. The vision lasted an hour and a half, and it left Teresa with an even deeper love for Gracián and the conviction that he was meant to be with her and her nuns.

Another time, "I was very distressed because it had been a long time since I had heard from my Father, and he hadn't been well when he last wrote." She felt a light appear within her soul, then had a vision of him coming toward her on the road, looking very pleased. His face was white, just like the souls in heaven, and she understood that he would succeed at what he was trying to do.

She actively supported him, even though she wished he hadn't been made visitor to the Calced friars of Andalusia—that was simply asking for trouble. When he had first received the commission, she had convinced him to turn it down, which he had tried (maybe not so wholeheartedly) to do. The nuncio wouldn't hear of it, and Gracián began making plans for his visitation, asking advice from Teresa, Mariano, Antonio de Jesús, Gregorio Nacianceno, and anyone else he could get his hands on. Teresa thought he should move slowly and cautiously with the friars, making sure they understood how he derived his authority and assuring them (as she had once assured the nuns of the Encarnación) that he would wield it to their advantage. "Even if they don't obey, your paternity should hold off from issuing them letters of excommunication so that they can carefully consider their actions. That's what I think. Others know better, but I wouldn't want the friars to feel like they're being checkmated." She also advised him to write to Rubeo, "flattering him as much as possible. . . . It's enough that all these things are being done against his will, without anyone telling him, or giving him the time of day. Look at it this way, my father: we did promise him our obedience, so we can't lose anything."

Mariano thought otherwise. He had always circumvented Rubeo and wasn't about to stop now. As for the Andalusian friars, an iron fist was what he recommended, and that was what Gracián decided to employ. He stormed into the friary barking orders and brandishing his commission from the nuncio, but the friars shouted him down. He yelled back that they were all excommunicated, at which point they threw him out, with his companion Antonio de Jesús (the newly appointed prior of Los Remedios), so roughly that it was rumored that Gracián had been murdered. A locution told Teresa not to be concerned, that everything would be all right. And it was, though Gracián wasn't spared by any charitable sentiments of the friars. Andalusians weren't famous for their restraint. They had simply decided to rely on other means of getting rid of the intrusive visitor who seemed so bent on reforming them. The prior had already sent his emissary, Pedro de Cota, to the pope to obtain a brief voiding Gracián's authority, and he expected results at any moment. He was disappointed, as it happened; the pope was inclined to take a wait-and-see approach, which put Gracián in an even more precarious position.

Teresa worried about him constantly: whether he was keeping warm, whether he was managing to keep his seat on his mule ("I really am annoyed about these falls of yours. It would be good if they'd tie you on, so that you *couldn't* fall"), whether he was being careful about what and where he ate. The friars weren't above settling their disputes with poison, so she arranged for Gracián to take his meals at the convent as often as possible. When he had to eat out, he confined himself with difficulty to a hard-boiled egg, served in the shell. "Fear," he was heard to grumble, "makes a bad sauce."

She had other reasons to be anxious. Some of the nuns that she and Seville's prioress, María de San José (Doña Luisa's former lady-in-waiting had some talents, it seemed, after all), had chosen for this difficult foundation weren't holding up very well: Isabel de San Jerónimo, for example, was having supernatural experiences again and showing renewed signs of melancholy. And some local acquisitions were causing trouble. A charismatic *beata* named María del Corro—a forty-year-old woman prone to *abobamientos*, as Teresa had once labeled silly raptures—had been admitted to the convent, thanks to her powerful friends in the city, whose demands Teresa was in no position to refuse. But convent life was not what the *beata* had expected. She disliked enclosure, hated the menu, the routine, the prioress, and the competition (Isabel de San Jerónimo). Soon María del Corro, along with another disgruntled nun, began telling tales about life in the convent to the Inquisition. She claimed that the founder wouldn't let the nuns see a priest, but made them confess to her; that she had taught the nuns strange devotional practices, like the Jewish custom of praying facing a wall (they were actually trying to avoid the blinding sun); that to discipline them, Teresa tied them up by their wrists and ankles and suspended them upside-down from the ceiling. These accusations were too outlandish even for the inquisitors, who decided to take no action against the founder. María del Corro left the convent in a rage.

It wasn't long, though, before she tried a fresh approach. Gracián, she now told the inquisitors, was Teresa's lover, though hardly her first. The two of them had corrupted the other nuns with their bizarre sexual practices—Gracián even used to dance naked in front of them—while encouraging them in heretical modes of prayer like those of the *alumbrados*. Isabel de San Jerónimo was entertaining who knew how many diabolic paramours.

This was steamy stuff, and one day in the middle of February, a cohort of inquisitors descended on the convent. They read the charges against Teresa and, as was customary, examined her at length for many days. She, in turn, provided a written defense of her life and religious practices, which now appears among her *Cuentas de conciencia*. What the inquisitors saw, both in person and in her written account (a kind of drastic condensation of the *Vida*) was not what they had been led to expect. This was clearly a woman who, mistrusting her own experience, had examined herself from every possible angle, as had numerous prominent *letrados* (she emphasized her friendship with Bartolomé de Medina). She was hardly the sexpot they had been imagining: at sixty-one, she was a fairly old woman, and anxiety and illness had taken their toll. Her nuns (though terrified by the inquisitorial invasion) were obviously devout, even Isabel de San Jerónimo, who seemed at worst a little unbalanced. The inquisitors gathered up their documents and rode away, leaving Teresa and her daughters in whatever passed at that convent for peace.

After the crisis was over, things began to look up for the foundation. A merchant freighter brought Teresa's brother Lorenzo home from Peru, which must have seemed like a godsend—she was more remote from her family and friends than she had ever been in her life. Lorenzo, a religious man, agreed to give his sister the infusion of funds she needed to buy a better house, just as soon as he could take care of the necessary paperwork at Madrid. Teresa had reason to trust him: he was the most reliable of her remaining siblings. (Several of her brothers, including Rodrigo, had died overseas.) Since Lorenzo's wife was also dead, Teresa agreed to shelter his boys at Los Remedios during his absence and place his amusing eight-year-old daughter, Teresita, in the hands of her own nuns.

She soon found a house to buy in a very good neighborhood. It couldn't have been more appealing: white walls ("like frosted sugar"), an orchard, and a splendid view of the galleons sailing along the Guadalquivir. Unfortunately, the beautiful new house came furnished with problems—proof once again that every blessing was balanced by trials. Lorenzo had returned from Madrid with only a tiny part of what the crown owed him for his services in Peru, and all he could do for his sister now was guarantee a loan. This should have settled the matter, but it soon became apparent that because of an error in drafting the contract, a tax would be levied on the property. As the guarantor, Lorenzo was legally responsible for payment, and to avoid arrest, he had to take sanctuary at Los Remedios until the problem could be ironed out.

It was Gracián who broke it to Teresa that at Piacenza she had been declared apostate and excommunicate, and ordered to choose a convent in Castile where she would permanently enclose herself, making no more foundations. She was hurt that Rubeo hadn't bothered to tell her this directly, letting the judgment trickle down via Angel de Salazar and make the rounds at court before she had a chance to hear of it. She decided to write to the prior general again, showing more remorse and pain. She also steeled herself to leave Seville, a prospect that upset María de San José— though not for the obvious reason. The socially ambitious prioress had actually been trying to distance herself from the controversial founder ever since their arrival in the city, annoying Teresa by her aloofness and indirection. But María soon realized that if Teresa left and the inquisitors returned, she herself would become their target. She confessed to these ignoble sentiments later on, describing how the founder laughed when asked what would happen if the Inquisition came to take her and didn't find her there. "Sister," Teresa replied, "you have a peculiar way of reassuring me when I'm in so much trouble: you tell me that the Inquisition will lock me up!"

As it happened, Gracián countermanded Rubeo's orders and told her to stay at Seville, ostensibly for her health, until at least the end of winter. Then she could go north to her permanent convent, to be decided at a future date. She would stop first at Toledo, where the climate agreed with her, and where, because of its central location and reliable couriers, she would have easy access to her other Castilian foundations. She also had important friends in Toledo: Doña Luisa, for one, was very close with Gaspar de Quiroga, who was archbishop as well as inquisitor general. So Teresa overcame her qualms and stayed in Seville throughout the winter, which extended into late spring. During that time she sent off surrogates to complete the foundation that had been stalled at Caravaca until the necessary documents arrived.

She also supervised the work on the Seville convent. A priest called Garciálvarez helped with the construction and added some Andalusian flourishes, such as highly imaginative altars and, in the cloister, a fountain perfumed with orange water. It was at about this time that Teresa sat for her portrait by Juan de la Miseria, at Gracián's insistence. (If she ever regretted her vow of obedience to him, it had to be then.) She was forced to sit still for hours, with her palms together in an attitude of prayer, until Fray Juan produced a painting for the convent wall that even today has a sobering effect on everyone who stands before it. Gracián said it was a good likeness. María de San José said it resembled the founder, but also that Gracián had commissioned it as a mortification.

That winter Teresa wrote again to Rubeo, as she had planned, in an effort to set the record straight. "When we are both standing before God, your lordship will see what you owe to your loyal daughter Teresa de Jesús," she writes. The truth is that Gracián (who loves him so much) tried hard not to be appointed visitor to Andalusia, but without success. He and Mariano also tried to write and account to Rubeo for their actions, but the devil made them botch the job. Maybe Antonio de Jesús, who is about to pen his version of events, will have less diabolic interference. In the meantime, she, Teresa, can help Rubeo make sense of the Andalusian enterprise, because "even though women aren't good at giving advice, sometimes we're right on the mark."

As far as her permanent enclosure is concerned, she wishes Rubeo had told her the news himself in a letter; then she would have been very grateful for his thoughtfulness. That's how much she needs a rest. But under the circumstances, she's hurt; he has treated her "like a very disobedient person," even though she has never dreamed of disobeying him or any other superior. In fact, her dogged obedience has brought her no end of grief, and she can't imagine how Angel de Salazar (who really knows better) can say otherwise. But then, the provincial has never been her friend.

So Rubeo must see that she is staying in Seville not because she wants to; she is staying for her health and once again obeying orders (from Gracián), but she will go to her new convent in the spring. "I beg your lordship not to stop writing to me, wherever I may be; since I'll no longer be doing any business (which is bound to make me very happy), I'm afraid that your lordship will forget me." But even if he's too tired to write, she assures him, she'll keep her letters coming. That alone will bring her joy.

Winter turned to spring, and it was time for Teresa to move on. The Calced were still on the warpath, but thanks in part to María de San José's brilliant networking, the convent now had powerful supporters, not the least of whom was the archbishop, Don Cristóbal. In early June, to celebrate the new foundation, the city held lavish festivities, with singing and dancing and cascades of flowers. There were also fireworks, and one of the rockets whizzed up to the vaults of the cloisters, setting a small fire, but miraculously the silk wall hangings were spared. After the service, in the kind of theatrical moment that Teresa had become famous for, she knelt before the archbishop to ask for his blessing, and he (not to be outdone) knelt to ask for hers. Everyone in the chapel was elated, though Teresa knew that the devil must be furious. And he wasn't the only one.

Chapter 17: *Going In*

—

Rubeo's only interest now was in dismantling the Andalusian reform. He began by appointing a Portuguese friar named Jerónimo de Tostado to the position of vicar general, giving him the mission of ousting Gracián and dissolving all the Discalced monasteries, as per the Piacenza agreement. Tostado was at Barcelona, patents in hand. Angel de Salazar, weighing in, summoned a chapter to formally endorse the Piacenza decisions. The wheels of political intrigue were turning quickly. Teresa, through her well-placed spies, had been following Tostado's movements as well as those of the emissary Pedro de Cota, who had secretly returned from Rome and was hiding out at the home of Agustín Suárez, the Calced provincial, until the time for his emergence was right. The only thing that had made sense was for Gracián to disappear until the nuncio Ormaneto could be apprised of what was happening. The Calced had spread rumors that Gracián was living at the convent, but in fact, he had left Seville, wearing around his neck the bezoar stone that Teresa had given him as an antidote against poison. As she prepared for her own journey north, Gracián was already tiptoeing through Castile and was as safe, for the time being, as his protector's foresight could make him.

The day after the festivities at the Seville convent, Teresa began making her way to Toledo, a journey she seems to have enjoyed. Her brother Lorenzo insisted that she travel by coach, and at this point, worn out as she was, she didn't mind a little luxury. No broken-down wagons, no filthy inns and spoiled provisions, but good food and pleasant company, including Lorenzo himself, along with his sons and the adorable Teresita in her miniature nun's habit; Teresa's ne'er-do-well younger brother Pedro, who had joined Lorenzo on the boat back from the Indies; the reliable Gregorio Nazianceno; and a lay companion named Antonio Ruiz. Their one adventure came during lunch in a granary full of corn, as Teresa later wrote to Gracián: "A giant lizard slipped between my tunic and the bare flesh of my arm and, thanks to God's mercy, nowhere else—I thought I would die. My brother grabbed it and flung it away—and it hit Antonio Ruiz in the mouth!" Give that sweet, patient fellow the habit right away, she tells Gracián. He has definitely earned it.

After a stop at Malagón to deal with problems at the convent there, she reached Toledo and settled in. "I'm feeling better than I have in years," she writes to Lorenzo, who has gone on to Avila. "I have a very pretty, secluded little cell with a window that gives onto the garden. I'm not bothered with many visitors, and if I didn't have to deal with all this correspondence, I'd be so happy that it couldn't possibly last—which is what always happens when I'm feeling good." She had some reason to be hopeful. Tostado had arrived at Madrid, where he had had a less than cordial meeting with the ailing Ormaneto and been booted back to Portugal. This would buy the Discalced some time. On the other hand, Teresa knew that Ormaneto was very ill and that Tostado's cousin Filippo Sega was in line for the job. The Calced friars were in Rome drumming up support for their cause by spreading rumors about the Discalced, and she urged Gracián to send his own representatives there as quickly as possible, for damage control if nothing else.

Gracián dragged his feet on this, but he did pursue her goal of creating a separate Discalced province and called a meeting at Almodóvar to discuss possible strategies. It was probably when he was passing through Toledo on his way to this meeting that he and Teresa sat down to figure out how they might safely trade information in their letters to one another. Corresponding was no simple matter: a person had to make use of any available courier—with luck, a reliable muleteer, but otherwise some friend or acquaintance who happened to be traveling in the right direction. Letters were more than likely to be opened and read by interested parties, so Teresa sometimes had to enclose them in mail addressed to other people, with instructions for their delivery. Sometimes the letters reached their destinations, and sometimes they didn't. Though it might be tempting to suspect, for example, that she had received but ignored the letters Rubeo had sent her the year before, they could easily have been intercepted by someone who wanted to cause trouble between them and did.

Teresa and Gracián agreed on code names for themselves and their adversaries, calling the Calced friars "cats" or "owls" (because they moved in darkness) and the Andalusian friars "Egyptians." The too vocal Calced nuns were "crickets" or "night birds," while the Discalced nuns, beautiful in their simplicity, were "butterflies." The Discalced friars, boldly rising above their earthly trials in service to God, were "eagles." The sick old nuncio Ormaneto was "Metusalem," Tostado "Peralta," Salazar "Melchisadech." The all-seeing inquisitors were "angels" and the inquisitor general was the "archangel." Teresa was usually "Angela" or "Laurencia," and Gracián was usually "Paul" or "Eliseo," though other names were used. God was "Joseph," and his rival, the devil, was (in the closest translation possible) "Hoofy."

Teresa made ample use of these aliases. She loved a secret and must have enjoyed writing a private language that only Gracián could read. After hearing about how, during one of his visitations, he made a slandering Calced friar wear a habit sewn with tongues, she informs him that "I wrote Paul a letter last week . . . about that matter of the tongues. When I was talking to Joseph, He told me to warn him that he had a lot of enemies, visible and invisible, and that he should take precautions. This is why I didn't want him to confide so much in the Egyptians—your paternity must tell him this—or in the 'night birds.' " Because she sees Gracián so seldom and can't count on having him as her confessor, she makes a point of reassuring him—and perhaps herself—that in his absence, a Toledan prelate, Dr. Alonso Velázquez, is doing an admirable job: "And so, my father, she is very happy to have made her confession to him, the more so because, since she first met Paul, her soul hasn't felt at all contented or con- soled by anyone else. Now, even though she's not as happy as she was before, her soul is content to subject itself to him, and that's a big relief. . . . Ever since she's been apart from Paul, she's been discontented, and hasn't been able to do a single thing right, or subject herself to anyone else, even when she wanted to."

An argument might be made that Velázquez, by all reports an intelli- gent and levelheaded man, suited Teresa's needs at this moment better than did Gracián, who had so much to distract him. She herself was over- whelmed with monastic business, in effect running a small empire from the ledge in her cell that she used as a writing desk, and must have been grateful for the hours when she could open her heart to someone with time to listen. Velázquez, a true Castilian gentleman, said that being her confessor would delight him as much as if he were made a bishop. Later on, as luck or divine justice would have it, he was.

If Rubeo had thought about it when he mandated Teresa's enclosure, he would have realized that she could travel as efficiently through her correspondence as she could on the back of a mule. She had always kept in constant touch with her prioresses, involving herself in every detail of convent life—right down to which locks and bolts were needed for the grilles. She wrote to María de San José, who deftly sidestepped her business questions (that prioress was such a "fox"), but also entertained her with gossip and shrewd observations. Teresa's responses ranged from caustic and furious to contrite and softly importunate. Writing to María shortly after her own arrival at Toledo, Teresa apologizes for an outburst of temper at her dear but sometimes oddly distant prioress: "I promise you that I'm touched at the loneliness you say you feel at my absence. . . . I was so delighted to hear from you that I calmed down and was ready to let you off the hook. If you will just love me as much as I love you, I'll forgive you everything you've done and will ever do, because my main complaint against you now is that you had so little interest in being with me at Seville."

With María Bautista, the Valladolid prioress who had once docilely planted a cucumber and had hardly obeyed an order since, she was generally less forgiving. She slammed María more than once for her greed (a prioress had no business angling for postulants' inheritances) and her pretensions: "You make me laugh when you say that one day you'll give me your opinion about certain matters. What valuable advice you must have for me!"

María's close relationship with Domingo Báñez was also a constant irritant. Báñez was justifiably angry at Teresa: he had written his defense of her *Vida*—and her character—for the Madrid tribunal, deflecting harm, and then she had gone on to invite more scandal in Andalusia. As far as the Dominican could see, she had ignored his advice and deferred to a man with singularly bad judgment, if nothing worse. Báñez had never been able to fathom what Teresa saw in Gracián. María Bautista, who liked to be on Báñez's good side, often made snide remarks about Gracián and the reform, which Teresa found intolerable. "It's bad to think you know everything, and then say that you're humble," she snaps. "No prioress has ever acted this way with me, and neither has anyone else. Keep it up and you'll lose my friendship."

She wrote to Gracián as often as she could—sometimes three or four letters in a day. She wouldn't let him out of her range for a minute and asked everyone who ran into him for detailed reports. She heard that he wasn't being careful about what he ate, that he was fasting too much, that he was confessing unbalanced women—these days any priest had to watch out for that, and he more than most. She heard, to her horror, that he occasionally read her letters out loud: the man had no idea whom to trust. "Time will cure your paternity of some of that naïveté, which I'm sure is that of a saint," she assures him. "But since the devil tries to keep all of us from becoming saints, people who are nasty and wicked—like me—want to rob him of his chance."

It was a wonder, given the complexities of her personal and business transactions, that Teresa had any spiritual life at all. But as she writes to Lorenzo, she can't stem the tide of favors that the Lord has been sending her:

> You should know that for more than eight days I've been in such a state that, if it were to continue, I would not be able to attend to business. Since before I last wrote to you I've begun having raptures again, and they've been a problem because they've happened several times in public, and even during matins. It is no use resisting them, or pretending that nothing is happening. I get so embarrassed that I want to hide, anyplace at all. I pray wholeheartedly to God to stop making this happen to me in public, and you have to pray too, because it's a real nuisance, and it doesn't seem to help me at all in prayer. Lately I've been seeming almost as if I were drunk.

For some days before this last bout of raptures, she had felt a spiritual dryness, or emptiness, that she actually welcomed because she felt so drained. How could she get any work done when she kept having to excuse herself and lock herself up in her cell, sometimes for hours, until she felt recovered enough to come back out? Sometimes she became so rigid that she couldn't even sit down, as the sacristan discovered one day when he found her tilted against a wall. An old woman like her could only take so much physical abuse.

Lorenzo had begun having irresistible impulses too. Sometimes they left him trembling (he had to control that, his sister said); at other times, he felt nothing afterward. That, Teresa explained, was no problem. Wasn't it Saint Augustine who had said that God's spirit passed without a trace, just as an arrow left no trace in the air? In any case, Lorenzo needed to be patient. She was sending him a *cilicio* for those times when he needed a little help in prayer. He couldn't sleep in it, but he could wear it any way he wanted, just as long as it felt uncomfortable. "It makes me laugh," she writes to him, "that you send me sweets, gifts and money, and I send you hair shirts."

It occurred to Teresa that this might be a good time to expand her *Vida,* since she was always readjusting her ideas about prayer. It had been some time since she'd been able to focus on the subject: the book of her *Fundaciones,* completed at Gracián's request, was very savory ("*es cosa sabrosa . . .* see how well I obey you?" she writes to him), but hardly an inspired piece of work. She could do more, now that she had a little time—provided, of course, that God lent a hand. Gracián agreed with her but thought she should leave the *Vida* alone (why ask for more trouble?) and begin a new book, one that would be tailored to the needs of her nuns. So Teresa threw herself into it just about a year after her arrival in Toledo, and worked steadily for over a month. She had finished most of it when events forced her to leave Toledo and attend to some business in Avila. By late fall, after only another month or so of writing, the book she called *Moradas* (literally, "Dwellings" but most often translated as *Interior Castle*) saw the light of day.

This was the precious volume that, as her nuns reported with wonder, she wrote as if in a trance, her pen skimming along the page as her face grew more and more radiant and her eyes looked away toward heaven. And that seemed right for a book as deeply, confidently spiritual as this one was: "As I was praying to our Lord today to speak for me—because I had nothing to say and had no idea how to obey the order to write this—something came to me, which I'll tell you now, so that we'll have a place to start. Imagine that the soul is a castle, made entirely from a diamond or very transparent crystal, where there are many chambers, just as in heaven there are many mansions. If we think about this carefully, sisters, we see that the soul of a just person is nothing but a paradise in which, He says, He delights."

Where else, she asks, would such a powerful, wise, pure king, one so completely good, take up residence? The beauty and dignity of the soul—its wonderful capacity—are beyond anyone's comprehension. It strikes her as a shame that people have so little self-knowledge that they don't know who they are and what their own souls are made of. It's like not knowing what country you come from or who your parents are. We flawed human beings have no idea how to conserve this treasure, but "focus only on the diamond's rough setting, the outer walls of the castle—in other words, these bodies of ours."

It is hard to conceive of a metaphor that would be more dazzling to a small group of nuns living in seclusion behind the grim stone walls of their convent and in silence behind their impenetrable black veils. Teresa was tapping into their dreams of spiritual rewards and riches—and showing them that these could be found, quite soon, in a place where they might never have thought to look. She was building them a perfect enclosure, one where if they moved slowly, carefully, toward the innermost recesses, they could find God:

> Well then, let's imagine that this castle has—as I've said—many chambers, some above, others below and at the sides, and in the very center, the middle of all the rest, is the most impor-tant one, which is where the most secret exchanges take place between God and the soul. It's important that you keep this comparison in mind, and maybe He will make it useful in explaining some of the favors He gives, and the differences among them—as far as I've been able to understand the possi-bilities. Nobody can fully grasp them, numerous as they are, much less someone as worthless as I am.

She goes on to explain how a person might receive no favors but still be glad to know that such things happen, even to others: unselfish gratitude is no small gift. Having established this, she invites her daughters into the castle while acknowledging how silly that must seem. How can they be inside the castle, when the castle is inside them? "You have to understand the different ways of being inside. Many souls stay in the courtyard of the castle—which is where the guards are—and couldn't care less about going inside. They don't even know what is in that very precious place, or who inhabits it, or even how many chambers there are. You've heard about books of prayer that advise the soul to enter within itself: well, that's what I mean."

Teresa guides her daughters from the first, or outermost, chambers all the way to the seventh, or innermost, warning them of obstacles and illusions along the way. The first dwellings are full of snakes and vipers and other poisonous creatures that slink in and befoul the soul with mundane concerns. (Teresa has very exact knowledge of how a reptile behaves.) These chambers are dark, somehow—as if mud were flung against the walls—though not as dark as when the soul descends into the darkness of sin. "I know a person," she begins in time-honored narrative style, referring obliquely to her vision of herself in hell, "whom our Lord wanted to show what it was like to live in mortal sin. That person says it seems to her that if people really understood what that state was like, they would never be able to sin again." It woud be as if the luminous crystal were shrouded in a black cloth—blacker than the blackest thing on earth. The devil, she warns, will try everything to get the soul into that state, tempting it to practice too much mortification, for example, against the orders of superiors, or to judge its imperfect companions harshly, putting charity aside. These are subtle temptations, and only frequent and persistent prayer, with a view toward self-understanding, can help the soul resist them.

In the second chambers the soul has blocked out the world enough to hear God's voice, not directly but through sermons or pious conversations or words in books. This is a torment because the soul isn't yet capable of responding and the devils are making such a tremendous racket that it's hard to hear anything at all. But it is important to keep listening: people who are further inside the castle can pull the soul toward them. Even so, it might slip back. God might let the reptiles bite once or twice, the soul experience dryness and bad thoughts, so that it will learn and grow stronger for the coming battles. "It has to be manly . . . determined to fight all the devils, knowing there are no better weapons than those of the cross."

As she leads her readers toward the third chambers, Teresa pauses to reflect on the struggle. ("It's a great misery to have to live as if the enemy were always at the gate, so that we can't eat or sleep without weapons.") She also reflects on her own wretchedness, as an example and a guide: "One thing you can be sure of, my daughters, is that I'm so terrified as I'm writing this that I don't know how I can write it, or even live. . . . Pray that His Majesty will always live within me, because if He doesn't, what security can there be in a life as badly spent as mine?" This ends up, like many of her apologies, as an argument for humility, which even those who have reached the third dwellings by devoting themselves to prayer and ascetic practices so often lack. They want consolations, the sweet relief that comes from prayer, and when God gives them dryness of spirit instead, they get impatient and start to mope. "Oh humility, humility," Teresa sighs, "I don't know what temptation I'm undergoing, because I can't help thinking that someone who makes a big deal of this dryness is running a little short on humility." It might help to realize that sometimes consolations are for the weak—they can't handle more—and trials, like dryness, are for the strong, to test their mettle. Still, she admits, given a choice, most people wouldn't take the trials. "We like our consolations better than the cross." But unless we can quietly accept whatever comes to us, these third chambers are as far as we'll ever get.

That isn't far enough, because the fourth chambers are where supernatural experiences begin. There the soul may experience the prayer of quiet, tasting spiritual delights, *gustos de Dios,* that expand its capacity, enlarging it for God. Consolations don't expand the soul but, if anything, constrict it. That is why, when she's weeping over the Passion, for example, Teresa gets such terrible headaches. Spiritual delights, on the other hand, seem to perfume the soul, as if there were a brazier inside it, and "the sweet, smoky warmth pervades the soul and often—as I've said before—the body too." Here Teresa guesses quite rightly that her readers will be longing for this favor and asking her how to achieve it. Her advice is: don't try. It doesn't come through effort. Sometimes women, in particular ("since we are weaker") try so hard that they further weaken themselves, then mistake their light-headedness for spiritual favors, even rapture. They'd do better to get some sleep.

Going In

It takes more skill than Teresa can muster, she says, to tell about the riches found in the fifth chambers. Like an epic poet about to describe a battle, she summons supernatural help: "Send light from heaven, my Lord, so that I can share it with these your servants—because it's been your pleasure to let some of them taste these delights often enough—and so they won't be deceived by the devil's transforming himself into an angel of light. For all they desire is to please You." The fifth chambers are where the soul receives the prayer of union, which brings it together with God, though not yet indissolubly, as in spiritual marriage. In the prayer of union the soul loses its senses and can't even think: "It loves (if it does love) without understanding how or what it loves, or what it might be after. In sum, it is like someone who has died to the world in every possible way, in order to live more fully in God. So this is a savory death, a ripping out from the soul of all the functions it can have while it's in the body; delightful, because it seems the soul has to be outside the body to be more fully in God."

In the other chambers, the soul was always worried about the devil getting in. There was no stopping some of those little lizards, the ones with the small heads that they could poke in just about anywhere. But there are no lizards in these fifth rooms, because if this union with God is genuine, the devil won't even come close.

How does a person tell what's real and what isn't? For one thing, there is a very distinct and deep-rooted sensation: if it were physical, it wouldn't be felt on the surface of the body but in the marrow of the bones. And there's a feeling of certainty afterward that only God can put there. Still, it is important to get a second opinion. But (here Teresa gives an important tip) when the nuns tell their confessors about what is happening to them, they should always say—as she does when she discusses delicate matters— "it seems to me." That way they can still defer to men who have more knowledge than they do. "I've had lots of experience with learned men, and also with half-learned, fearful men, who have cost me plenty," Teresa ruefully informs her readers. Real men of learning are never surprised by the power of God.

As if she is trying even now to get through to a confessor, Teresa searches for a more exact and detailed description of the soul's progression from sense to spirit. Without this she won't be able to go on to the next stages, which are even harder to explain. She looks to nature for her imagery, as usual, and this time comes up with the silkworm—not exotic, but common in Spain, where farmers fattened their worms on mulberry trees and collected their silk for textile production. Teresa reviews the silkworm's short and productive life:

> You will have heard about the marvelous way silk is created—an invention no one but God could have come up with—how it all begins with a germ as tiny as a grain of pepper. . . . As the weather gets warm, and the leaves begin appearing on the mulberry trees, the germ begins to quicken and eat. Until it gets this nourishment, it's as good as dead. The worms get big on the mulberry leaves, and when they're grown, twigs are put down for them. There with their little mouths they begin spinning the silk and making the tight little cocoons in which they enclose themselves. Then this big fat ugly worm dies, and out of this same cocoon comes a graceful white butterfly.

Would anyone believe this if no one had ever seen it? But it is exactly what happens to the soul, which is virtually dead until it's quickened by the warmth of the Holy Spirit and nourished by good books, sermons, and confession. Then it starts spinning its silk and building a house to die in, which is Christ. "Well, we see here, daughters, what we can do with God's help: His Majesty will become our dwelling place, constructed by us, just as in the prayer of union." To get the building materials for this house-tomb, she explains, we subtract from ourselves, weaving the cocoon by sloughing off our love and willfulness, and all our attachments to earthly things, through penance, prayer, mortification, obedience, and so on. "Let this worm die, let it die, as it does when it finishes doing what it was created to do."

When the soul is dead to the world, out comes the little white butterfly. This is how the soul, so close to God in the prayer of union, comes to be so transformed that it doesn't even recognize itself. "Think of the difference between an ugly worm and a white butterfly—that's the difference here." The soul knows it didn't deserve a blessing like this and wants to do something for God in return, to suffer and do penance. And the little butterfly becomes restless, not knowing where to alight—because having rested in God and having been given wings, it can't find rest anywhere in the world.

Going In

It can't go back to its former life; settling for the drudge work of the worm is impossible: "How can it be happy walking step by step when it can fly?"

Teresa had reached this point in the *Moradas* when she had to stop: the world, as usual, got in her way. Ormaneto had died in June, after summoning Gracián to his deathbed. (Gracián had arrived in Madrid at almost the last minute; he had never been quick on his feet.) Filippo Sega, the new nuncio, was on his way there from Palencia, and Tostado had returned from Portugal to catch Ormaneto's dying words, which he claimed were an excoriation of Gracián. The persecution of the Discalced was heating up again.

Teresa had to rely on Mariano for information; under normal circumstances, he would probably have been her last choice. Mariano was in Madrid trying to found a Discalced monastery, even though he had no authorization, and he was getting advice from, of all people, Teresa's longtime enemy Valdemoro, the prior of Avila, who now claimed to be in favor of the reform. Mariano thought that Teresa and Valdemoro should get together. "I think he's telling the truth when he says he is our friend now," Teresa writes, laconic as she often is in her letters to Mariano, "because it serves his purposes." What better way to spy on the Discalced? The only way she can possibly help Valdemoro will be to pray for him. Meanwhile, she'll do her best to advance Mariano's cause, ill-considered as she thinks it is, because "I am such a good bargainer—just ask my friend Valdemoro."

In July of 1577 she went to Avila. Her friend Alvaro de Mendoza was leaving to become bishop of Palencia, so Teresa proposed to transfer the San José convent from the jurisdiction of the bishop to that of the order—since Gracián was still apostolic visitor to Castile, that seemed the safest course. God had suggested it to her in a locution, and Teresa's confessor had confirmed it. Armed with these authorizations, she went to Bishop Alvaro, who was adamantly against the transfer. Eventually he did give in, though not without extracting written promises from the order that he would one day be buried by the founder's side in the chapel he had sponsored at San José.

While Teresa was working out the details of the transfer, Sega arrived in Madrid and began asserting his authority—with some caution, given the mood at court. He didn't immediately depose Gracián (who offered to resign his commission), but warned him to watch his step and do nothing without Sega's express approval. It wasn't a friendly interview. Fearful and hesitant about returning to Andalusia, Gracián went to Toledo to consult Archbishop Quiroga, whose response was withering. "Let them kill you," he'd said, adding that Gracián had the courage of a fly.

Left to twist in the wind, the visitor avoided the question of visitations for as long as he could. In fact, he went back to Pastrana, where he had camped out during the summer, to stay in one of the hermitages there. Teresa had always admired Gracián's ability to focus on prayer even at a time of political chaos, and presumably he succeeded again. He may have hoped that his absence would defuse the tensions in Andalusia, but it did exactly the opposite. His apparent passivity made his enemies hungry for blood, especially one enemy he didn't even know he had.

Teresa had been wondering where Baltasar Nieto had disappeared to. Having had the foresight some years before to rejoin the Calced, Nieto, who had attached himself to Tostado in Madrid, had now jumped to the forefront of the persecution by attacking Gracián, the man who had out-paced him in his own reform. Nieto sent King Philip a rumor-packed doc-ument from Seville that he hoped would settle the score and put Nieto himself in a position of power. It was the usual fare—Gracián's indecent behavior with the women he confessed, not to mention the founder—and the king wasn't particularly interested. Teresa, though, was horrified at yet another open invitation to the Inquisition. She wrote a frantic letter to the king: "I am astonished at the ruses of the devil and of these Calced fathers, who don't consider it enough to slander this servant of God . . . but have tried to ruin the reputation of those monasteries where the Lord is so well served." She begs Philip to protect Gracián, who is doing so much good in the king's reform and who is (a gentle reminder, here) from a family that has served the crown well. She and her nuns will, if necessary, write a testi-monial to Gracián's unimpeachable character.

It turned out not to be necessary. Nieto's document, signed by him and another friar (who later disavowed it), was examined by the royal council and thrown out, as was Nieto himself. He spent the rest of his life at a monastery in Portugal, far from the chaos he had helped to instigate.

Teresa, meanwhile, faced another nightmarish situation at the Encar-nación. The nuns were again voting for a prioress, and the vast majority of them wanted her. Teresa writes to María de San José, who is always eager for stories:

> I have to tell you what's been going on at the Encarnación, the likes of which I'm sure no one has ever seen before. At Tostado's orders the provincial of the Calced [now Juan Gutiérrez de la Magdalena] came here to hold an election—that was two weeks ago—and threatened terrible censures and excommunications against anyone who voted for me. He might as well not have said a word, because fifty-five nuns voted for me, and as each one handed her vote to the provincial he hurled abuse at her and excommunicated her, pounding the ballots with his fist again and again, and finally burning them. And for exactly a fortnight he hasn't let them take Communion or hear Mass. . . . The funniest thing is, the day after this election-by-pounding he called for another vote. The nuns said they didn't need another, they'd already had one. And with that he excommunicated them again and called in the ones who were left—forty-four of them—picked out a new prioress and sent her off to Tostado for confirmation.

It didn't take long for the excommunications to be voided through an appeal to the king, and for Teresa—as if she had nothing else on her mind—to return to her *Moradas,* the only place she could find a little peace.

Trials are to be expected, she tells her readers, as she prepares to lead them into the sixth chambers, where the soul is wounded with love for God. "I know a person who, since the Lord began to give the favor just mentioned, can't honestly say that she's passed a single day without physical pain and other kinds of suffering. . . . It's true that she had been very wicked, and that these trials were insignificant compared to what she had deserved." Still, that soul had had to deal with the sharpest pains, worse than any martyrdom; with malicious gossip ("those she thought were her friends reject her, and they're the ones who take the biggest bite out of her, the one that hurts the most"); with timid, inexperienced confessors who doubted whatever they couldn't understand—and then accused her of giving in to the devil or to melancholy. Worst of all, the soul had been tormented with self-doubt.

When these things happen, Teresa advises, there's nothing to do but wait for God to come to the rescue. It's hard to concentrate on prayer when there are so many distractions, but then God approaches the soul "as swiftly as a comet, or a clap of thunder, and even though the soul hears nothing, it understands that God is calling to it." The soul feels wounded in the most delightful way imaginable and has no desire to heal. It strains toward God, who loves it enough to wound it. This is called spiritual betrothal. The soul is swept away and, after it returns, is so consumed with longing that the smallest stimulus sends it flying back up again. "And so in this dwelling place the raptures are more frequent, and there's no avoiding them, even in public." The embarrassed soul wants nothing more than to be alone. On the other hand, it wants to plunge into the world to help save souls. A woman in this stage of prayer has to deal with "natural constraints." No wonder she's envious of men.

A couple of caveats: too much longing, and especially uncontrolled weeping, can be the sign of a weak constitution. Some people are mushy, though not Teresa herself. ("I'm not a bit tender, but have such a hard heart that it sometimes upsets me.") A person needs to try to keep functioning in the world, "because to be removed from everything corporeal, and always burning with love, is for angels, not for physical beings."

When the time comes—and not a minute before—God invites the soul into the seventh chambers. Here is where the king lives, the inner sanctum of the castle, where He will make the soul his bride. But first He gives her a strange new experience. "Our kind Lord now wants to remove the scales from the soul's eyes so that it can see and understand something of the favor He is bestowing on it. . . . And having brought it into this chamber by means of an intellectual vision, a special way of revealing the truth, He shows it the Most Holy Trinity, all three Persons." The soul, illuminated from within, not only understands that "all three Persons are one substance and one power and one knowledge and one single God," but "sees" that truth with its own eyes. And having seen it, the soul can never lose sight of it again. Just as a person standing with others in a very bright room can't see anyone else when the lights are off but knows the others are there, so "in the interior of her soul, the very, very interior, and in a very profound way—I don't know how to explain this, because I'm not learned—this person senses within herself this divine company."

Readers might expect that anyone who reached this state would go around in a daze, unable to pull herself together. Quite the contrary: she becomes more alert, more capable, and ready to accomplish great things. "The person mentioned earlier found that she was improved in every way, and it seemed to her that—in spite of her trials and the business matters that pulled her away—her soul, her very essence, never left that room." Sometimes it even seemed her soul was split down the middle, with Martha complaining to Mary about having to be in the world, while Mary kept company with God.

One day, just after this person received Communion, she saw Christ as He appeared after his resurrection, "in great splendor and beauty and majesty, and He told her that it was now time she consider whatever was his as hers, and that He would make whatever was hers, his own." This delicate exchange was how God took the soul to be his bride. "Understand that there is the greatest difference between what happens in this chamber and everything that happened before, between spiritual betrothal and spiritual marriage: one occurs between those who are betrothed, and the other between those who can no longer be separated." The soul is not rushed away, as in a rapture, but moves gently inward to rest with God.

Once it has received this favor, the soul becomes much more sensitive to God's honor and more afraid than ever of offending him. It wants to do penance, the more the better. In fact, the truest penance comes when God takes away the soul's health, so that it cannot do penance anymore. Another paradox is that the soul is beside itself with happiness when it is being persecuted by others, and it develops a special fondness for its persecutors, who are helping the soul to serve God better. "It is worth enduring so many trials, I believe, to enjoy this gentle and penetrating love."

At the end of November, Teresa finished her *Moradas.* She must have been in a cheerful mood, judging by what she wrote in her epilogue. When she began the book, she sounded exhausted and depressed: "Few things that obedience has demanded of me have been as difficult as writing about the subject of prayer. For one thing, I don't think God has given me the spirituality or the desire to do this. For another, these past three months I've been hearing noises in my head and feeling such weakness there that it's hard for me even to write about important business matters."

She was afraid that she would have nothing new to say. "I'm exactly like those birds that they teach to speak, that don't know anything but what they hear or are told, and repeat that over and over." Less than six months later she writes:

> Although when I began to write this book I was very unwilling to do it, as I said at first, now that it's finished I'm quite glad I did, and think it was well worth the trouble—though I confess it wasn't much. Considering how strictly you are enclosed, and how little you have to entertain you, my sisters, and how your houses aren't always fit to be convents, I think you will find consolation and delight in this interior castle, where without having to ask permission from your superiors you will be able to go inside and walk around whenever you want.

Freedom had always been essential to Teresa. The desire for it had propelled her out of her father's house and into the liberating confines of monastic life. The freedom that the soul could discover in prayer was the secret weapon of her reform. So it was ironic that as she opened the castle doors for her sisters, a prison door was closing on someone else.

Chapter 18: *The Prince in the Tower*

—

While Teresa was still at Seville warding off the Inquisition, the Calced prior of Avila thought he saw a window of opportunity. In her absence the only thing that stood between Valdemoro and the nuns of the Encarnación was their confessor, Juan de la Cruz. The nuns were devoted to him and now had no use for Valdemoro's much less competent henchmen. But he was not a man to give up power easily. His violent and badly thought-out solution was to kidnap Juan, along with his assistant, Germán de San Matías, and transport them to the friary at Medina. Of course Teresa was outraged, and she complained to Ormaneto, who ordered the fathers to be returned and threatened the friars with excommunication if they didn't stay away from the convent.

That settled matters for the time being. But after the death of Ormaneto, all bets were off. Sega and Tostado were furious when the nuns rejected Gutiérrez's choice for prioress, and they were convinced that their confessor had egged them on. (In fact, Juan had tried to keep peace in the convent and had advised the sisters of the Encarnación to obey their provincial; that was better than being adrift and compromised, as they now were.) Teresa, in Avila making her arrangements with the bishop, sensed that the Calced might try another surprise attack, so she arranged for some neighbors to guard the confessors' cottage. But the men left their posts after a few nights of deceptive quiet.

In the early hours of December 3, 1577, a gang of friars and constables descended on the cottage. Valdemoro's men caught Fray Germán and dragged him off to a monastery between Avila and Medina. Juan was snatched by the forces of the Toledan prior Fernando Maldonado, but the next day he somehow escaped and made his way back to the cottage. As

An anonymous seventeenth-century bust of the poet and mystic Juan de la Cruz, at the Discalced Carmelite convent at Alba de Tormes

his pursuers bashed in the door, Juan set fire to all his papers. Legend has it that whatever he couldn't burn, he ate. And then they took him away to prison in Toledo.

Just three days earlier, Teresa had finished her *Moradas,* with its serene encomium on the usefulness of trials and of forgiving one's enemies. But when she wrote to King Philip from Avila the day after the abduction, she must have been struggling with less generous impulses. "This whole place is scandalized," Teresa tells the king. "As for me, I'm extremely upset that they're in the clutches of those people, who have been after them for ages. I think they'd be better off with the Moors, who might take more pity on them." She provides a more graphic account to María de San José: "I hear that the day they were abducted they were flogged twice and subjected to the worst treatment possible. Maldonado . . . took Father Juan de la Cruz, to deliver him to Tostado. And the prior from here [Valdemoro] took Fray Germán to San Pablo de la Moraleja. When he came back, the prior told those nuns who are in his camp that he had left the traitor well-guarded. I hear that when they took [Fray Germán] there was blood pouring out of his mouth."

Germán escaped, but Juan was imprisoned in Toledo for nine months. Teresa wrote to everyone she could think of, begging for help and depicting Juan as a saint, "which in my opinion he is and always has been." His behavior while in captivity drives home the point. Though confined in a tiny, dark, airless cell with a pinhole window, fed almost nothing, and tortured regularly (scars from his lashings were seen on his shoulders after he died), he suffered quite literally in silence, enraging his jailors even more. He felt that God was punishing him in the most terrible way imaginable: by withdrawing his love. It was out of such concentrated blackness of sense and spirit—the state referred to in mystical theology as the dark night of the soul—that he created the first thirty verses of his *Cántico espiritual,* or *Spiritual Canticle.*

The *Cántico* is Juan's intensely lyrical recasting of the Song of Songs, the same text that inspired Teresa to write her *Meditaciones* and Luis de León to write the treatise that, along with his biblical teachings, cast him into the arms of the Inquisition. Juan composed his verses, filled with longing for his absconded God, in the darkness of his cell and wrote them down only after his release. He set a scene that any reader of the biblical text would recognize: a pastoral landscape filled with sensory delights, through which the desperate bride, the soul, roams in search of her vanished bridegroom.

Juan's verses almost always suffer in English translation. Their note of longing is played out in cascades of mournful Spanish vowels:

> *¿Adónde te escondiste,*
> *amado, y me dejaste con gemido?*
> *Como el ciervo huiste,*
> *habiéndome herido;*
> *salí tras ti, clamando, y eras ido.**

The bride calls out to the shepherds in the fields, then to the groves and meadows themselves, to ask if they have seen the bridegroom:

* Where have you concealed yourself, my love, and left me moaning? Like the stag you ran away, having wounded me; I came out crying for you, and you were gone.

¡Oh bosques y espesuras,
plantadas por la mano del amado!
¡Oh prado de verduras,
de flores esmaltado,
decid si por vosotros ha pasado! *

The bride is stricken to hear that the bridegroom has just been there, leaving tantalizing hints of his presence: it's as if he has plunged an arrow into her heart. She cries out to him:

¿Por qué, pues has llagado
aqueste corazón, no le sanaste?
Y pues me le has robado,
¿por qué así le dejaste,
y no tomas el robo que robaste?

Apaga mis enojos,
pues que ninguno basta a deshacellos,
y véante mis ojos,
pues eres lumbre dellos,
y sólo para ti quiero tenellos.†

The bride is swept away on the current of her passion, and at last the bridegroom responds:

Vuélvete, paloma,
que el ciervo vulnerado
por el otero asoma,
al aire de tu vuelo, y fresco toma.‡

---

* Oh woods and thickets, planted by my beloved's hand! Oh grassy meadow enameled with flowers, tell me if he has passed near you!

† Since you've wounded my heart, why haven't you healed it? And since you've stolen it from me, why have you left it behind, not taking away what you've stolen?
Ease my fierce longings—no one can do away with them—and let my eyes gaze at you, who are their light; I only want them because of you.

‡ Come back, dove, the wounded stag appears on the hill, cooled by the soft fanning of your wing.

The wounded heart, the restless searching and sudden flight, the sweet relief when the lover unites with the beloved—these are all stages of prayer that Teresa, with her scientist's passion for accuracy, had to struggle to articulate. She was less fluent than her confessor at describing the soul's anxious longing for an absent God: the spiritual dryness, characterized by profound weariness and self-contempt, that results from such total deprivation. Juan's poem known as "En una noche oscura" ("On a Dark Night") goes to the heart of this condition, a black hole of desire where the soul, all but extinguished by its misery, discovers the source of light:

> *En una noche oscura,*
> *con ansias en amores inflamada,*
> *¡oh dichosa ventura!,*
> *salí sin ser notada,*
> *estando ya mi casa sosegada:*

The soul searches, and the darkness conveys it to its destination:

> *¡Oh noche que guiaste!,*
> *¡oh noche amable más que el alborada!,*
> *¡oh noche que juntaste*
> *amado con amada,*
> *amada en el amado transformada!* †

Riding the cadences of this poem, a reader might get an inkling of how, at the moment of union, the soul flows out of itself and God rushes in to fill the void. But as Teresa often remarks, there is really no describing it. No wonder that late at night, after convent business was done, some of Encarnación's nuns claimed to have seen the two mystics deeply immersed in conversation, the chairs they sat in floating gently up toward God.

Juan's imprisonment by the Calced ended thanks to a sympathetic prison guard, who apparently looked the other way while the friar crawled

---

* On a dark night, anxious and inflamed with love (oh lucky chance!) I slipped away from my house unnoticed, all being quiet at last.

† Oh night that guided me! Oh night more gentle than the dawn! Oh night that joined the lover with the beloved, transforming the beloved into the lover!

through a tiny window and eased himself down a sheer wall on a rope made of old blankets and pieces of his ragged tunic. He made his way to the Toledo convent and not long afterward returned without fanfare to his work for the reform. His completed *Cántico espiritual* became so popular among the Discalced nuns that Juan had to explicate it so that they could be saved from their own potentially dangerous interpretations. As a result, his readers today can find his exquisite verses embedded in page after page of relentless prose—the verbal image of a perfectionist in theology, poetry, and life.

By mid-December the excommunications of the Avila nuns had been lifted (as every *letrado* Teresa consulted had assured her they would be). That was a consolation, though the turmoil at the convent hadn't died down. Teresa was not feeling well. "I'm having a horrible time with this problem in my head—I don't know why people seem to think I've recovered," she writes to María de San José. "And so many troubles all coming down on me at once make me exhausted at times." On Christmas Eve, Teresa misjudged a step and fell down a flight of stairs, breaking her left arm. Though the doctors set it, it healed badly, so a *curandera* was called in to rebreak it and repair the job. Teresa never had the use of that arm again. She could no longer dress herself or do the simplest tasks, and a devoted lay sister named Ana de San Bartolomé—later one of the staunchest promoters of the reform—became her constant companion and nurse.

Gracián poked his head out of his cave from time to time. He couldn't resist giving a sermon and went off to Alcalá during Lent, much to Teresa's annoyance. (There are souls to be saved everywhere, she writes, so why does he have to put himself in danger by searching out more? "Please God, let this zeal not turn out to be a temptation in disguise that we'll all end up paying for.") Gracián also met with Mariano and Antonio de Jesús and hatched a plan to hold another meeting at Almodóvar and elect a provincial, even though the Discalced were not yet a separate province. Teresa thought the idea was foolish and dangerous, but no one was listening. The meeting convened in the fall, in spite of her efforts and those of Juan de la Cruz, who shook off the ill effects of nine months of imprisonment and torture to go to Almodóvar and make his reasoned arguments—all for nothing, as it turned out. Antonio was elected provincial of the nonexistent province, and Sega's anger at the reform was fueled once again.

Gracián had resumed his visitations in Castile during the summer at the royal council's insistence, just as Sega was producing a counterbrief revoking the apostolic visitor's authority and putting the Discalced under his own control. But the king retorted with a royal order reinstating Gracián and forbidding the Discalced to obey the nuncio. Then it was Sega's turn again, and he sent emissaries to confront Gracián, who this time gave up his commission and all the documents that pertained to it without a fight. When the king heard that Gracián had done this, he was furious, and Gracián found himself in the unique position of being offensive to almost everyone.

Teresa had written to Gracián when she first heard about the nuncio's brief to tell him how blessed he was to have so many trials. "When I think about how our Lord Himself and his saints traveled along this road, I can only envy your paternity, because I don't merit such trials now—except for feeling what someone dear to me suffers, which is much more painful." He needs to straighten things out in person, and she has a strategy: first Julián de Avila will go to Madrid—just as he once went to Medina and Segovia—to herald Gracián's arrival. She, Teresa, will write letters to important people urging them to tell Sega how obedient Gracián habitually is. (He only resumed his visitations because the royal council ordered it, and also because he heard that Tostado meant to obliterate the reform.) She'll make it clear how happy all the Discalced are to obey the nuncio. All Gracián has to do is to pull himself together. He is prone to attacks of melancholy, and as much as Teresa loves him, her patience for that sort of thing has always been limited. "Don't go around expecting the worst—God will make everything all right. . . . If you are this melancholy with things going as well as they are now, what would you have been like if you'd had Fray Juan's troubles to cope with?"

As it turned out, Gracián was right to worry this time. Despite Teresa's careful preparations, nothing worked out as planned. Sega, who had shown a flicker of interest in letting the Discalced form a separate province, was fed up when he heard about the meeting at Almodóvar. Once Gracián had officially surrendered his authority, Sega made no more gestures toward the Discalced, but he immediately began to clean house, excommunicating all the friars who had attended the meeting, dissolving their new province and their communities, and imprisoning Antonio, Mariano, and Gracián at separate Calced monasteries. Gracián was held at Madrid, which was not the disaster it seemed at first: he readily admitted that the friars there treated him with every courtesy.

The very mention of Teresa, at this point, tried Sega's patience; it was when he was speaking to her emissary, a persuasive priest called Juan de Jesús Roca (whom he also imprisoned) that Sega famously characterized her as "an unstable, restless, disobedient and contumacious female who, in the name of devotion, devised false doctrines, leaving the enclosure against the orders of the Council of Trent and her superiors, and teaching as if she were a master, in spite of Saint Paul's order that women should not teach." Teresa heard what the nuncio had said about her and was insulted. "They're saying that I'm a restless vagabond, and that the convents I've founded are unlicensed by either the pope or the general," she complained to a former confessor who had influence with the royal council. "What more damning or unchristian thing could they say?"

Again and again in her letters, she held up as her standard Rubeo's original commission—to found as many convents as the hairs on her head. She didn't know it yet, but Rubeo had died that fall, and his commissions had expired with him. This signaled not only the end of her bargaining power with Sega but also the end of her hopes for the prior general's forgiveness and renewed support. When she heard the news, she was deeply upset and blamed Mariano and other advisers for Gracián's failure to approach Rubeo directly about his foundations in Andalusia. "You must have been counseled by someone who couldn't care less how much your paternity suffers," she writes to him. "Now, I'm glad to say, you've learned from experience to steer your affairs in the direction they have to go, and not against the current, as I've always told you." Keeping herself on a straight course had been difficult enough; keeping Gracián and the others on it had proved virtually impossible. Word had it that while in captivity Gracián had seriously considered becoming an Augustinian. Teresa urged him to stay the course; his mother told him she'd never speak to him again if he left the order; and the count of Tendilla, a gallant friend of the reform, proposed to run him through with his dagger. Whatever plans he might have had, Gracián quickly rethought them.

Teresa was never put off by his obvious weaknesses. She had always admired his spirituality, his intelligence, and his talents at preaching and writing, florid as they were. She saw him as a martyr, envied by the devil and favored by God, and she was sure his suffering could only strengthen him. It wasn't long before God favored him again.

Beatriz de la Madre de Dios (formerly known as Beatriz Chávez) was an attractive and flamboyantly pious Sevillian woman with a large following in town. In spite of a miserable childhood (Teresa writes about it at length in the *Fundaciones*), Beatriz had survived her abusive parents to realize her dream of entering a Discalced convent. By the time she got there, she was, according to the laconic María de San José, "forty, very authoritative, and had a clever way of getting out of every difficulty" by claiming that she was ill. She was disruptive and increasingly annoyed by the demands of convent life, as well as by the unsympathetic attitude of the prioress. (María had seen through her from the start.) Beatriz also resented Gracián, who, following Teresa's advice for once, had stopped hearing her wildly dramatic confessions. With another nun as her accomplice, Beatriz accused him of seducing all the nuns in the convent, as well as an assortment of local women. Her accusations of debauchery extended, of course, to Teresa and María, whom she portrayed as abetting Gracián while indulging their own unnatural desires.

Garciálvarez (the priest who had helped design the chapel and sweetened the cloister with the fragrance of orange water) became Beatriz's confessor and acolyte, and he helped her take her claims to the Inquisition. As a result María de San José was deposed as prioress, and Beatriz was installed in her place. Gracián was tried and sentenced to confinement at Alcalá, where his humility and long-stated desire for mortifications were put to the test. So were Teresa's: Sega sent a delegation to Avila to inform her that she would now be permanently enclosed in a convent of *his* choice. This was a frightening prospect. She was probably correct in predicting that if the Calced got their hands on her, they would treat her even worse than they had Juan de la Cruz.

Juan had set the standard for bearing up under persecution; Teresa was not about to subject him to a repeat performance. She arranged that during this crisis, he be sent to Beas, close to one of her least visible convents. The usually supportive prioress, Ana de Jesús, received him grudgingly, and Teresa promptly rewarded her with a letter that would turn up as testimony at Juan's canonization proceedings:

> You amuse me, my daughter, by complaining for no reason whatsoever, when you have with you my father, Fray Juan de la Cruz, who is a divine, heavenly man. I'm telling you, daughter, that since he left us I haven't found anyone else in all of Castile who so passionately inspires souls on the road to heaven. You wouldn't believe how lonely I am without him. Think what a great treasure you have in this saint, and make sure everyone in that house interacts with him and reveals their souls to him— they'll find themselves greatly advanced in spirituality and perfection, because our Lord has given him that particular grace.

It took a great deal of hardship and the threat of losing him to make Teresa fully realize what she had in Juan de la Cruz.

She saw the catastrophe at Seville, like most other catastrophes, as a spiritual challenge. In a rousing letter to the Sevillian nuns, she challenges them to exploit their suffering for the sake of their souls. She understands that they are frightened and confused; some of them may have cracked under the pressure from the inquisitors and signed whatever was put in front of them. That shouldn't defeat them, Teresa says; it was just God's way of revealing that they weren't quite ready for those trials they had always prayed for. "Courage, courage, my daughters," she trumpets. "Remember that God never gives more trials than a person can bear, and is always with those who suffer." She reminds them that they haven't *really* shed their blood in martyrdom—it's not as if they're among the Moors— and that God will protect them by revealing the truth. But since the devil is also trying to entrap them, they will have to be very careful. "Prayer, prayer, my sisters, and let your humility and obedience be brilliantly displayed"—especially toward the new prioress and especially by María de San José.

The crisis was relatively short-lived. The scuffles between the nuncio and the king subsided when Sega began to realize that the persecution of the Discalced was doing his own career no good. The king and the royal council were growing more hostile to him by the minute. So bowing to necessity, Sega agreed to the appointment of four assessors to help resolve disputes within the order, one of whom was Pedro Fernández. This was really the first good news Teresa had heard in years. And there was more: the Calced were to be divested of their authority over the Discalced, and a new vicar general was to be appointed to make visitations and oversee reforms. By midsummer the Seville debacle would be reexamined, and María de San José would be reinstated as prioress.

At this point, another woman might have begun to relax. But Teresa had lived too long, and through too much trouble, to fold her tents at the first sign of détente. A letter to María de San José and Isabel de San Jerónimo outlines tactics for dealing with Beatriz, who is no longer prioress but again a nun. Pray for her by all means, Teresa advises them, so that the devil will stop sending her hallucinations. ("I consider her partially insane.") Don't let her leave the convent; she can do much less harm inside it. Try to forget the past, because the devil will blame her for his failure, and "he might use her to commit some crime that would make her lose her soul and her reason—the latter probably wouldn't take much." Don't leave her alone with anyone from outside the convent. In fact, give her some job to do that has nothing to do with outsiders. Be aware that the devil may try to convince her that the other nuns dislike her and treat her badly, and "I would be very annoyed if there were any basis for that." Teresa signs off with a friendly greeting to Beatriz: "Tell her how pleased I am that her troubles are over, since she told me in a letter what a tremendous burden that office was to her."

Having dispatched this letter, Teresa went on to her next order of business: pursuing her goal of creating a separate province for the Discalced. Fray Juan de Jesús Roca and a companion were already on their way to Rome. Nicolás Doria, a friend of Mariano's (always a dubious recommendation), a Genoese banker-turned-friar with connections at Rome and Madrid, was facilitating the negotiations. Doria had been managing the affairs of the Discalced since Gracián's confinement at Madrid, and at this point, Teresa was pleased with his efficiency and good sense. She wouldn't live to witness his betrayals.

There was every reason to be optimistic. The cats, as Teresa called the

Calced, had been declawed by Sega himself. The nuncio was even beginning to favor the idea of making the Discalced a separate province. Gracián had served his time and would soon regain his freedom. (Mariano and Antonio had been released already.) There was just one catch, and it can't have been a complete surprise to Teresa, who had always said that every blessing came with its trial: the Discalced's new vicar general was Angel de Salazar.

Chapter 19: *Campaigns and Conspiracies*

The new vicar general wanted Teresa to get back on the road, beginning with a trip to Malagón. The obvious reason was that the Malagón convent was in trouble, as usual. Doña Luisa had never adequately supported the nuns and after years of promises still hadn't provided them with a suitable house. There were also political problems: the prioress, Teresa's friend Brianda de San José, had had to be removed because of a tenacious illness (and, even more debilitating, years of mismanagement and scandal). Salazar suggested that Teresa herself should become Malagón's next prioress, but she took that as just another of his half-baked efforts to get her out of the way. (She'd go to the ends of the earth if he ordered her to, she wrote to him; it was just that the need to visit her other convents would prevent her from staying long at Malagón.) It seemed clear that Salazar wanted her nowhere near Avila, where the Encarnación was again about to hold elections—and she certainly didn't want to be there. Malagón was also a good safe distance from Seville, which made her journey there seem a blessing to the Calced.

She planned a tour of Valladolid and Salamanca too, with stopovers at Medina and Alba de Tormes—a remarkable itinerary for a chronically ill sixty-four-year-old with a permanently broken left arm. She didn't want to go to Valladolid, but the trip was unavoidable: María Bautista had orchestrated an urgent plea from María de Mendoza and her brother. "Your reverence is . . . getting what you want, God forgive you," Teresa writes to her prioress. "Pray to Him that my coming will improve your reverence, and make you less insistent on getting your own way. I personally think this is impossible, but God can do anything."

It was much more important for Teresa to get to Salamanca, where Pedro de la Vanda was still wrangling with the nuns about improvements, even though the house was a complete disaster. Teresa refused to waste more time, so she located a better house with a much more trustworthy seller. Everyone assured her that this man was as good as his word, but, she admitted ruefully, "there's no trusting these sons of Adam." She had not only his word but his signature on a contract, when his relatives somehow changed his mind. It was, Teresa knew, the devil's work. She had to leave Salamanca without resolving the crisis.

At Malagón, Doña Luisa finally honored her promise, providing a decent house for a new convent. Teresa, by jump-starting the masons and supervising each day's work, managed to have the place ready for occupancy before Christmas. She also warded off an insurrection by the nuns, who were resisting her choice for their new prioress. The Sevillian nuns had urged them (at María de San José's instigation) to insist on having Brianda back again. "They're saying that since it worked there, it would work here, too," Teresa writes Nicolás Doria. "Your reverence should give the prioress a good penance. She should have realized that I'm not such a bad Christian that I would take a step like that without a very good reason. . . . If it had pleased God to show me that it wouldn't do any harm, I would have brought her back myself, as I did there." This is one of the few times Teresa takes credit for her own behind-the-scenes manipulations.

More and more she relied on Doria to help her handle the internal business of her convents, as well as negotiations with Madrid and Rome. She wasn't very taken with him personally, but she was glad to have finally found someone as competent as she was. Doria had visited Teresa while she was still at Avila, and they had gone over all the matters that couldn't then be handled by poor Gracián, still under house arrest at Alcalá and forbidden to write to Teresa. She, however, managed to write to him—a letter that is remarkable for its ingenuousness:

> Father Nicolás spent four days with me in Avila. It's a great comfort to me that your paternity now has someone you can talk to about business, and who can be a help to you. . . . It's troubled me quite a bit to see you alone in the order, as you have been. I certainly found him sensible, full of good advice, and a servant of God—even though he doesn't have Paul's charming and peaceful manner. . . . But he really is a man of substance, very humble and penitent and direct, and good at winning peo-

ple over. He's sure to see how valuable Paul is, and to follow his lead in everything—it was a comfort to know that.

Doria was assiduous, for the moment at least, in reporting back to her from her convents. That was how she found out that María de San José was busy making trouble, now that things were more or less status quo at Seville. After Beatriz had been put in her place, María had made a show of no longer wanting to be prioress, eliciting a snappish letter from Teresa. Now María was insisting, as she had in the past, that their house was unhealthy for the nuns, and she was demanding a new one. She was also cleverly avoiding repaying Lorenzo's loan while assuring Teresa that the money was on the way. "I have written her some terrible letters," Teresa complains to Gracián, "but it was like banging an anvil." The sad truth about María, she suspects, is that "she's never been frank with me."

Teresa couldn't help wondering if that might be the case with Gracián himself. Using the confidential voice that she reserves for him, she writes: "I want to tell you about a temptation I had yesterday—and I'm still having it. It seemed to me that sometimes Eliseus is careless about telling me the whole truth about things. I know that these are minor matters, but I would like him to be very careful. For charity's sake, will your paternity get this across to him from me, because such carelessness undermines perfection. See how I meddle, as if I had nothing better to do?"

She was concerned that after his release Gracián would make plans without consulting her, as he had in the past, putting himself and the Discalced in danger. Sega was still opposed to him, and it was important to proceed with caution. She wrote to Doria about whether, in fact, Antonio de Jesús might make a better (or less controversial) choice for provincial once the new province was established; Antonio had already been elected, albeit prematurely, at the Almodóvar meeting. Gracián could serve as apostolic visitor, something he did very well when no one interfered. She broached the idea with him a little later, assuring him that it was a minor matter, because whatever his position in the order, "you would be everything."

Antonio had been after Teresa to make a foundation at Villanueva de la Jara, close by La Roda, where he had been confined during Sega's recent attack on the reform. Teresa resisted the idea of founding at Villanueva: trying to turn seven eccentric *beatas*—all of them intoxicated by the example of Catalina de Cardona, who had died a few years earlier—into Carmelite nuns sounded like more trouble than it was worth. Even though the down-at-heels *beatas* wrote to her often, imploring her to come, as did the current prior of La Roda, Teresa hesitated. She did ask for permission from Angel de Salazar, but in such a way that he would be inclined to refuse (something he usually did without any prompting). But then she was surprised by a locution in which God told her that He wanted to see this foundation made. "Later I understood that the devil had mixed me up," she writes in the *Fundaciones*, "because even though the Lord had given me so much courage, I had become so timid, I didn't seem to be trusting God at all." Luckily, as she notes, God knocked some sense into her.

As soon as Salazar gave his go-ahead, Teresa recruited some sensible nuns to work with the *beatas*. She also arranged for Ana de San Bartolomé to accompany her—as she would on all future journeys—and for Fray Antonio and the prior of La Roda to escort the group from Malagón. Antonio looked (she remarked) very plump and healthy: his severe trials must have agreed with him. Teresa had been ill herself, but after receiving her locution, she perked up, the sun shone gaily, and the group set off for Villanueva de la Jara.

This journey, as reported by Ana de San Bartolomé, had little in common with Teresa's usual bumpy, inconvenient, and dangerous ride. On the way she was besieged by admirers, who would barely let her stop and eat; some of the more enthusiastic among them had to be carted off to prison. She would lean out of her carriage from time to time to greet the adoring throngs who lined the road and held up their children and even their sheep to receive her blessings. At one inn where they stayed, Ana was awakened in their room by a beautiful, unearthly music that could only have been made by angels' harps. Teresa, though, slept through the night.

As she approached the monastery at La Roda, she was treated to the kind of scenario she might have choreographed herself: "The house stood in a delightful, desert solitude, and as we arrived, the friars emerged to meet their prior, in solemn procession. Since they went barefoot and wore their coarse woolen mantles, they filled us all with devotion. I was very moved, because I felt as if I were back in those palmy days of our holy fathers. The friars appeared, in that field, like fragrant white flowers."

The processional turned toward the church, with its clever underground entrance, and this was when Teresa found herself wishing she could be as uncompromisingly holy as Catalina de Cardona herself. The two had never met during the ascetic's lifetime, but for Teresa, death had never been much of an obstacle. "One day," she writes,

> when I had just taken Communion in that holy church, I became very recollected, and was caught up in a suspension that transported me out of myself. In an intellectual vision, this holy mother appeared to me, her body glorified and accompanied by some angels. She told me not to grow weary, but to try to press on with these foundations. I understood—though she never said it in so many words—that she was helping me before God. She told me something else, which there's no reason to bring up here. I was left feeling very consoled, and eager to get to work.

It is tempting to speculate about what else Catalina told her—something she didn't already know about prayer and penance, or something she had always suspected about Mariano or Antonio? Whatever that communication was, Teresa apparently never divulged it.

Continuing on to Villanueva—where the townspeople were so happy to see her that they hung decorations from the trees and set up little altars to line her path—Teresa arrived at the hermitage where the nine *beatas* lived and began cleaning up ferociously (something those women had never felt inspired to do). Most of them couldn't even read, but they approximated their prayers and lived as piously as they could, using their asceticism as a hedge against their ignorance. With Antonio's help Teresa and her nuns taught the *beatas* how to adhere to the Carmelite rule, and within a month they transformed the primitive enclosure into something resembling a Discalced convent. Teresa left Villanueva feeling spiritually refreshed and determined to keep on with her foundations, no matter what happened next.

What happened, once again, was trouble and heartbreak. After she left Villanueva de la Jara, she and her companions passed through a small town where they stopped to visit the church. Teresa's fame had preceded her here too, but all the townspeople knew about was her reputation for immorality, which had led the Inquisition to her door. The citizens were outraged that she presumed to enter their sanctuary, and they were becoming increasingly violent when Antonio fended them off, allowing Teresa to retreat to her coach. Soon after she arrived at Toledo, she became seriously ill, with pain in her joints and chest, and a high fever. The *catarro universal*—the influenza epidemic that was sweeping the country—almost killed her that spring, as it did many of her friends. Among them were the *caballero santo* Francisco de Salcedo, and her former confessor Baltasar Alvarez.

As she began to recover physically and emotionally, she tried to focus on her next foundations. Salazar had ordered her to make one in Palencia, where Alvaro de Mendoza was now bishop. She didn't expect that to be much of a challenge. But she also wanted to make a foundation in Madrid, which would require permission from Quiroga, the "archangel" who was also archbishop of Toledo. Gracián, as it happened, was in town preparing for his upcoming trip to Seville. (He had been made prior of Los Remedios but was understandably not in a rush to get back to Andalusia.) The two reformers hounded Quiroga until he granted them an audience, and though he had been stalling for months, when he finally saw them, he couldn't have been more accommodating. Not only did he give Teresa the go-ahead for her foundation but he told her that he had read the *Vida*—the princess of Eboli's copy, still in the hands of the Inquisition—and found nothing at all wrong with it. In fact, he had found it very enlightening. He would release it to her whenever she asked.

As it turned out, Quiroga never did send Teresa the license for Madrid; her successors had to make that foundation for her. And he never returned her manuscript. Luckily, enough copies of the *Vida* were extant so that she could lay her hands on one if she ever needed it. María de Mendoza had one; the duchess of Alba had another, which she loaned to her husband to read while he was in prison for his son's indiscretions. The aged warrior was casting his weary eye over Teresa's pages and presumably learning something he didn't know about spiritual soldiering, when the king released him so that he could back up Spain's claim to the Portuguese throne with a show of force.

In June, Teresa headed north to Segovia—one of her scheduled stops on the way to Palencia—where she pored over the *Moradas* with Gracián and a theologian named Diego de Yanguas. The two *letrados* made surprisingly few revisions, though more were made by Luis de León in later years. But

Yanguas was disturbed by her *Meditaciones sobre los Cantares*—her little disquisition on the Song of Songs. The subject matter was dangerous, to say the least, and so was her apparent desire to teach theology to her nuns. He ordered her to burn the book, and she did—signal proof, when it was later called for, of her obedient nature. When Yanguas ordered the sisters of Alba to burn their copy, they behaved like true daughters of their resourceful founder, by making a gift of the manuscript to the duchess.

While in Segovia, Teresa learned of the death of her brother Lorenzo. He had written to her before he died, and his letter had been so glum that she had written back scolding him for giving in to what was clearly just a bout of melancholia. "I can't imagine how you could know that you are about to die," she wrote, "or why you have these silly thoughts or are upset by something that's not going to happen." For once, her prescience failed her; her brother died only a week after she wrote that letter. She was already worn down by illness and loss, and this was a hard blow to sustain. As she explained to María de San José, "Everything seems to pass so quickly, my daughter, that we have to focus more on how to die than on how to live. Please God, since I'm left here, that I'll be able to serve Him somehow, because I'm four years older than my brother was, and I never manage to die. I've recovered from my illness, though I still get the usual attacks, especially in my head." It was getting harder for her to manage her correspondence, and she now almost always used Ana de San Bartolomé, one of the few people she trusted implicitly, as her amanuensis.

The gentle sister lived up to that trust, in later years not only providing intimate details for the canonization hearings but founding Discalced convents in France. Though her fidelity to Teresa's Constitutions pitted her against the saint's less scrupulous followers and subjected her to persecutions, for almost another half century Ana nursed the fragile ideals of the reform.

As executor of her brother's estate, Teresa had to return to Avila and begin untangling his affairs. This included calling in debts, both from Spain (María de San José, for example, still hadn't repaid his loan) and from abroad. It is possible that one reason Teresa objected so strongly to María's purchase of a new convent was that the current one looked out on the harbor. The prioress could tell her—if she would only remember to—whether the ships arriving from the Indies had brought the money that was owed her brother. Teresa also had to make sure that Lorenzo's children, especially the youngest, Teresita, got their inheritance. Even for an estate as relatively modest as his, claimants were likely to come out of the woodwork, as they later did. Pedro de Ahumada, the blacksheep brother, was already complaining that he hadn't been left enough to live on (though he had), and Teresa had her hands full trying to settle him down. In addition, she had to make arrangements to build a chapel in Lorenzo's honor, which his will provided for. It was when she was about to leave Avila, having worked things out for the time being, that she heard that the brief making the Discalced a separate province had just arrived from Rome. Exhilarating as this news was, it signaled a lot of backbreaking work for her, and she prayed for the strength to tackle it.

She was bone weary when she got to Valladolid. Too much business had depressed her, she thought, and possibly also her catastrophic illness, from which she hadn't entirely recovered. Soon after she arrived, she had a relapse, which drained her so much that she wrote to María de San José, "I don't know why God leaves me here, except to see so many of his servants die this year, which is a torment to me." She was also tormented by María Bautista, who involved herself in the growing disputes over Lorenzo's will, siding with relatives who resented his bequest to the Avila convent. Teresa had come to Valladolid in the first place to plan the Palencia foundation with Bishop Alvaro, who lived nearby, but now she didn't have the heart for it. Whether the devil or her illness was responsible for this, she couldn't tell. "The truth is that I'm surprised and saddened," she writes in the *Fundaciones*. "I often complain to our Lord about how much the poor soul takes part in the body's infirmity, so that it seems the soul can't do a thing but obey the body's laws, and cater to its needs and whims." She didn't want to rest now, physically or spiritually; she just wanted to serve God. And yet she felt incapable.

This failure of *determinación* was something that Teresa had never expected. She hadn't thought that her body could break down her spirit. The Palencia foundation suddenly didn't seem important, and neither did a proposed foundation at Burgos, a much larger city to the north. As usual, she consulted *letrados,* but this time they were no help. Master Ripalda, her former confessor from Salamanca, informed her that she had lost her nerve because she was getting old. This didn't make sense to her: she had often worked through worse infirmities than she had now, and more pain. One day after receiving Communion, she brought up the question with God, who didn't bother with explanations. The point was that she had a job to do, and she wasn't doing it. He had never let her down, so why was she disappointing Him? That locution set her straight, as usual. It turned out that all she needed was the treatment she often recommended for melancholic nuns: firm direction and a dose of useful activity. Though she was no stronger physically than before, she suddenly had the impetus to move ahead.

Taking four other nuns, plus Ana de San Bartolomé, she made the trip from Valladolid to Palencia, arriving as per her custom very quietly and saying Mass first thing in the morning. But there turned out to be no need for secrecy: Alvaro de Mendoza had greased the necessary wheels, and all she had to do was find the right house for the nuns to live in. Aside from some wrangling about real estate (resolved, as she could easily tell, through God's intercession), she had very little trouble with the foundation. This actually made her a little nervous; the devil might be trying something new. But the more time she spent in Palencia, the more satisfied she was with the people she met and with the house she had bought—right in town and felicitously named Nuestra Señora de la Calle, Our Lady of the Street. By the time she wrote to Gracián in January 1581, Palencia was no longer on her mind.

Something had changed for Teresa. Her anxiety was gone, and she felt sure that God was with her, even though her life was as turbulent as ever. She was (as she writes in a *cuenta* addressed to Dr. Velázquez, her former confessor and now the bishop of Osma) like someone who knew she would come into a fortune at some future date and felt cautiously grateful. She also felt a healthy desire to serve God, which made her take better care of herself than she would ever have dreamed of doing in the past. She was more careful about what she ate and less eager to do penance. "Often, as a great sacrifice, the soul offers Him the care of the body, and this care wearies it quite a bit."

Her ecstasies had stopped years before. But the sense that the three persons of the Trinity lived in her and the sense of Christ's humanity—the intellectual vision that she described in the *Moradas*—never left her. She still received locutions, which were necessary to keep her from making stupid mistakes. Her desires were muted, even the desire for martyrdom and the yearning to see God. What was more amazing, she wasn't deeply upset the way she used to be when she saw souls being lost or when she felt that someone was offending God. "It seems to me I live only to eat and sleep, and to suffer from nothing, and even this doesn't bother me, except sometimes, as I say, when I'm afraid I might be deceived." But she wasn't really concerned, because nothing in the world attracted her anymore, and the one thing that thrived in her was her love for God.

It was a relief that she had stopped fearing the devil, and her own wickedness, "and so I no longer need to meet with *letrados,* or to tell anybody anything. I just need the satisfaction of knowing if things are going all right, or if I need to do something." She understood that God needed her to live, so she couldn't even wish for death. After so many years of strenuous effort, a lifetime filled with conflicts, persecutions, and dire illnesses, she felt that she had finally done what her own proud (and therefore wretched) nature had urged her not to do. She had surrendered her will to God's.

It must have felt strange, given what had happened inside her, to be surrounded by men and women who could still be driven by personal motives. She continued to believe in Gracián's spirituality, but now she clearly saw his weaknesses. More than ever she needed to correct them, since the elections for the new province were coming up and he would most likely become provincial. Teresa was as honest as possible in her letters, telling him that she knew his election would benefit the Discalced, even though she'd rather see Doria get the job: he was more suited for it and wouldn't get into so much trouble. Gracián could work hand in hand with him— that would be an ideal arrangement. But either way, he should make sure to keep Doria by his side at all times, as "his advice is always good, and anyone who has suffered because of others as your reverence has will be glad to be with someone who won't cause you to suffer at all."

Mariano, always a few steps behind everyone else, was lobbying hard for Antonio de Jesús' election as provincial. Teresa had given up the idea, having discussed it with Pedro Fernández before his death that year. The two had decided that Antonio should have some authority, but that he had too many limitations to be entrusted with the job. Antonio was miffed: he had long resented Gracián and felt that his own age, experience, and lifetime of serious networking should have won him more prominence. Teresa wrote him a letter, but apparently, he never answered it. Send Antonio her kind regards, she instructed Gracián, because she had no intention of writing to him again.

As plans for the new province began to take shape at Alcalá, Teresa wrote Gracián a slew of letters telling him what to watch out for in the governance of the Discalced convents. Extraneous conversations between nuns and their confessors, for example, should be discouraged, and so should overtures from friars who might become corrupting influences. She advised him on reasonable changes to her Constitutions: for example, he should consider deleting the part about her convents not having incomes, since in spite of her best efforts, most of them had them now. He should find out if the papal brief severely limiting the nuns' movements, the *motu proprio,* was still in force. "A constricted soul can't serve God well, and so the devil may tempt it," she writes. "When souls have freedom, on the other hand, very often they couldn't care less about it, and aren't attracted to it."

He could now delete Pedro Fernández's rule about the nuns not eating eggs or bread at collation (heaven knew she had tried to talk Fernández out of it), and he could omit any mention of whether the nuns' stockings should be wool or hemp—that was just asking for trouble from over-scrupulous sisters. Gracián might think such points were trivial, but "I've seen many things turn out to be disastrous which at first seemed like they mattered very little." It almost went without saying that he should burn these letters from her—which, posterity can testify, he never did.

Even as she was advising Gracián, Teresa was making plans to go to Soria, where Velázquez, the bishop of Osma, wanted her to make a foundation. She knew she would also have to make a trip to Avila, where the convent of San José was on a downhill slide—worse than she could ever have imagined. This was partly because of its poverty (Lorenzo's bequest hadn't been received yet, since the will was still being contested and Francisco de Salcedo, who had had some bad financial luck, had been able to leave the convent only a token amount), and partly because of bad management. Julián de Avila had been too lenient with the nuns, and they had developed some bad habits that would be hard to break. The sisters wanted Teresa as their prioress—from hunger, as she said.

She left for Soria in early summer and actually enjoyed her trip. There were river views all the way, and water always refreshed her spirits. Gracián disappointed her by not coming along, but with his usual naïveté, he sent Nicolás Doria in his place. It was in this city, where she was received very warmly, thanks to the bishop, that witnesses first began remarking on the lovely scent that emanated from the aged nun; children noticed it on her clothes. A sense of well-being, or more likely a certain impatience, soon had Teresa writing to Archbishop Quiroga, pressing him about the Madrid foundation. With her usual finesse, she injected into this letter the news that his niece Doña Elena de Quiroga—the patron of Medina—was anxious to join the Madrid convent if it could be founded soon. This strategy backfired: Quiroga was appalled that his niece wanted to join the Discalced, and he blamed Teresa for talking her into it. Suddenly she found herself mounting a defense of her motives, another difficult and nerve-racking campaign.

She was in Avila by September, trying to salvage what was left of the convent of San José. Family dissention and scandal (rumors about one of her nieces) pursued her there, and the squabbles over Lorenzo's will continued. She was also worried about the upcoming elections: at this stage of her life, the taxing job of prioress was the last thing she wanted. Padre Julián, old and sweet and incompetent, was driving her crazy: "God deliver me from ancient confessors!" she wrote to Gracián.

There was some good news. The duchess of Alba loaned Teresa her copy of the *Vida*, which the founder was pleased to have back in her possession. It was a nice coincidence that García de Toledo, who had first commissioned the book, returned from Peru at around this time and was about to visit María de San José at Seville: a real treat for the prioress, Teresa assured her. (She herself could not manage to see him.) Having the *Vida* in hand must have confirmed Teresa's impression that she had made a lot of progress since she had written the book, and she now understood some things much better than she had at the time she wrote it. She asked María to read the last chapter of the *Moradas* (surely she wouldn't be interested in the whole thing) to Teresa's former defender at Seville, Rodrigo Alvarez, and to let him know that the writer had reached the state described there and attained the peace that went along with it.

The bad news—and it seemed God always wanted her to have some—was that during Doria's visit, he and María had put their heads together and figured out a way for the prioress to weasel out of her debt to Lorenzo. She would send the money to Doria's brother, to whom Teresa owed a similar amount. This was awful news, especially since the money from the Indies had never come (and wasn't likely to, now that word of Lorenzo's death had spread overseas). Lorenzo's chapel would never be built. And Teresa, from then on, would know that in addition to his other talents, Doria had a flair for conspiracy, which he would later exercise to the fullest—not only against Gracián but against María de San José herself. She was a brilliant and subtle woman, and after Teresa's death she extended the reform to Portugal. But because she sided with Gracián against Doria, she was embattled for much of her later life, and died in exile, refusing all attempts to rescue her.

By December of 1581, Teresa was still in Avila, and she didn't have a lot to look forward to. She was likely to find herself in Castile for the winter, which in her weakened state would be almost unbearable. She had been elected prioress of San José. ("You would think I had nothing else to keep me busy!") And she was exchanging nasty letters with her nephew Francisco's mother-in-law, who was challenging Lorenzo's bequest to the convent, partly on the grounds that the will had been torn in half. (No one ever proved who had done it.) Teresa expected to have to take the mother-in-law to court, which was a grueling prospect.

Juan de la Cruz, now prior (against his better judgment) of Baeza in Andalusia, had made the long trip to Avila in order to persuade Teresa to go with him to Granada and make a foundation there. He had been very alone at Baeza, feeling, he said in a letter, as if a whale had swallowed him up and disgorged him on a foreign shore. The thought of having Teresa with him in Andalusia gave him as much joy as he ever allowed himself. He had brought mules and everything else they would need for the journey. But Teresa refused him, saying that the trip would be too tiring. And she had to make her foundation at Burgos, even though this was in every way a chilling proposition. The archbishop of Burgos had said he would give his approval, but Teresa had nothing in writing, and she would have to go there to make the arrangements. Burgos was very far north, its climate even more brutal than Avila's. She would have to travel in the dead of winter, in spite of her recurring illnesses. But God had told her, she explained to Juan, that the devil was just using the dreadful weather to dissuade her: she had no choice but to make the trip.

Juan was stricken, though quietly as always. "Affliction," he had written sometime earlier, "is like a file, and we are storing great joys for ourselves by suffering in darkness." At dawn the day after their meeting, he left Teresa for the last time and made his way back to Granada. Ana de Jesús, the strong-willed prioress of Beas, was ordered to join him in making the new foundation. She must have come through for him: while they were together in Granada, Juan wrote his little treatise on the dark night of the soul (an exegesis of his poem "En una noche oscura") at her request. After Teresa's death the two made the foundation at Madrid. In later years Juan, who had the nerve to challenge Doria's takeover of the reform, was sent into exile at an Andalusian monastery—a punishment he thoroughly appreciated. He died a painful death in 1591, was canonized in 1726, and two centuries later became a Doctor of the Church.

Teresa was not impressed by Ana de Jesús' formidable personality, and after hearing the details of the Granada foundation, she wrote its prioress a scathing letter, accusing her of disobedience. Ana had brought more nuns with her than Teresa had directed her to, and now the convent was so crowded that she had to send some back where they had come from, much to their embarrassment and everyone else's. Ana hadn't communicated either with Teresa or with Gracián, and she was following her own direction, as usual. She had allowed her nuns at Beas to become too attached to her, and as a result, they had been insubordinate with Teresa when she had assigned their prioress to Granada. Ana had also stood on ceremony about titles and had sniped at Teresa in her letters. In short, she had broken every rule in the book. Unusually for Teresa, who laced even her sharpest criticisms of María de San José with endearments, she had nothing good to say about this rebel prioress. Still, it was Ana de Jesús who, after Teresa's death, was largely responsible for the spread of the reform into France and Flanders. She collected Teresa's manuscripts and gave them to Luis de León, who would edit the first collection of her works. Later, Ana de Jesús worked with Gracián to publish the *Fundaciones* at Brussels, where she died in 1621. She was beatified in 1876.

Teresa was almost always feeling sick now, with a chronic sore throat that made it hard to speak and impossible to eat solid food; but she left on her journey anyway, accompanied by Gracián and Teresita (Teresa was whisking her niece away from a relative who wanted to remove her from the convent), a group of nuns, and (of all people) Angel de Salazar. She arranged with Catalina de Tolosa, her benefactor at Burgos, for a secret late-night arrival: this foundation had all the earmarks of becoming a problem. The journey was possibly the worst yet, with sleet and then driving rain all the way (peculiar for that time of year), and flooded roads that threatened to carry the coach away. At one point, she got fed up and complained to God, who answered that this was how He treated his friends. That, she retorted, was why He had so few of them.

By the time she reached Burgos, she was vomiting blood and had to be put to bed. Meanwhile, Gracián went to see the archbishop in hopes of a quick approval for the foundation. But the archbishop had changed his mind. Teresa had offended him, he said, by bringing so many nuns to his city, as if the foundation were a given when all he had told her was maybe. If she could get a house and an endowment, he might reconsider. When Doña Catalina had offered her house and her fortune to Teresa, the archbishop softened, but his vicar—inspired by the devil, Teresa was sure— made even more problems. It felt like Seville all over again. Gracián was discouraged and wanted to leave, and Teresa told him to go ahead: she didn't want to have to worry about him on top of everything. She felt shaky about this enterprise, but God strengthened her. *"Ahora, Teresa, ten fuerte,"* He instructed in a locution. "Now, Teresa, hold fast."

The nuns decided to leave Doña Catalina's house in order to give the poor generous woman a little relief. While searching for a place to buy, they moved temporarily into the top-floor rooms of a local hospital for the poor, where Teresa healed some invalids (according to Ana de San Bartolomé) and called in favors from as many people as she could think of. A letter from Bishop Alvaro, judiciously edited by Teresa and then rewritten, apparently turned the archbishop around. The resident Jesuits had been upset about the diversion of Doña Catalina's fortune, but they settled down after Teresa renounced it (secretly, so the archbishop wouldn't get nervous about her funding). The foundation was made, and Gracián, who had lingered in Burgos much longer than he had expected, departed for Soria and points south. He said good-bye to Teresa for the last time.

Like her, he was destined to spend his life as a *romero*, except that he was seldom where he needed to be to further his own interests. After the founder's death he sent Doria as his emissary to Rome, where Doria so ingratiated himself that he was soon in a position to challenge Gracián's authority—and Gracián, naive as ever, responded by nominating Doria to succeed him in the office of provincial. Juan de la Cruz warned him that he was promoting the man who would someday strip him of everything he had, and he was right: Doria thanked Gracián for his efforts by first exiling him to Portugal, then getting him expelled from the order. Gracián appealed to Rome with no success, then set off for Naples, but had the bad luck to be ambushed by Barbary pirates, who dragged him off in chains and tattooed his feet with crosses. He saw his captivity as a divinely ordained chance to convert the infidel, which he tried to do until his ransom in 1595. He was never readmitted into the order, but joined the Calced, and died in Belgium in 1614.

A flood that invaded the walls of the convent kept Teresa in Burgos longer than she would have liked; repairs were necessary, and she had to be there for them, even though she was confined to her bed. She planned to make more journeys as soon as possible: to Valladolid, where María Bautista was plotting with the evil mother-in-law; to Salamanca, where the frantic prioress was overdoing her penances and making foolish business deals; to Avila, where a lawsuit and a chaotic convent waited for her; to Madrid, where Quiroga would have to capitulate, if only to get rid of her.

She had made it as far as Medina del Campo, where she was doing battle with a dogmatic prioress, when she was waylaid by an order to go straight to Alba. It came via Antonio de Jesús, who had jurisdiction in Castile during Gracián's absence. The daughter-in-law of the duchess was about to go into labor, and both Antonio and Doña María Enríquez thought that the holy woman's presence would set the perfect tone for the event. There was no room for argument: the priest and the duchess made a formidable alliance. So on a September day in 1582, Teresa forced herself into the coach sent for her from Alba and began the most anticipated journey of her life.

Everything else belongs to legend: the slow and painful ride with no provisions (no one had thought to supply them), and Ana de San Bartolomé's desperate search for some eggs to give the ailing founder; she had to make do with a few dried figs instead, for which she expressed her profoundest gratitude. The night spent at the wretched inn, and the passage through a town where she was given nothing except some onions seasoned with herbs; the news from Alba that the duchess's daughter-in-law had gone into labor prematurely and had given birth to a son, and Teresa's wry reaction, "Thank God, now they won't be needing this old saint."

Once inside the convent, a flurry of activity: fine linen sheets for her bed and an unsoiled habit for her to wear. The sisters knew what must be happening. There had been signs: unearthly lights in the chapel and strange moans with no apparent source. A dying saint was a treasure, so it must have startled everyone when Teresa got up the next morning and went to Mass, then scolded Teresa de Laíz, who had been bullying the nuns, and quibbled with a rector from Salamanca about a new house she didn't want him to buy. She spoke with the outgoing prioress, whose laxity had allowed the nuns to abuse the freedoms she had given them, and made arrangements for the election of a new prioress. She finally collapsed a few days later, hemorrhaging vaginally, and was taken to her room to die.

She called the nuns to her bedside so that she could convince them of her wickedness. "My daughters and my ladies," she said, "for the love of God, I ask you to pay close attention to the observance of the Rule and the Constitutions, and not to follow the example that this bad nun has given you, which I ask you to forgive." She took Communion and offered prayers to her divine bridegroom. She thanked God for letting her die a daughter of the church. When Antonio de Jesús asked her if she wanted to be taken back to Avila after her death, she famously answered him, "Padre, what kind of a question is that? Do I have anything at all of my own? Can't they be kind enough to give me a bit of earth here?"

Weakened by agonizing pain, she drifted into a state that looked like rapture. Ana de San Bartolomé never left her side, except to get something to eat, and then the dying woman became so restless that the lay sister had to come back and hold her head. As long as her lips would move, Teresa kept repeating words from the psalm: "A sacrifice to God is an afflicted spirit. . . . A humble and contrite heart, Oh God, thou wilt not despise." Her face became smooth and radiant. The fragrance in her room was overpowering. Even in the kitchen the sisters smelled it, and realized it came from a saltshaker she had touched.

She died on the night of October 4 in Ana's arms, in the presence (the sister said) of Christ and an angelic host. Earthly witnesses said that she died in ecstasy, her soul ripped away from her body by the force of God's love. The blood on her sheets, her biographer Yepes wrote, was proof of that holy consummation—and his opinion was borne out years later, when her coffin was reopened and some drops of blood on a cloth that had been buried with her were still fresh.

What remained of the woman, once the saint emerged from the cocoon of her earthly existence, was by her own standards immaterial. All she had ever been was a wretched creature whose only virtue was her determination to reach God. Of course she had been restless, *muy andariega:* how else could the butterfly find its home? After her death, which could only be construed as a triumph, there was little need for others to remember her flawed humanity. If María de San José and Ana de Jesús still smarted from her rebukes, they never revealed it, but each of them cast herself as *la santa's* favorite daughter, the one who would fully realize her plans for the reform. If Gracián remembered some warmth that was fully human, he didn't let it interfere with his perception of her sanctity, as evidenced by his cool and detailed appraisal of her corpse. If Juan de la Cruz was sometimes wary of her passionate nature, he never doubted the force that propelled her spirit. He understood the logic of her love.

Glorification of St. Teresa by Giovanni Battista Tiepolo. Ceiling fresco, c. 1725, in the Church of Santa Maria degli Scalzi, Venice

Epilogue: *Swordplay*

—

Teresa's posthumous battles were fought in many arenas. After the publication of her writings, edited by Luis de León in 1588, a number of theologians who had never known her began sending *memoriales,* or briefs, denouncing her work to the governing council of the Inquisition. A Dominican preacher named Alonso de la Fuente (her most unrelenting critic and a well-known persecutor of *alumbrados*) launched a crusade against her. He mistrusted her approach to prayer, claiming that it gave the devil every opportunity to deceive her. Her spiritual progress was so swift, he said, that it had to be unholy. If her confessors had misunderstood her, that was because she was traveling a forbidden path, one that excluded the church by positing an exclusive relationship between the soul and God. The fact that this deluded, uneducated woman presumed to teach others struck Fuente and other critics as an obvious contradiction: women couldn't reason or teach, and so Teresa couldn't possibly transmit Christian doctrine. If (as her supporters claimed) educated men were inspired by her teaching, that proved the devil was working through her to reverse the natural order.

Thrusts like these were parried by theologians who had known and worked with her, including Gracián, who wrote a treatise in her defense. Luis de León revised the "Apologia" that prefaced his edition of her writings, locating her squarely in a venerable tradition of mystical literature. Others made the case for her right to teach, pointing out that her ability to do so effectively, even though she was a woman, was a certain sign that God was working through her—which is what Teresa herself believed.

Except for one anonymous champion, who wrote that women, fuzzy-minded and emotional as they were, *might* be more receptive to divine inspiration than dusty *letrados,* the men who evaluated Teresa's life and work believed she triumphed over her femininity. (Yepes, for example, declared that even when she was a little girl, "her desires were manly.") This was also the opinion of the nuns who knew her and testified at her canonization proceedings. She had urged them to be *varoniles* and had set an example through her own manly behavior. Women like her who, "with fortitude, overcome their passions and subject themselves to God, must be called men," wrote her biographer Francisco de Ribera, "and men who let themselves be vanquished by [their passions] are women. This isn't based on the body's difference, but on the soul's strength." As Gillian T. W. Ahlgren points out in her study *Teresa of Avila and the Politics of Sanctity,* "The canonization of a sixteenth-century woman [involved] quite a bit of reconstruction."

After she was canonized in 1622, having been praised in the papal bull for "overcoming . . . her female nature," the sparring resumed with a vengeance, both in and out of the cloister. Discalced Carmelites proposed to Rome that Teresa be made patron saint of Spain. It seemed to them that the martial talents of the Apostle Saint James (Santiago the Moorslayer) had become irrelevant, because there weren't any more Moors to slay. Spain was in a serious political and financial decline, and what it needed most, Teresa's partisans claimed, was potent spiritual intercession. King Philip IV couldn't help but agree. When the brief arrived from Rome, allowing her to share the honor of patronage with the Moorslayer, his proponents—led by the militant Knights of Santiago—rallied behind him, claiming that it was humiliating for the sword-waving champion of the Spanish people to have to share his title with a woman. In his furious tract *Su espada por Santiago,* Francisco de Quevedo (whose talents were much better employed as a poet and satirist) protested that Teresa had never wielded any weapon but her spindle, whereas Santiago, "fighting personally and visibly" on his white charger in four thousand seven hundred battles, killed "numberless enemies." (Quevedo actually rounded off the number at eleven million fifteen thousand; no one knows how he arrived at the figure.) The conflict escalated in literary jousts—at that time, as in Teresa's own, a popular entertainment in Spain—as rivals tried to slash one another with clever verses. But the real battle lines were drawn between social classes, with the general population favoring Santiago and the elite favoring Teresa. "One might say, without the slightest intention of impropriety," writes historian Américo Castro, "that the salons favored Teresa and the people favored the Apostle."

In 1629 Pope Urban VIII revised the earlier brief and allowed the faithful to make up their own minds: they could choose whether or not to recognize Teresa as co-patron saint of Spain. Most Spaniards chose not to, putting their money instead on the old soldier—just in case the sword really was mightier than the pen.

Appendix: *Last Views*

———

The first English translation of Teresa's *Vida* was published in London in 1623; the second, translated by Sir Toby Mathew, in Antwerp in 1642. It was Mathew's version, entitled *The Flaming Hart or the Life of the Glorious S. Teresa*, that caused a sensation in England and inspired Richard Crashaw to write his cycle of Teresa poems in 1646 and 1648. The third poem in the cycle, below, is Crashaw's baroque interpretation of the words and prevailing image of the Spanish saint.

The flaming Heart. Upon the booke and picture of *Teresa*. As she is usually expressed with a *Seraphim* beside her

> Well meaning Readers! you that come as Friends,
> And catch the pretious name this piece pretends,
> Make not so much hast to admire
> That faire cheek't fallacie of fire.
> That is a *Seraphim* they say,
> And this the great *Teresia*.
> Readers, be rul'd by me, and make,
> Here a well plac't, and wise mistake.
> You must transpose the picture quite,
> And spell it wrong to reade it right;
> Read *Him* for *Her*, and *Her* for *Him*,
> And call the *Saint*, the *Seraphim*.
> *Painter*, what dids't thou understand
> To put her dart into his *Hand*?
> See, even the yeares, and size of Him,
> Shew this the Mother *Seraphim*.
> This is the Mistrisse *Flame*; and duteous *hee*

Her happier *fire-works,* here, comes down to see.
O most poore spirited of men!
Had thy cold Pencill kist her Pen
Thou coulds't not so unkindly err
To shew us this faint shade for Her.
Why man, this speakes pure mortall frame,
And mocks with Femall Frost Love's manly flame.
One would suspect thou mean'st to paint,
Some weake, inferior, *Woman Saint.*
But had thy pale-fac't purple tooke
Fire from the burning Cheekes of that *bright booke,*
Thou would'st on her have heap't up all
That could be form'd *Seraphicall.*
What e're this youth of fire wore faire,
Rosie Fingers, Radiant Haire,
Glowing cheekes, and glistring wings,
All those, faire and flagrant things,
But before All, that fierie Dart,
Had fill'd the *Hand* of this great *Heart.*
Do then as equall Right requires,
Since *his* the blushes be, and *hers* the fires,
Resume and rectifie they rude designe,
Undresse thy *Seraphim* into *mine.*
Redeeme this injury of thy art,
Give *him* the *veyle,* give *her* the *Dart.*
Give *him* the *veyle,* that he may cover,
The red cheekes of a rivall'd Lover;
Asham'd that our world now can show
Nests of new *Seraphims* here below.
Give *her* the *dart,* for it is *she*
(Faire youth) shoot's both thy shafts and *thee.*
Say, all ye wise and well pierc't Hearts
That live, and dye amids't Her darts,
What is't your tast-full spirits doe prove
In that rare Life of *her,* and Love?
Say and beare witnesse. Sends she not,
A *Seraphim* at every shot?

What *Magazins* of imortall armes there shine!
Heav'ns great *Artillery* in each *Love-spun-line.*
Give then the *Dart* to *Her,* who gives the *Flame;*
Give *Him* the *veyle,* who kindly takes the shame.
   But if it be the frequent *Fate*
   Of worst faults to be *Fortunate;*
   If all's *prescription;* and proud wrong,
   Hearkens not to an humble song;
   For all the *Gallantry* of *Him,*
   Give me the suff'ring *Seraphim.*
   His be the bravery of all those Bright things,
   The glowing cheekes, the glittering wings,
   The *Rosie* hand, the *Radiant Dart,*
   Leave her alone the *flaming-Heart.*
   Leave her that, and thou shalt leave her,
   Not one loose shaft, but *loves* whole quiver.
   For in *Love's* field was never found,
   A nobler *Weapon* than a *wound.*
   Love's Passives, are his *activ'st* part,
   The *wounded* is the *wounding-heart.*
   O Heart! the equall *Poise,* of *Love's* both *Parts,*
   Big alike with *wounds* and *Darts,*
Live in these conquering *leaves;* live all the same,
And walke through all tongues one triumphant flame.
Live here *great heart;* and Love, and dye, and kill,
And bleed, and wound, and yield, and conquer still.
Let this imortall Life, where e'er it comes,
Walke in a crowd of *Loves,* and *Martyrdomes.*
Let *Mystick Deaths* waite on't; and wise soules bee,
The *love-slaine-witnesses,* of this life of *Thee.*
O sweet incendiary! shew here thy art,
Upon this carcasse of a hard, cold, hart,
Let all thy scatter'd shafts of light, that play
Among the leaves of thy larg Books of day,
Combin'd against this *Brest* at once break in
And take away from me my self & sin,
This gratious Robbery shall thy bounty be;

And my best fortunes such fair spoiles of me.
O thou undanted daughter of desires!
By all thy dowr of *Lights* & *Fires;*
By all the eagle in thee, all the dove;
By all thy lives & deaths of love;
By thy larg draughts of intellectuall day,
And by thy thirsts of love more large then they;
By all thy brim-fill'd Bowles of feirce desire
By thy last Morning's draught of liquid fire;
By the full kingdome of that finall kisse
That seiz'd thy parting Soul, & seal'd thee his;
By all the heav'ns thou hast in him
(Fair sister of the *Seraphim!*)
By all of *Him* we have in *Thee;*
Leave nothing of my *Self* in me.
Let me so read thy life, that I
Unto all life of mine may dy.

Louis L. Martz, ed., *The Anchor Anthology of Seventeenth-Century Verse,* vol. 1, rev. ed. of *The Meditative Poem* (Garden City, N.Y.: Doubleday Anchor Books, 1963), pp. 278–81.

Notes

—

Introduction

ix **baroque theater:** Bernini was famous not only for his architecture but also for his unconventional and often startling theatrical productions; once he emptied a theater by setting a fire onstage. The connections between architecture and theater in Bernini's work are explored by Rudolf Wittkower in his classic *Bernini: The Sculptor of the Roman Baroque,* 4th ed. (London: Phaidon Press Limited, 1997), pp. 159–60, and in the section entitled "Bernini and the Theater" (pp. 146–57) in Irving Lavin's two-volume *Bernini and the Unity of the Visual Arts,* which is unfortunately out of print.

    The marble gentlemen: These were members of the Cornaro family, the chapel's patrons. Bernini represented Cardinal Federico Cornaro and deceased family members as witnesses to Teresa's transverberation. See Lavin, pp. 92–103.

x **ecstasy, or rapture:** Teresa generally used these words interchangeably, as I do here, but many mystics made careful distinctions between them. See E. W. T. Dicken, *The Crucible of Love,* p. 396. For basic information about mystic states, presented with the enthusiasm of a fellow traveler, see Evelyn Underhill's *Mysticism.* For a discussion of ecstasy as interpreted by Bernini and other artists, see Lavin, pp. 107–24.

xi **Doctor of the Church:** Saint Catherine of Siena, following hard on Teresa's heels, was also declared a Doctor of the Church by Pope Paul VI in 1970.

    saints are not angels: Phyllis McGinley's *Saint-Watching* (New York: The Viking Press, 1969) is an eclectic reading of the lives of selected saints.

xi **Sainthood is not gender-neutral:** Much work has recently been done on the subject of female sanctity. See Jane Tibbetts Schulenburg, *Forgetful of Their Sex: Female Sanctity and Society, Ca. 500–1100* (Chicago: The University of Chicago Press, 1998); also Gillian T. W. Ahlgren, *Teresa of Avila and the Politics of Sanctity*. For discussions of the transformative power of virginity, see the introduction to Jo Ann Kay McNamara's *Sisters in Arms: Catholic Nuns Through Two Millennia* (Cambridge: Harvard University Press, 1996); and the section entitled "Sexuality, Language and Power" (pp. 11–13) in Electa Arenal and Stacey Schlau's *Untold Sisters: Hispanic Nuns in Their Own Works.*

xiii **one laconic eighteenth-century Frenchman:** This was the President de Brosses, cited in Howard Hibbard, *Bernini* (Hammondsworth, England: Penguin Books, 1965), pp. 241–42.

"Su espada por Santiago": See Américo Castro's analysis of Francisco de Quevedo's 1628 polemic in *The Structure of Spanish History,* pp. 189–201.

La Santa de la Raza: See the discussion of Teresa's Spanishness in Carlos M. N. Eire, *From Madrid to Purgatory,* pp. 379–82; and, for an exhaustive treatment of the subject, Gabriel de Jesús, *La Santa de la Raza: Vida gráfica de Santa Teresa de Jesús,* 4 vols. (Madrid, 1929–35).

culture as cul-de-sac: See Carlos Fuentes, *The Buried Mirror,* pp. 33–4.

The Black Legend: "The basic premise of the Black Legend is that Spaniards have shown themselves, historically, to be *uniquely* cruel, bigoted, tyrannical, obscurantist, lazy, fanatical, greedy, and treacherous. . . ." See Philip Wayne Powell, *Tree of Hate: Propaganda and Prejudices Affecting United States Relations with the Hispanic World* (New York: Basic Books, 1971), p. 11.

the word *desesperado:* For a discussion of despair and heroic hope, see Miguel de Unamuno, *The Tragic Sense of Life in Men and Nations,* pp. 351–52.

"Those Spaniards, those Spaniards!": Nietzsche reportedly made this remark to his sister, Madame Nietzsche Forster. See José Ortega y Gasset, *Invertebrate Spain,* p. 208.

The Spanish tragedy: The uniquely Spanish approach to death is the subject of Eire's *From Madrid to Purgatory.* See especially bk. 3, "The saint's heavenly corpse: Teresa of Avila and the ultimate paradigm of death," pp. 371–510.

Notes

xiv **"We apprehend here":** Quoted in Eire, pp. 262–63.

the king's collection: Andrew Wheatcroft catalogues some of King Philip's holdings in *The Habsburgs* (London: Penguin Books, 1996), pp. 145–46. For more on relics and saintliness, see Kenneth L. Woodward, *Making Saints* (New York: Simon & Schuster, 1990), pp. 405–6. For early history of the veneration of saints, see Peter Brown, *The Cult of the Saints* (Chicago: The University of Chicago Press, 1981), especially pp. 69–127.

xv **"the saner Protestant":** This particular jab and the one that follows it (on "celestial billing and cooing") appear in Hugh E. M. Stutfield's *Mysticism and Catholicism* (London: T. Fisher Unwin Ltd., 1925), pp. 89–91. Equally diverting is Stutfield's discussion on p. 45 of saints as "spiritual pointers: if evil spirits were about, they scented them as a dog scents partridges. Their noses could detect the odour of sanctity . . . no less than the stench of concealed sin."

George Eliot: She discusses the fate of latter-day Saint Teresas in her Prelude to *Middlemarch* (Hammondsworth, England: Penguin Books, 1965), p. 26: "Here and there is born a Saint Theresa, foundress of nothing, whose loving heartbeats and sobs after an unattained goodness tremble off and are dispersed among hindrances, instead of centering in some long-recognizable deed."

"the prototype of the hysterical": See V. Sackville-West, *The Eagle and the Dove: A Study in Contrasts*, pp. 7–8.

the findings of Jean-Martin de Charcot: For an excellent discussion of Charcot and his influence, see Cristina Mazzoni's *Saint Hysteria: Neurosis, Mysticism and Gender in European Culture*, chap. 1, "The Ecstasy of Saint Hysteria: Women's Mysticism in Medical Writings," pp. 17–53.

"the patron saint of hysteria": This witticism appears in Breuer's section on unconscious ideas. See *Studies on Hysteria*, Basic Books' reprint of vol. 2 of the Standard Edition of the *Complete Psychological Works of Sigmund Freud* (Hogarth Press, 1955), p. 232.

the "French Freud," Jacques Lacan: Quoted in Mazzoni, p. 46.

xvi **It took a modern feminist theorist:** Carole Slade quotes Irigaray in the epilogue to her study *St. Teresa of Avila*, p. 134: " 'In Rome? So far away? To look? At a statue? Of a saint? Sculpted by a man? What pleasure are we talking about? Whose pleasure?' "

xvi **"That magnificent and terrible saint"**: J. K. Huysmans, *En Route*, translated by C. Kegan Paul (London: Kegan Paul, Trench, Trübner & Co. Ltd., 1897), p. 70.

"She is not the slave": Simone de Beauvoir, *The Second Sex* (New York: Vintage Books, 1974), p. 747. Reprint of 1952 edition by Alfred A. Knopf.

"the ludicrous contradictions": Slade, p. 5.

Prologue: *First Views*

4 **the same sweet scent**: After Teresa's death the scent became so strong that the nuns reported it gave them headaches; they had to open a window. Whatever she had touched was redolent of this scent, which couldn't be washed off. See the account in Eire's *From Madrid to Purgatory*, pp. 419–21.

5 **The Jesuit Ribera**: His *Vida de Santa Teresa de Jesús* was first published at Salamanca in 1590 and circulated widely throughout Europe. An edition edited by Jaime Pons was published at Barcelona in 1908.

The authorized version: The physical woman who emerges in this description is ideal from a sixteenth-century Spanish point of view—which may explain why biographer Kate O'Brien, writing in 1951, remarks that the elements of her beauty "do not overmuch persuade a twentieth-century taste." From *Teresa of Avila* (New York: Sheed & Ward, 1951), p. 21.

6 **the sculptor's visceral image**: See Lavin, pp. 108–10.

Chapter 1: *Expeditions*

9 *La vida es sueño:* Teresa would have encountered this theme in the *Amadis de Gaula* and elsewhere. For background see Otis H. Green, *Spain and the Western Tradition*, vol. 4 (Madison, Wisconsin: The University of Wisconsin Press, 1968), pp. 40–42.

11 **but here revisionists**: Misconceptions about Teresa's ancestry persisted for centuries and inspired paeans to her aristocratic heritage:

for example, Alexander Whyte, D.D., wrote in his *Santa Teresa: An Appreciation* (Edinburgh and London: Oliphant, Anderson & Ferrer, 1898), p. 4, that "no one who ever conversed with her could for a moment fail to observe that the oldest and best blood of Spain mantled in her cheek and shone in her eye." Nevertheless, in the 1940s the truth about her *converso* background finally emerged and has since been the subject of numerous studies. See Francisco Márquez Villanueva's essay "Santa Teresa y el linaje" in his study *Espiritualidad y literatura en el siglo XVI* (Madrid: Alfaguarra, 1968).

Convivencia: Américo Castro developed the idea of *convivencia* (literally, "living-togetherness") as a key to understanding Spanish civilization after 711, when Muslims occupied the peninsula: "I wish to submit that that which is most original and universal in the Hispanic genius has its origin in a living disposition forged in the nine centuries of Christian-Jewish-Moorish interaction." See *The Structure of Spanish History,* p. 96.

12 **the *pleito* vouchsafed him:** For details of Juan's petition and a discussion of ideas about honor and lineage, see Jodi Bilinkoff, *The Avila of Saint Teresa,* pp. 18–22.

14 **Avila was a lively, though still semirural:** See Bilinkoff, pp. 4–14.

17 **"She was beautiful":** From the introduction to Louis Bertrand's *Sainte Thérese d'Avila, racontée par elle-même* (Paris: J. de Gigord, 1939), p. 35. Alison Weber remarks on the frequency with which critics comment on Teresa's beauty and charm: "This tendency to define Teresa in terms of a feminine mystique almost constitutes a critical school in itself." See *Teresa of Avila and the Rhetoric of Femininity,* p. 7.
a flirtation: Victoria Lincoln believes that Teresa lost her virginity at this point, but Teresa's own explanation is more convincing.

18 *Honra* **was always fragile:** From Lope de Vega's *La estrella de Sevilla,* quoted in Marcelin Defourneaux, *Daily Life in Spain in the Golden Age,* p. 34. See his discussion of the concept of honor, pp. 32–45.

Chapter 2: *Perils*

21 **"mitigated" convents:** In 1432—twenty years before women were admitted into the Carmelite order—Pope Eugene IV issued a bull

allowing the friars to live somewhat less austerely, eating meat and leaving their cells at specified times. By the time Teresa arrived at the Encarnación in 1535, Carmelite nuns were enjoying even more liberties, partly due to the influx of well-off postulants and partly because of overpopulation in the convents, which strained their resources and led them to allow extended visits to friends and relatives, as well as visits from potential benefactors.

22 **the posture he calls** *altanería:* See Ortega y Gasset, *Invertebrate Spain,* p. 148.

all but escaped his past: See Bilinkoff, pp. 64–7. For a full discussion and documentation of the Cepedas' *pleito,* see Teofanes Egido, *El linaje judeoconverso de Santa Teresa (Pleito de hidalguía de los Cepeda)* (Madrid: Editorial de Espiritualidad, 1986).

26 **Osuna's homespun prose:** A very readable recent translation of Osuna is *Francisco de Osuna: The Third Spiritual Alphabet,* translated by Mary E. Giles (New York: Paulist Press, 1981), p. 48.

27 **the vogue of private, interior devotion:** Américo Castro theorized that this widespread interest in mysticism and private prayer was a particularly Spanish version of the discovery of the individual elsewhere in Europe: "The mystical phenomenon can only be explained as the fruit of the restless individualism of the Renaissance." See *Teresa la santa y otros ensayos* (Madrid: Alianza, 1982), p. 53.

31 **Under the circumstances:** In his *Hours with the Mystics: A Contribution to the History of Religious Opinion* (London: Strahan and Company, 1856), Robert Alfred Vaughan, one of Teresa's more entertaining critics, writes that "it is significant that the miraculous manifestations of the Romish Church should have been vouchsafed only to women whose constitution . . . was thoroughly broken down by years of agonizing disease." William James takes a different approach: "Saint Teresa might have had the nervous system of the placidest cow, and it would not now save her theology, if the trial of the theology by these other tests [i.e. "immediate luminousness," "philosophical reasonableness," and "moral helpfulness"] should show it to be contemptible." See *The Varieties of Religious Experience* (New York: Macmillan, 1961), p. 33.

32 **an olive twig:** See Rudolf M. Bell, *Holy Anorexia,* p. 18.

32 **her most assiduous twentieth-century biographers:** See Efrén de la

Madre de Dios, O.C.D., and Otger Steggink, O. Carm., *Tiempo y vida de Santa Teresa*, pp. 124–34.

"a painful stimulant": In *The Saints That Moved the World: Anthony, Augustine, Francis, Ignatius, Teresa* (New York: Thomas Y. Crowell, 1946), René Fülöp-Miller embellishes this theory with references to the illnesses of Saint Francis, Oliver Cromwell, Vincent Van Gogh et al. To his romantic mind, "illness and sainthood appear at times merely as two different manifestations of one and the same creative force," p. 356.

Chapter 3: *Discoveries*

35 **"pure *coquetry* of humility"**: Bertrand, p. 137.

37 **Modern readers have wondered:** Weber's and Slade's persuasive studies, which appeared, respectively, in 1990 and 1995, were joined in 1996 by Ahlgren's analysis of the complex situation of religious women in Counter-Reformation Spain.

38 **essential for her to be *desengañada:*** See Green, vol. 4, chap. 3, "Desengaño," for ramifications of this idea in Spanish and European literature.

Chapter 4: *Gold*

47 **"the royal way"**: See Osuna, translated by Mary E. Giles, p. 223.

53 **the "religion" of courtly love:** See C. S. Lewis, *The Allegory of Love* (London: Oxford University Press, 1936), pp. 29–43.

58 **what Teresa means by love:** For a discussion of visual representations of ecstasy, see Lavin, text volume, pp. 113–24.

Saint Bernard's painstaking explication: See vol. 2 of *The Works of Bernard of Clairvaux, On the Song of Songs I*, translated by Kilian Walsh, O.C.S.O. (Kalamazoo, Michigan: Cistercian Publications, 1981), p. 58.

The *Dialogue* of the Italian saint: Catherine of Siena, *The Dialogue*, translation and introduction by Suzanne Noffke, O.P. (New York: Paulist Press, 1980), p. 30.

Notes

Chapter 5: *A Glimpse of Hell*

71 **he presented a *Dictamen:*** Carole Slade includes this document, in its entirety, in *St. Teresa of Avila*. See Appendix B, *Judgment*, attributed to Pedro Ibáñez, pp. 149–52.

72 **The politically astute Dominican:** This is Victoria Lincoln's theory, and though plausible, it also makes sense that Ibáñez would sequester himself following this complex spiritual and intellectual endeavor.

Chapter 6: *The Conquest of Toledo*

80 **the established norms:** See Bilinkoff, pp. 139–40.

Chapter 7: *Paradise*

94 **"an angel's banquet":** See Marcelle Auclair, *Saint Teresa of Avila*, p. 138.

Chapter 8: *Cultivating Souls*

102 **wrote Alejo Venegas:** Quoted in *Spain and the Western Tradition*, vol. 2, p. 159.

104 **Whether or not she was a natural:** Teresa herself claimed that she didn't have time to fine-tune her writing, and until recently most critics backed up that claim. Ramón Menéndez Pidal theorized in the essay "El Estilo de Santa Teresa," in *La Lengua de Cristobal Colón y otros estudios sobre el siglo XVI* (Madrid: Espasa Calpe, 1958), that she intentionally rusticated her language as a way of identifying herself with simple souls—an exercise in humility. Américo Castro argued in *Teresa la santa y otros ensayos* that she was reacting against a racially and socially unjust society—though he still maintained that she wrote spontaneously and with feminine élan. Alison Weber, in *Teresa of Avila and the Rhetoric of Femininity*, considers the elements of Teresa's

style—use of diminutives, digressions, sentence fragments, etc.—
then, building on the work of the Spanish critic Victor G. de la Con-
cha, who wrote *El arte literario de Santa Teresa* (Barcelona: Ariel, 1978),
introduces her own reasoned explanation: that the politically astute
Teresa was manipulating her readers via a "rhetoric of femininity."

Chapter 9: *Strategies*

113 **the unedited first draft:** Teresa submitted her original draft of the
Camino de perfección to García de Toledo, who ordered substantial
revisions. The first draft, called the "Escorial" (which is where the
manuscript is housed) was written exclusively for Teresa's nuns and
has a more personal flavor than the revision, called the "Valladolid"
(and housed at the Discalced Carmelite convent there). Translators
of the *Camino* generally rely on the Valladolid text but make judgment calls on which parts of the Escorial text to include.
114 *La perfecta casada:* Quoted in Green, vol. 2, p. 21.
118 **"footloose pilgrim":** The standard translation, introduced by E. Allison Peers, is "restless gadabout," but I wanted to preserve Teresa's wry
comparison of herself with specifically religious wanderers.
119 **Writing about their arrival:** Julián de Avila's lively account of his
travels with Teresa can be found in the Appendix to the 1919 translation of Teresa's letters by the Benedictines of Stanbrook. See *The Letters of Saint Teresa*, vol. 1, pp. 287–308.

Chapter 10: *Alarms and Diversions*

125 **"womanly weakness":** Quoted in E. de la M. de Dios and O.
Steggink, p. 371.
"she liked girls": Lincoln, p. 119.

Chapter 13: *Dueling Saints*

160 **Teresa's French biographer:** Auclair, p. 362.

Notes

Chapter 16: *A Season in Seville*

189 **that quintessential Castilian landscape:** Frances Parkinson Keyes, *The Land of Stones and Saints*, p. xxvi (London: Peter Davies, 1958).
"the air is heavy": Jan Morris, *Spain* (London: Penguin Books, 1982), p. 67.

Chapter 18: *The Prince in the Tower*

221 **"En una noche oscura":** For a brilliant explication of this poem in relation to two other masterpieces, see Leo Spitzer, *Essays on English and American Literature* (Princeton: Princeton University Press, 1962), chap. 9, "Three Poems on Ecstasy: John Donne, St. John of the Cross, Richard Wagner," pp. 139–79.

224 **"unstable, restless, disobedient":** See *Santa Teresa de Jesús, Obras completas*, p. 935.

Chapter 19: *Campaigns and Conspiracies*

242 **"Affliction," he had written:** Quoted in Auclair, p. 385.

245 **She died on the night of October 4:** As if once again upsetting the natural order, Teresa died right before the first full day of the new Gregorian calendar. So October 5, the morning after her death, officially became October 15, the date that now marks Saint Teresa's feast day.

her soul ripped away: In Yepes's own words, "The knife that killed her was God's great impulse of love, so powerful and strong that it not only ripped the spirit from the soul but also the soul from the body. In all that time she was so absorbed and enraptured (a period of fourteen hours . . .) that she caught fire and burned with love for what she saw, with delight in what she had desired. . . . Like the phoenix, she died in that happy conflagration in which she had always lived." From *Vida de Santa Teresa de Jesús por Fray Diego de*

Notes

Yepes, in bk. 1 of *Tesoro de escritores místicos españoles* (Paris: Garnier Hermanos, 1847), p. 316.

Epilogue: *Swordplay*

247 **Teresa's posthumous battles:** For a detailed discussion of these and their relevance to gender ideology in Spain, see Ahlgren, especially pp. 114–66.

248 **"her desires were manly":** Yepes, *Escritores místicos,* p. 8.
Women like her who, "with fortitude": P. Francisco de Ribera, *Vida de Santa Teresa de Jesús,* 3rd ed. (Barcelona: Gustavo Gili, 1908), p. 88.
"quite a bit of reconstruction": Ahlgren, p. 146.
"fighting personally and visibly": Quoted in Castro, *The Structure of Spanish History,* p. 193. For Castro's discussion of Santiago's role in Spanish culture, see the chapter headed "Apogee and Decline of the Belief in Santiago," pp. 181–201.
the real battle lines: Castro, p. 197.

Appendix: *Last Views*

251 **prevailing image of the Spanish saint:** Crashaw was living in Italy while Bernini was working on the Cornaro Chapel, but the poet died two years before the chapel, with its flamboyant sculptural group, came into public view. Crashaw would have been familiar, though, with engravings of Teresa and the angel that illustrated English editions of her works, as well as with Fray Juan de la Miseria's portrait.

Selected Bibliography

———

Translations of Saint Teresa's Writings

The most accessible English translation of the *Vida* is *The Life of Saint Teresa of Avila by Herself,* translated by J. M. Cohen (London: Penguin Books, 1957), and reissued as a Penguin paperback in 1987. Cohen's translation has a more modern flavor than the more widely known translation by E. Allison Peers in *The Complete Works of Teresa of Avila,* 3 vols. (London: Sheed and Ward, 1944–1946). The most recent translation, by Kieran Kavanaugh, O.C.D., and Otilio Rodríguez, O.C.D., *The Collected Works of St. Teresa of Avila,* 3 vols. (Washington, D.C.: Institute of Carmelite Studies, 1976–1985), is somewhat less fluid than Peers's but is very faithful to the original Spanish text and also contains extremely useful front and back matter.

It is understandably hard for lay readers to find a compelling version of the *Camino de perfección;* best, even now, is Peers's *The Way of Perfection* (in *The Complete Works*), which gracefully blends the Escorial and Valladolid autographs while faithfully observing Teresa's own preferences and those of her original editors. Kavanaugh and Rodríguez have also produced a viable synthesis of the two autographs (in *The Collected Works*). Peers's translation of the *Moradas,* called *Interior Castle,* remains the standard version of Teresa's much more popular mystical work, currently available in several editions, though in 1995 Fount Paperbacks, an imprint of Harper-Collins Religious, resuscitated the long-out-of-print translation by the Benedictines of Stanbrook, revised by Benedict Zimmerman, O.C.D.

The Kavanaugh and Rodríguez translation of the *Fundaciones* (*The Foundations,* in *The Collected Works*) is accompanied by an extremely detailed and helpful introduction and a chronology. Teresa's Constitutions for her convents are interesting to read alongside the *Fundaciones,* as are curiosities like the *Vejamen,* or *Response to a Spiritual Challenge,* a literary joust in which Teresa and her nuns match their piety against that of their challengers—probably Gracián and his friars. The translators have also taken a crack at her poetry, which seldom transcends its origin as recreational reading for her nuns.

Teresa's letters are badly in need of a fresh translation. Peers's two-volume, 1950 edition of *The Letters of Saint Teresa* is long out of print; so is the four-volume, 1919–1927 edition by the Benedictines of Stanbrook. The Benedictines, in particular, provide some enlightening—and occasionally startling—annotations.

I confess to leaning on the expertise of every one of these translators in order to produce my own translations from the Spanish text of *Santa Teresa de Jesús, Obras completas,* edited by Efrén de la Madre de Dios, O.C.D., and Otger Steggink, O.Carm. (Madrid: Editorial Católica, 1977), which are an attempt to let Teresa speak in a contemporary voice. A new translation of her works would be nothing short of a godsend.

Other Works Consulted

In the early 1980s, when I first asked the librarian at Columbia University for a printout of available material on Saint Teresa, she and I were both astonished to see hundreds of entries scroll out of her then primitive computer. The number is, of course, much greater now that Teresa's life and work have attracted the interest of a diverse group of modern readers, from feminist scholars to adherents of new-age spirituality.

By far the most entertaining biography of Teresa in English is still Vita Sackville-West's eccentric *The Eagle and the Dove: A Study in Contrasts. St. Teresa of Avila, St. Thérese of Lisieux* (New York: Doubleday, Doran & Company, Inc., 1944), which for some reason has never been reissued. It ranks with G. K. Chesterton's *St. Francis of Assisi* as one of the truly original saints' biographies. Victoria Lincoln's *Teresa: A Woman. A Biography of Teresa of Avila,* edited with introductions by Elias Rivers and Antonia T. de Nicolás (Albany: State University of New York Press, 1984) is worth reading, even if Lincoln sometimes gets bogged down in detail; Teresa's history is an intricate jigsaw puzzle to which Lincoln, a novelist, devoted many years of her own life and, unfortunately, died before she could see her book published. Stephen Clissold's *St. Teresa of Avila* (New York: The Seabury Press, 1982) is solid, pretty up-to-date, and has the virtue of clarity. Marcelle Auclair's 1950 biography *Saint Teresa of Avila*, translated by Kathleen Pond (Petersham, Massachusetts: St. Bede's, 1988), is shrewd and provides a considerable amount of detail about Teresa's social and religious milieu (though Auclair turns a blind eye to *converso* issues). While assembling my own version of Teresa's story, I often referred to these works, along with the more or less definitive Spanish text of Efrén de la Madre de Dios and Otger Steggink's biographical study, *Tiempo y vida de Santa Teresa*, 2nd ed. (Madrid: BAC, 1977).

To get a sense of what life was like in Teresa's Spain, two good books to consult (other than *Tiempo y vida*, which has not yet been translated into English) are Jodi Bilinkoff's *The Avila of Saint Teresa: Religious Reform in a Sixteenth-Century City* (Ithaca: Cornell University Press, 1989), and Marcelin Defourneaux's *Daily Life in Spain in the Golden Age* (London: George Allen and Unwin Ltd., 1970). The Spanish approach to death is the subject of Carlos M. N. Eire's fascinating study, *From Madrid to Purgatory: The Art & Craft of Dying in Sixteenth-Century Spain* (Cambridge: Cambridge University Press, 1995), which contains detailed accounts of the deaths of both Saint Teresa and King Philip II. For a masterful account of the political, social, and religious life of Spain, see Henry Kamen's biography *Philip of Spain* (New Haven: Yale University Press, 1997). Also see B. Netanyahu's *The Origins of the Inquisition in Fifteenth-Century Spain* (New York: Random House, 1995).

Américo Castro's *The Structure of Spanish History*, translated by Edmund L. King (Princeton: Princeton University Press, 1954), is an essential source book for anyone interested in Spanish culture and identity, as are Miguel de Unamuno's *The Tragic Sense of Life in Men and Nations*, translated by Anthony Kerrigan (Princeton: Princeton University Press, 1972); and José Ortega y Gasset's *Invertebrate Spain*, translated by Mildred Adams (New York: W. W. Norton & Company, Inc., 1937). Other works with distinct points of view are Carlos Fuente's *The Buried Mirror: Reflections on Spain and the New World* (Boston, New York, London: Houghton Mifflin, 1992); John A. Crow's *Spain: The Root and the Flower* (Berkeley, Los Angeles, London: University of California Press, 1963); and V. S. Pritchett's *The Spanish Temper: Travels in Spain* (New York: The Ecco Press, 1954).

Selected Bibliography

Studies of the writings of religious women have proliferated in recent years. Among works on Teresa herself, two of the most original, in my opinion, are Alison Weber's *Teresa of Avila and the Rhetoric of Femininity* (Princeton: Princeton University Press, 1990), and Carole Slade's *St. Teresa of Avila: Author of a Heroic Life* (Berkeley, Los Angeles, London: University of California Press, 1995), both of which analyze Teresa's *Vida* in light of sixteenth-century expectations (her prospective readers' and her own). A worthy successor to these two, and valuable for its author's insights into the role of women in the Spanish church, is Gillian T. W. Ahlgren's *Teresa of Avila and the Politics of Sanctity* (Ithaca: Cornell University Press, 1996). A rare and important study is Electa Arenal and Stacey Schlau's *Untold Sisters: Hispanic Nuns in Their Own Works* (Albuquerque: University of New Mexico Press, 1989), which includes and analyzes selections, in both the original Spanish and in English translation, of writings by two of Teresa's daughters in religion, Ana de San Bartolomé and María de San José.

Among numerous twentieth-century studies of the psychology of religious women—Teresa in particular—a brilliant new arrival is Cristina Mazzoni's *Saint Hysteria: Neurosis, Mysticism, and Gender in European Culture* (Ithaca: Cornell University Press, 1996). Also see Rudolph M. Bell's ground-breaking *Holy Anorexia* (Chicago and London: The University of Chicago Press, 1985).

For a general background in Christian mysticism, a good place to start is Evelyn Underhill's *Mysticism: A Study in the Nature and Development of Man's Spiritual Consciousness* (New York: E. P. Dutton & Co., Inc., 1961). For Teresan mysticism in particular, see E. W. T. Dicken's *The Crucible of Love: A Study of the Mysticism of St. Teresa of Avila and St. John of the Cross* (New York: Sheed and Ward, 1963)—one of the few books in English that explains the difference between (say) an *arrobamiento*, or trance, and an *arrebatamiento*, or rapture. For more on Spanish mysticism, see Marcel Bataillon, *Erasmo y España*, (Mexico: Fondo de Cultura Económica, 1950) and Gaston Etchegoyen, *L'Amour divin: Essai sur les sources de Sainte Thérèse* (Paris: Féret, 1923). To discover where art and mysticism intersect, see Robert T. Petersson, *The Art of Ecstasy: Teresa, Bernini, and Crashaw* (New York: Atheneum, 1970)—or go directly to heaven with Irving Lavin's two-volume *Bernini and the Unity of the Visual Arts* (New York and London: Oxford University Press, 1980).

Acknowledgments

—

I first met Saint Teresa more than twenty years ago at Columbia University, in a graduate seminar on comparative Renaissance literature. The professor's enthusiasm for Richard Crashaw's poetry (at a time when many Renaissance scholars approached his work gingerly, if at all) led me to the Teresa poems and to the saint's own work. Professor James V. Mirollo may be surprised to see this book finally come to light. I'll always be grateful to him for his early encouragement.

Robert Gottlieb, then editor at Alfred A. Knopf, took a leap of faith when he accepted my book proposal, as did Peter Matson, my agent, who has been almost supernaturally patient. Jane Garrett became my editor at a time when my contract had been (as Peter once put it) "in pickle juice" for about a dozen years, and she agreed to take me on anyway. It was a long shot, and I'm very grateful. Her meticulous attention to detail has guided the manuscript (and its author) through the difficult stages of editing and publication.

Professor Angel Alcalá, a gentleman and a scholar, did me the favor of reviewing the manuscript. I can't thank him enough for the time he took, the insights he provided, and the lunch he prodded me to eat as I chewed on his suggestions. Professor Ciriaco Morón Arroyo provided valuable corrections, and gave me answers to questions that I couldn't find in books.

Wendy Gimbel performed numerous rescue missions—always with the graciousness that is her particular trademark. Frank Cantor, Esmeralda Santiago, Rachel Abram, Amy Goldberger, and Amy Gross were generous with their time and their expertise. Professor Marcia Welles loaned me volumes I might not otherwise have found—and waited almost ten years to get them back.

Two of the people who believed in this book didn't survive to read it. Leo Lerman encouraged me from the start, and the thought of him cast-

Acknowledgments

ing his practiced eye on my manuscript kept me going when I didn't think I could. My father, Maury Medwick, always said that willpower (Teresa would call it *determinación*) could accomplish anything, and I'm beginning to think he had a point.

My mother, Lucille Medwick, died long before I began this project. But she has always been behind it, as much for her love of saints as for her appreciation of spirited women and difficult books.

When I began my research, I was in my mid-thirties and the mother of a toddler. Now I'm fifty-one and the mother of two teenagers. Lucy and Peter Silberman have my love and gratitude for growing up so well, even though a saint kept muscling in on their time. Jeff Silberman, my husband, who has taught me nearly everything I know about human kindness, knows how much I owe him.

Index

—

Index

Index

Index

Mendoza, Alvaro de, 119, 128, 234, 237, 243; foundations supported by, 129, 140, 149; raptures witnessed by, 93; and San José convent, 73, 83–4, 88, 211

Mendoza, Ana de, *see* Eboli, princess of

Mendoza, Bernardino de, 124, 125, 128, 130

Mendoza, María de, 99, 119, 125, 129–31, 139, 143, 167–8, 177, 229, 234

Mendoza, Pedro de, 149

Menéndez Pidal, Ramón, 262

Moors, 8, 10–12, 15, 16, 123, 189, 218, 226, 259; Christian recapture of Spain from, 13; Granada rebellion of, 132, 140; St. James and, xiii, xiv, 248

Moradas del castillo interior (*The Interior Castle*), x, 205–11, 213–16, 218, 234, 237, 240

Morris, Jan, 189

Muslims, 14; *see also* Moors

Nacianceno, Gregorio, 4, 183, 194, 200

Narduch, Giovanni, *see* Juan de la Miseria

Nieto, Baltasar (Baltasar de Jesús), 141, 146, 158–61, 179, 184, 192, 212

Nietzsche, Friedrich, xiii

O'Brien, Kate, 258

Ocampo, Leonor de, 67

Ocampo, María de, *see* María Bautista

Ordóñez, María, 89

Ormaneto, Nicholas, 168, 180, 193, 200–2, 211, 217

Ortega, Isabel, *see* Isabel de Santo Domingo

Ortega y Gasset, José, xiv, 22

Ortiz, Diego, 132, 133, 149

Osuna, Francisco de, 26, 28, 38, 47, 49

Ovalle, Juan de, 69, 83–5, 151, 153, 172

Padilla, Casilda de, 182

Pardo, Arias, 122, 126

Paul, St., 224, 230

Paul VI, Pope, 255

Peña, Isabel de la, *see* Isabel de San Pablo

Pérez Núñez, Bartolomé, 155

Peso, Catalina del, 12, 13

Philip II, King of Spain, x, xiii, xiv, 17–19, 112, 125, 193, 212, 218; Netherlands rebellion against, 172; reforms supported by, 115, 158, 161

Philip IV, King, 248

Pius IV, Pope, 84

Pizarro, Francisco, 19

Polonia (subprioress), 125

Prádanos, Juan de, 43, 44, 61

Protestants, xiv, 27

Quesada, Teresa de, 153–4, 164

Quevedo, Francisco de, xiii, 248

Quiroga, Elena de, 122, 240

Index

Index

Illustration Credits

A Note About the Author

Cathleen Medwick, who was born in New York City, has a B.A. from Sarah Lawrence College and an M.A. and M.Phil. (in English and comparative Renaissance literature) from Columbia University. She has worked as an editor for a number of magazines, most recently *Mirabella* and *House & Garden,* for which she is now a contributing editor. Her feature articles and book reviews have appeared in the *New York Times Magazine,* the *Washington Post Magazine, Mirabella, Vogue, House & Garden, Vanity Fair,* and *Elle.* She lives on a small farm in northern Westchester with her husband and two children.

A Note on the Type

This book was set in a modern adaptation of a type designed by the first William Caslon (1692–1766). The Caslon face, an artistic, easily read type, has enjoyed over two centuries of popularity in our own country. It is of interest to note that the first copies of the Declaration of Independence and the first paper currency distributed to the citizens of the newborn nation were printed in this typeface.

Composed by North Market Street Graphics,
Lancaster, Pennsylvania
Printed and bound by Quebecor Printing,
Fairfield, Pennsylvania
Designed by Soonyoung Kwon